MW00791683

Liability Hedging and Portfolio Choice

Liability Hedging and Portfolio Choice

By Bernd Scherer

Published by Risk Books, a Division of Incisive Financial Publishing Ltd

Haymarket House
28–29 Haymarket
London SW1Y 4RX
Tel: +44 (0)20 7484 9700
Fax: +44 (0)20 7484 9800
E-mail: books@riskwaters.com
Sites: www.riskbooks.com
    www.incisivemedia.com

ISBN 1 904339 66 2

British Library Cataloguing in Publication Data
A catalogue record for this book is available from the British Library

Managing Editor: Laurie Donaldson
Development Editor: Steve Fairman
Designer: Rebecca Bramwell

Typeset by Mizpah Publishing Services Private Limited, Chennai, India

Printed and bound in Spain by Espacegrafic, Pamplona, Navarra

Contents

About the Author

Dr. Bernd Scherer heads Deutsche Asset Managements Research Centre in New York. He is widely published in both academic and practitioners journals and (co)authored several books on modern asset management. He holds a PhD in finance as well as MSc and MBA degrees and is adjunct professor of finance at the European Business School as well as the University of Augsburg.

Introduction

Corporate pension plan sponsors have one thing in common: a set of more or less complicated pension liabilities. The management of pension assets in the presence of pension liabilities gained increasing attention due to poor performance of corporate pension funds (the current underfunding of US defined benefit plans is about US$400 bn.[1]) that forced additional contributions by plan sponsors, changes in accounting rules, the increasing awareness of rating agencies and the development of wider corporate risk management frameworks.[2] Let us exemplify the development with a brief review of the UK experience.

The aggregate pension funding position of FTSE 350 companies at the beginning of 2005 is a deficit of GBP85 bn which translates into a funding of 76% on a FRS 17 basis.

The largest deficits are found in industrial sectors such as airlines, auto components, or aerospace and defence with a large exposure to equity markets (above 60% on average). Asset portfolios are largely invested into non-cash flow matched bond portfolios with a large mismatch in real and inflation duration, leading to a significant exposure to unexpected changes in inflation and interest rates. Equity and bond investments have been compared against an index of passively held bonds and equities (benchmarks). When equity markets started to sell off in 2000 and interest rates were rising these allocations led to a deteriorating surplus that eventually led to the above deficit. As a consequence the cash flows to equityholders of a local saucepan manufacturer, became sensitive to global equity and bond markets. Hardly a value generating strategy.

Table 1 Funding deficit for FTSE 350 companies in January 2005. Pension fund balance sheet for FTSE 350 companies. The funding deficit is a direct consequence from large equity exposures

Pension fund balance sheet

Assets		Liabilities	
General assets (66.5% average equity exposure)	GBP275 bn	Projected benefit obligation (PBO)	GBP360 bn
		Funding deficit	−GBP8.5 bn

Source: Own calculations.

At first, asset managers have been blamed by their clients for their flawed benchmark approach. What was truly required in the eyes of pension fund managers was a total return approach.

> "We see a trend to give asset managers more room to move within a total risk budget. Sometimes even the traditional guidelines are abolished, as long as the manager makes more return and total risk is kept within the boundaries".[3]

However there was nothing wrong with benchmarking assets in order to measure performance, compensate managers and root investments in risk-return space. It was not the problem that benchmarks and hence assets dropped in value, but that assets and liabilities showed little relation. After all the only reason we need assets is that we have liabilities. In a world without liabilities (Adam and Eve's paradise) we don't need assets (however we know that did not last forever, even though some might say that Eve was the liability).

As a consequence from the above mismatch that triggered the worldwide pension crisis, asset managers, consultants and corporate sponsors became more liability sensitive. Still they tend to focus on an asset management centric approach as described in Figure 1. Briefly reviewing this approach will provide an impression of this books line of reasoning.

The traditional approach starts correctly with the valuation of pension liabilities and the search for a liability replicating asset.

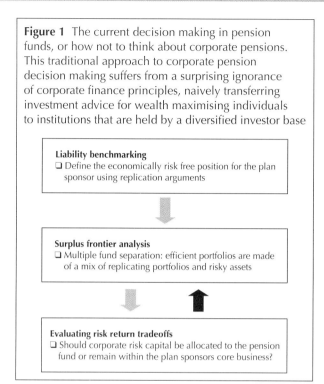

Figure 1 The current decision making in pension funds, or how not to think about corporate pensions. This traditional approach to corporate pension decision making suffers from a surprising ignorance of corporate finance principles, naively transferring investment advice for wealth maximising individuals to institutions that are held by a diversified investor base

Given specific liability characteristics either perfect replication or more or less perfect hedging methodologies will be used to find a portfolio of investable assets that will track the movements in pension liabilities as closely as possible. All remaining risks are by definition orthogonal to capital markets. From the treasurers point of view some additional practical questions arise. How perfect is the liability hedging asset correlated with liabilities and at what costs does replication come? How flexible is my hedging policy if positions need to be unwound in case projected cash flows do not materialise due to actuarial risks?

After having established the hedging position (and also approximately the value of liabilities) current asset management practice begins to miss the point. It starts with running a surplus optimisation (active, ie, liability relative optimisation) that model the economic benefits from investing into higher yielding assets (credit, equity, emerging markets, etc) of alternative pension fund asset allocations. This trade-off simply does not exist as we know that all capital market investments have a net present value of zero. The effect of risk on corporate value comes through its impact on tax shields, bankruptcy and liquidity costs but not via a risk premium (never mind the subjectivity of those forecasts). Ignoring this basic principle shakes the foundations of corporate finance and valuation theory in general (which obviously is not a concern to some). At this stage the arguments for the asset management centric approach become increasingly opaque. Some arguments will be philosophic in nature. Is there more than economics for a shareholder value maximising firm? Actually there is not. Alternatively they get carried away with accounting arguments. What are the costs (accounting, funding, etc) to the plan sponsor of implementing a liability hedging strategy? What are the mismatch gains/costs (economic, accounting, funding, reputation, etc) to the plan sponsor of implementing such a strategy? Does it increase the value of the firm? Whatever is thrown up into the air has to pass the final test. None of these arguments will, unless we implicitly assume substantial market failure, ie, investors are blinded by accounting numbers.

After a spurious trade-off has been constructed, the traditional approach attempts to back out the plan sponsors risk aversion to determine the best, ie, utility optimising solution. We can surely find an allocation that reduces total company risk (volatility of free cash flow, cash flow at risk or any other corporate risk metrics) by diversifying away from its core business. But what does this mean to the shareholder? Let us take an airline company that is looking for an optimal asset allocation for its pension fund. The director working for the CFO argues that in deriving an optimal allocation for the pension fund, the asset manager presenting his ALM proposal should have focused on asset classes that are uncorrelated to the cyclical return of its core business. Cash flow volatility could have been reduced by diversification. Not only is it next to trivial that an airline company is undiversified and carries too much airline risk. After all it is meant to do so. It is not a global equity fund. However from the shareholders point of view, airline risk is diversifiable risk (at least from the point of view of a well diversified shareholder). Replacing this risk with undiversifiable market risk that is largely uncorrelated to the airline business, but quite correlated with the remaining wealth of diversified shareholders, does not seem a cunning plan.

All it achieves is to make the airline company more risky than before, requiring a higher discount rate. The net effect on corporate value is zero in a world without liquidity and bankruptcy costs and negative in a world with these costs. Despite the Modigliani-Miller irrelevancy principle, the typical actuarial argument has been in the past that equities will outperform bonds in the long term almost certainly, so that high equity allocations make pension promises (priced from bonds) cheaper to finance. More generally, investors still perform some kind of surplus optimisation trading off average pension fund contributions against contribution risk (risk of unexpected large contributions). While it is certainly true that average contribution falls with an increase in equity allocation, contribution risk increases. But this does not make it a trade off in the eyes of shareholders. Companies are not quasi individuals so firms do not buy Big Macs. The Modigliani-Miller arguments (that one presumes should be known to everyone working in finance) made it clear half a century ago, that managing a company in the interest of its shareholders does not include utility optimisation on their behalf. Utility optimisation is what individuals do best on their own. This book does not intend to demean equity investments. Its purpose is to redirect equity investments from company pension plans where they destroy shareholder value to portfolios of individual end investors.

Finally note that any deviation from the liability mimicking asset will create exposure to capital market risks. Consultants, investment banks and asset managers like to ask: how much duration mismatch is too much duration mismatch, how much credit is too much credit or how much equity is too much equity? The answer from reading this book will be simple: any, or as the Harvard business review put it :

> "Any deviation from a risk-neutral investment strategy represents a decision by management to enter into a separate, non-operating line of business – namely, investment speculation".[4]

Corporate value-at-risk should not be allocated to the pension fund. Instead it best remains within the plan sponsors core business, where it can increase corporate value. After all an investment in equities, diversified across regions and sectors, possibly with an add on in emerging markets is hardly core business for a car manufacturer. All these thoughts are organised in the following way.

Chapter 1 starts with a review of actuarial techniques to evaluate the value of pension liabilities; this chapter demystifies actuarial mathematics and serves as a starting point for later chapters. It will explain and address the main shortcomings of actuarial valuation: focus on real world instead of risk neutral distributions, smoothing and failure to account for contingent claims.

In contrast to this Chapter 2 introduces the financial economist's approach where market prices (prices of traded assets) reflect the best possible guess of economic value. This guess does not need an adjustment for the long run. To say that millions of market participants got it wrong and that the valuing actuary has a better insight into long term valuation is not only arrogant and will on average lead to valuation errors, but it will also yield to differing valuation depending on the actuaries involved. Market-based valuations, on the contrary, do not require subjective inputs as they can be derived from a pricing framework that is independent from the estimation of risk premia.

As valuation and hedging are essentially two sides of the same coin, Chapter 3 introduces the idea of replication to find a liability mimicking asset. The best way to hedge liability cash flows is to use the replicating assets. However this is sometimes not desired or feasible. The techniques in this chapter will show the best possible hedge, knowing that real-life replication is often imperfect and involves the hedging of interest rate and inflation exposures. It discusses the application of various derivative strategies including inflation derivatives to hedge liability risks.

Chapter 4 deals with asset-liability management as it is taught in asset-management classes. More precisely, it defines asset-liability management as the derivation of optimal asset-allocation policies relative to a set of exogenously defined liabilities that rely on risk premiums and risk preferences trading off expected surplus risk and surplus return. It will also explain why this asset management centric thinking is likely to fail in the real world.

The alternative framework is offered by corporate finance theory in Chapter 5. The impact of asset allocation decisions on debt capacity, taxation, liquidity costs is simply neglected in conventional asset liability analysis. Strange enough corporate leaders routinely underline the importance to invest into a companies core competences, while at the same time their pension funds seem to hold diversified global investment portfolios. This chapter demonstrates that the optimal asset allocation for externally financed pension obligations can not be answered by looking at the pension fund in isolation.

We finish with a critical view on external funding in Chapter 6. It shows that funding affects other debt like claims by shifting seniority towards pension beneficiaries. This is in stark contrast to the rating agencies that ignore the seniority shift, as they do not take into account the value of contingent claims that arise from outside funding.

1   Deutsche Bank, Global Markets Research, 11th February, 2005.
2   All views expressed in this book are solely the author's.
3   Brendan Naton in IPE, p 7, February 2005.
4   Harvard Business Review, June 2003, *"Pension Roulette: Have you bet too much on equities?"*

Actuarial Foundations

Actuaries are "mathematicians that take a bomb onto an airplane as the probability that there are two bombs in the plane is virtually zero". While this is certainly an unfair description of a highly skilful profession it makes the point that actuarial thinking has in the past been both too mechanic and too isolated from Nobel-winning financial economics. This chapter will review actuarial techniques to evaluate the value of pension liabilities. It serves as a starting point for later chapters and hopefully demystifies actuarial mathematics. The actuarial model generally calculates the expected present value (PV) of uncertain cashflows (C_{t_i}) from

$$E(PV) = \sum_i prob\left(C_{t_i}\right) \cdot C_{t_i} \cdot d_{t_i} \tag{1.1}$$

where d_{t_i} reflects the discount factor for the i-th payment and $prob$ (C_{t_i}) denotes its probability. This chapter will deal with each single element (mortality, benefit function and discount rate) and the differences between the actuarial approach and the financial economist.

MORTALITY TABLES

Corporate pension plans often specify death, disability and retirement benefits. In order to calculate the timing of expected cashflows we need to estimate the probability of each event occurring. Suppose we focus on death and retirement benefits only (simple decrement as opposed to multiple decrement, where plan members leave, say, or become disabled).[1] What we need to know is the probability that an individual plan member will die in any given year, which essentially is the distribution of the future lifetime. This information is summarised in a life table. A life table is essentially a table of one-year death probabilities q_x, where x denotes the current age of a male person. An example is provided in Tables 1 and 2. Here $q_{20} = 0.091\%$ means that the risk that a 20-year-old will die in this year is 0.091%. Interestingly enough, this probability is higher than for (on average more mature) 25-year-old men, which indicates that 20-year-olds engage in some silly risk taking. It is probably more optimistic to define the probability of not dying between your 20th and 21st birthdays, which is $p_x = 1 - q_x$ or 99.909%. Note that p_x is equivalent $_1p_x$ (probability that an x year old will live for another year), while $_0p_x$ stands for the probability that a life aged x will live up to age x, which obviously is 1.

How likely is it that a 20-year-old will become 40? Generally, actuaries write $_np_x$ for the probability that a (male) life aged x will live for another n years. We can also express this by the probability that a 20-year-old will become 21 times the probability that a 21-year-old will become 22 times ... times the probability that a 39 year old will become 40.

$$
\begin{aligned}
_np_x &= \prod_{i=0}^{n-1} p_{x+i} \\
&= p_x \cdot p_{x+1} \cdot p_{x+2} \cdot \ldots \cdot p_{x+(n-1)} \\
&= 0.99909 \cdot 0.99914 \cdot 0.99918 \cdot \ldots \cdot 0.99868 \\
&= 0.983288
\end{aligned}
\tag{1.2}
$$

How likely is it that a life aged 30 will become 40? As this is just a variation of the above example, we need to calculate $_{10}p_{30}$, which is 0.990704. Why is $_{10}p_{30} > {_{20}p_{20}}$? Simply because a 30-year-old has already survived the years between 20 and 30. The probability of becoming (at least) 40 after you have already become 30 is a conditional probability (conditional on survival).

How likely is it that a life aged x will survive the next s_1 years and subsequently die within the following s_2 years?

$$
_{s_1|s_2}q_x = {_{s_1}p_x} \cdot {_{s_2}q_{x+s_1}} = {_{s_1+s_2}q_x} - {_{s_1}q_x}
\tag{1.3}
$$

Table 1 Mortality table for active (male) employees.
The first column labelled by x denotes the age of the average male
employee. The male probability of dying at a given age x is given by
q_x while the corresponding female probability is q_y. The probability
of dying as a married man can be read from $h(x)$, while the age of
the average remaining wife is $y(x)$

[x]	q_x	q_y	$h(x)$	$y(x)$
20	0.091%	0.025%	3.870%	21
21	0.086%	0.026%	7.420%	22
22	0.082%	0.026%	11.370%	23
23	0.078%	0.027%	15.760%	24
24	0.074%	0.027%	20.390%	25
25	0.071%	0.027%	25.070%	25
26	0.069%	0.027%	29.600%	26
27	0.067%	0.028%	33.810%	27
28	0.066%	0.028%	37.600%	27
29	0.067%	0.029%	41.010%	28
30	0.068%	0.030%	44.090%	29
31	0.071%	0.032%	46.860%	30
32	0.075%	0.035%	49.380%	31
33	0.079%	0.038%	51.670%	32
34	0.085%	0.042%	53.780%	33
35	0.092%	0.046%	55.730%	34
36	0.100%	0.049%	57.560%	35
37	0.110%	0.053%	59.300%	35
38	0.120%	0.057%	60.980%	36
39	0.132%	0.062%	62.590%	37
40	0.146%	0.068%	64.120%	38
41	0.161%	0.075%	65.600%	39
42	0.177%	0.083%	67.010%	40
43	0.196%	0.092%	68.350%	41
44	0.216%	0.102%	69.620%	42
45	0.238%	0.114%	70.840%	43
46	0.263%	0.125%	71.980%	44
47	0.290%	0.138%	73.060%	45
48	0.319%	0.152%	74.090%	46
49	0.350%	0.166%	75.090%	47
50	0.384%	0.182%	76.080%	48
51	0.420%	0.199%	77.080%	49
52	0.460%	0.217%	78.130%	50
53	0.504%	0.236%	79.200%	51
54	0.553%	0.258%	80.230%	52
55	0.608%	0.282%	81.180%	53
56	0.671%	0.306%	81.980%	54
57	0.742%	0.332%	82.580%	55
58	0.820%	0.362%	82.970%	55
59	0.906%	0.394%	83.180%	56
60	0.980%	0.430%	83.210%	57

Table 1 (continued)

x	q_x	q_y	h(x)	y(x)
61	1.058%	0.472%	83.110%	57
62	1.145%	0.519%	82.890%	58
63	1.240%	0.573%	82.570%	59
64	1.348%	0.636%	82.140%	60

Table 2 Mortality table for retired (male) employees.
The first column labelled by x denotes the age of the average male employee. The male probability of dying at a given age x is given by q_x while the corresponding female probability is q_y. The probability of dying as a married man can be read from h(x), while the age of the average remaining wife is y(x)

x	q_x	q_y	h(x)	y(x)
65	1.465%	0.709%	81.918%	61
66	1.628%	0.793%	81.696%	62
67	1.809%	0.890%	81.474%	63
68	2.008%	1.003%	81.252%	64
69	2.225%	1.132%	81.030%	65
70	2.460%	1.281%	80.808%	65
71	2.746%	1.469%	80.587%	66
72	3.058%	1.684%	80.365%	67
73	3.397%	1.931%	80.143%	68
74	3.765%	2.210%	79.921%	69
75	4.162%	2.524%	79.699%	70
76	4.597%	2.878%	79.477%	71
77	5.075%	3.276%	79.255%	72
78	5.596%	3.714%	79.033%	73
79	6.175%	4.196%	78.811%	73
80	6.827%	4.727%	78.589%	74
81	7.546%	5.304%	78.367%	75
82	8.334%	5.929%	78.145%	76
83	9.191%	6.607%	77.923%	77
84	10.113%	7.339%	77.702%	77
85	11.097%	8.127%	77.480%	78
86	12.009%	8.971%	77.258%	79
87	12.959%	9.881%	76.370%	79
88	13.956%	10.856%	75.120%	80
89	14.995%	11.900%	73.750%	80
90	16.089%	13.013%	72.230%	80
91	17.229%	14.205%	70.540%	81
92	18.421%	15.467%	68.670%	81
93	19.675%	16.813%	66.590%	82

Table 2 (continued)

x	q_x	q_y	$h(x)$	$y(x)$
94	20.993%	18.238%	64.320%	82
95	22.385%	19.754%	61.910%	82
96	23.853%	21.356%	59.410%	83
97	25.398%	23.043%	56.860%	83
98	27.013%	24.810%	54.310%	83
99	28.700%	26.654%	51.780%	83
100	30.457%	28.570%	49.260%	83
101	32.250%	30.527%	46.700%	83
102	34.105%	32.548%	44.100%	83
103	36.013%	34.626%	41.440%	83
104	37.968%	36.754%	38.690%	83
105	39.964%	38.924%	35.880%	83
106	41.993%	41.131%	32.990%	83
107	44.049%	43.366%	30.050%	83
108	46.125%	45.622%	27.040%	83
109	48.215%	47.893%	23.970%	83
110	50.499%	49.267%	20.830%	83
111	52.782%	50.642%	17.620%	83
112	55.066%	52.016%	14.320%	83
113	57.349%	53.390%	10.930%	83
114	59.633%	54.765%	7.470%	83
115	100.000%	100.000%	4.000%	83

If we assume $x = 20$, $s_1 = 10$, $s_2 = 10$ we get $_{s_1 | s_2} q_x = 0.923\%$ for our assumed life table. Note that obviously

$$_{s_1 + s_2} p_x = {_{s_1}} p_x \cdot {_{s_2}} p_{x+s_1} \tag{1.4}$$

What is the reader's expected (remaining) lifetime? The probability that a life aged x will live for exactly another i years is the probability of living up to age $x + i$ and then dying within this year: $_i p_x \cdot q_{x+i}$. The expected remaining lifetime amounts to

$$\sum_{i=1}^{\infty} i \cdot {_i} p_x \, {_i} q_{x+i} \tag{1.5}$$

For a currently 40-year-old we find this figure to be 38.35. This corresponds to a life expectancy of, on average, 78.35 years. The whole distribution is shown in Figure 1. Note that for practical as well as biological reasons there is not even the tiniest probability of living for ever (not even for Dorian Gray, as we know). Hence actuaries

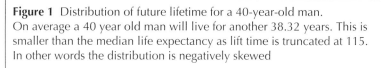

Figure 1 Distribution of future lifetime for a 40-year-old man. On average a 40 year old man will live for another 38.32 years. This is smaller than the median life expectancy as lift time is truncated at 115. In other words the distribution is negatively skewed

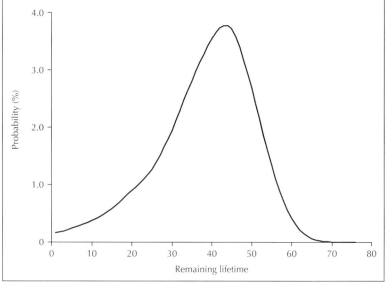

currently truncate death tables at $Z = 115$ (see Table 2). They also have separate tables for active lives and retirees. The tables 1 and 2 above assume a retiring age of $z = 65$.

How do we calculate probabilities for multiple (uncorrelated) lives? We assume 1,000 employees of age 40 (with equal health (that is, we can draw their death probabilities from the same life table). Apart from what happens in zombie movies, death is a binomial event (either you are or you are not dead). The probability of k deaths is then given by

$$\binom{1000}{k} q_{40} \left(1 - q_{40}\right)^{n-k} \tag{1.6}$$

For $k = 5$ we get 4.39%. The whole distribution is plotted in Figure 2. The expected number of deaths in the first year is given 1.46%.

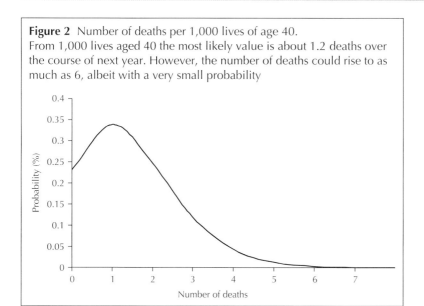

Figure 2 Number of deaths per 1,000 lives of age 40.
From 1,000 lives aged 40 the most likely value is about 1.2 deaths over the course of next year. However, the number of deaths could rise to as much as 6, albeit with a very small probability

So far we have been able to calculate the expected lifetime of male employees.

However pension benefits provided often also depend on the marital status, therefore also on the expected lifetime, of women. It is interesting to see that female mortality (q_y) is considerably lower at any age. For $y = 20$ it is 0.025%. Women simply live longer (on average). In case widows receive benefits from the pension plan of their diseased husbands, we also need the probability that a man of given age will be married in the year he dies. This probability is denoted by $h(x)$. The probability that a life aged 50 will have a surviving wife in case he dies is $h(50) = 76.08\%$. How old are the wives of 50-year-old men (on average)? We can again read this from Table 1. The respective number is given by $y(50) = 48$.

Finally, we can connect both lives. What is the probability that a man aged 65 dies when he is 70 and his wife lives for at least another 10 years? This is given by the probability of living up to 70, dying within this year, leaving a married wife and this wife (assuming how old wives of 70-year-old men typically are) surviving for at least another 10 years. In short

$$_sp_xq_{x+s}h(x+s)p_{y(x+s)} = {_5p_{65}}q_{70}h(70)\,_{10}p_{y(70)}$$
$$= 91.19\% \cdot 2.46\% \cdot 80.08\% \cdot 79.9\%$$
$$= 1.59\% \tag{1.7}$$

Note that this is not the probability for a corporate pension plan to provide pensions to a given married couple for at least 15 years. This probability would be higher, as the husband could well live another 15 years on his own.

So far we have familiarised ourselves with death probabilities. Actually, this is the only part of actuarial calculations that is unique to what has been called actuarial "science". Everything else is straightforward financial economics, as we will see throughout the book. Maybe not even that. For the financial economist mortality tables look strikingly similar to default tables, where a credit transitions through various states of the world. Both processes (mortality and default) have absorbing states (death or default), but people cannot become younger while credits can improve. Suppose we are interested in calculating survival probabilities for death benefits and hence are not interested whether an employee is at the retirement stage or not. In its simplest form we incorporate three states of the world. An employee aged x can survive with probability p_x, die married with a surviving wife with probability $(1-p_x)h(x)$, or die without a surviving wife $(1-p_x)(1-h(x))$. The survival and death probabilities for the associated spouse can be calculated accordingly. The final state is reached after the surviving wife passed away. In matrix form we can express this as Markov chain:

$$\mathbf{P}_x = \begin{pmatrix} p_x & (1-p_x)h(x) & (1-p_x)(1-h(x)) \\ 0 & p_{y(x)} & 1-p_{y(x)} \\ 0 & 0 & 1 \end{pmatrix} \tag{1.8}$$

Each entry exhibits the probability of transitioning from State 1 (row number) to State 2 (column number). Note that this is an inhomogeneous Markov chain, as the transition matrix depends on the age x. How do employees scatter across the states given a starting distribution of 1,000 living employees aged 40?

$$\begin{pmatrix} 0.9985 & 0.0009 & 0.0005 \\ 0 & 0.9993 & 0.00146 \\ 0 & 0 & 1 \end{pmatrix} \begin{pmatrix} 10000 \\ 0 \\ 0 \end{pmatrix} = \begin{pmatrix} 9985.42 \\ 9.35 \\ 5.23 \end{pmatrix} \quad \textbf{(1.9)}$$

From a cohort of 1000 lives aged 40, 9985 will remain alive, while about 15 will have passed away, of which 5 died without been married. The reader can extend the example above by providing a more elaborate chain, by allowing each age to be a separate transition state.

ACTUARIAL PENSION MATHEMATICS

Any pension claim can be written as the combination of two simple building blocks.[2] The blocks are pure endowments and (whole-) life insurance.

Whole-life insurance provides death cover for your whole life, that is to say the payment of the contractually agreed cover is made with certainty. What we do not know is when. Suppose the death cover agreed upon is 1 monetary unit. The expected payments for a life aged x can then be written as

$$\begin{aligned} A_x = {}& {}_0 p_x \cdot q_x \cdot d^1 \cdot 1 \\ & + {}_1 p_x \cdot q_{x+1} \cdot d^2 \cdot 1 \\ & + {}_2 p_x \cdot q_{x+2} \cdot d^3 \cdot 1 \\ & + \cdots \\ & + {}_{(Z-x)} p_x \cdot q_{x+(Z-x)} \cdot d^{(Z-x)} \cdot 1 \\ = {}& \sum_{i=0}^{(Z-x)} {}_i p_x \cdot q_{x+i} \cdot d^{i+1} \end{aligned} \quad \textbf{(1.10)}$$

Note that actuarial analysis applies a single flat (actuarial) interest rate. This rate is either constant (fixed by the regulator) for life insurance liabilities, or variable for corporate pension liabilities (under US GAAP, IFRS or FRS 17). More precisely $d = 1/(1 + s_{actuarial})$ pure endowments are paid conditional on survival at a prespecified point in time. Contrary to whole-life insurance, the payment date is known, but the payment is uncertain. Suppose an endowment of one monetary unit is paid at the end of s years. Its expected present value ${}_s p_x \cdot d^s \cdot 1$. A series of endowments (for the rest of your life) creates a life annuity.

$$\ddot{a}_x = \sum_{i=1}^{(Z-x)} {}_i p_x d^i \tag{1.11}$$

We can also defer a life annuity.

$$_s|\ddot{a}_x = d^s {}_s p_x \left(\sum_{i=1}^{(Z-x)-s} {}_i p_{x+s} d^i \right) = d^s \cdot {}_s p_x \cdot \ddot{a}_{x+s} \tag{1.12}$$

This is equivalent to a pension promise starting in s years, without death benefits. Hence without even realising we already calculated the (actuarial value) of a pension promise. All we need to now is to adjust s to reflect the time left to retirement, that is, set $s = z - x$.

How do we calculate the value of death benefits? After all, things look a bit more complicated as we also have to figure in the probability of leaving a surviving spouse. Essentially, we need to calculate the probability of dying in i years ahead with a wife still living, multiply this by the value of a life annuity for a women aged $y(x + i)$ that stretches out until $Z - y(x + i)$ and starts in year i and discount this back to reflect today's present value.

$$\sum_{i=0}^{(Z-1)} \underbrace{{}_i p_x \cdot q_{x+i} \cdot h(x+i)}_{\substack{\text{probability to die} \\ \text{with a surviving wife in year } i}} d^i \underbrace{\left(\sum_{j=0}^{Z-y(x+i)} {}_j p_{y(x+i)} d^j \right)}_{\substack{\text{life annuity for a widow} \\ \text{aged } y(x+i)}}$$

$$= \sum_{i=0}^{(Z-1)} {}_i p_x \cdot q_{x+i} \cdot h(x+i) d^i a_{y(x+i)} \tag{1.13}$$

So far we calculated the actuarial value of death and retirement benefits. Suppose we want to attribute the costs associated with a corporate pension plan to each single calendar year. These costs are called service costs (the costs associated with one year of service). Although there are many ways to spread the costs of pension benefits across years of service, I will focus on the projected unit credit method, since it is mandatory under most accounting regimes.[3] Under this method service costs are the present value of pension claims against the employer earned within a year of service. The benefit obligation for a particular date amounts to the present value of all pension claims earned by the employee up to that date. Suppose an employee of x is awarded a lifetime annuity, starting in $z - x$ years and paying one monetary unit for every year he survives. In that case, service costs are given by

$$SC_x = {}_{z-x|} a_x = {}_{z-x} p_x d^{z-x} a_z \tag{1.14}$$

If the whole annuity has been guaranteed in one year of service, the service costs associated with this particular year must reflect the full present value. In this scenario future service costs are zero. How will the present value of the employer's obligation evolve over time? We know that

$$BO_x =_{z-x|} a_x =_{z-x} p_x d^{z-x} a_z \qquad (1.15)$$

$$BO_{x+1} =_{(z-x)-1|} a_{x+1} =_{(z-x)-1} p_{x+1} d^{(z-x)-1} a_z \qquad (1.16)$$

Note that if we substitute $_{(z-x)-1} p_{x+1} \cdot p_x =_{(z-x)} p_x$ and $d^{(z-k)-1} d = d^{(z-k)}$ we get

$$BO_{x+1} = BO_x \frac{1}{p_x d} \qquad (1.17)$$

The benefit obligation grows with $d^{-1} = (1 + r)$, that is, with the actuarial rate as well as with the mortality adjustment p_x. Let us assume that only a fraction $1/(z - x_0)$ of a lifetime annuity is earned in the remaining $z - x_0$ years of service. Note that x_0 marks the year of pension plan entry. Service costs in any given year now become

$$SC_x =_{z-x|} a_x \frac{1}{z - x_0} =_{z-x} p_x d^{z-x} a_z \frac{1}{z - x_0} \qquad (1.18)$$

Applying the above generated logic we write

$$BO_x = \frac{1}{z - x_0} \left(SC_{x_0} \frac{1}{_{x-x_0} p_{x_0} d^{x-x_0}} \right.$$

$$+ SC_{x_0+1} \frac{1}{_{x-x_0-1} p_{x_0+1} d^{x-x_0-1}} + \cdots + SC_x \right)$$

$$= \frac{1}{z - x_0} \sum_{i=0}^{x-x_0} SC_{x_0+i} \frac{1}{_{x-x_0+i} p_{x_0+i} d^{x-x_0-i}}$$

$$= \frac{x - x_0}{z - x_0} {}_{z-x} p_x d^{z-x} a_z \qquad (1.19)$$

To check the above expression for a particular x we can write

$$BO_{x+1} = BO_x \frac{1}{p_x d} + SC_{x+1}$$

$$= \frac{x-x_0}{z-x_0} \, {}_{z-x}p_x d^{z-x} a_z \frac{1}{p_x d} + {}_{(z-x)-1}p_{x+1} d^{(z-x)-1} a_z \frac{1}{z-x_0}$$

$$= \frac{x-x_0}{z-x_0} \, {}_{z-x}p_x d^{z-x} a_z \frac{1}{p_x d} + {}_{(z-x)-1}p_{x+1} d^{(z-x)-1} a_z \frac{1}{z-x_0}$$

$$= \frac{x-x_0}{z-x_0} \, {}_{(z-x)-1}p_{x+1} d^{(z-x)-1} a_z p_x d \frac{1}{p_x d} + {}_{(z-x)-1}p_{x+1} d^{(z-x)-1}$$

$$a_z \frac{1}{z-x_0}$$

$$= \frac{(x+1)-x_0}{z-x_0} \, {}_{(z-x)-1}p_{x+1} d^{(z-x)-1} a_z \qquad (1.20)$$

The benefit obligation reflects accumulated service costs adjusted for survival and interest rate compounding (interest rate costs). So far we specified the simplest possible benefit function: a flat payment of $1/(z - x_0)$ monetary units for every period the employee is in service.

BENEFIT FUNCTION: FROM ACTUARIAL PRESENT VALUE TO EXPECTED CASHFLOWS

Formulas for calculating expected cashflows can become increasingly messy – particularly as we include multiple decrements or more complicated benefit functions. In the previous section, the benefit function was flat. However actuaries have been very creative in designing alternative benefit schemes. I will present two of the most common variations. Both are salary-related. The first benefit function arises from a so-called *final-salary* scheme. The liability payment in year t_i consist of a fraction (θ) of final salary $s(z)$ at retirement age z times years of service $z - x_0$, where x_0 denotes the year of pension plan entry.

$$l_{t_i} = s(z)\,\theta\,(z - x_0) \qquad (1.21)$$

Because (1.21) focuses only on last year's service it imposes large uncertainty on employees. All achievements during their career become largely irrelevant. It is the last year of service that counts. Therefore, final salary is sometimes replaced by an average of salaries prior to the retirement age.

$$\overline{s} = \frac{1}{n+1} \sum_{i=0}^{n} s(z-i) \tag{1.22}$$

The second benefit function focuses on *career average*. Each year of service leads to an increase of the benefit level depending on this year's salary (or more precisely pensionable income) as well as on a participation factor ϕ.

$$l_{t_i} = \sum_{j=0}^{z-x_0} s(x_0 + j)\phi \tag{1.23}$$

While these numbers are easy enough to calculate, we have to drop a couple of simplifying assumptions in (1.21) and (1.23). As death is random and can occur before z, we do not know in which year liability payments start. We therefore also don't know how many years of service take place before death occurs. Rather than try to work out the respective probabilities, I suggest following Monte Carlo simulation in order to calculate the distribution of expected cashflows. The beauty of Monte Carlo simulation is that it allows us to model arbitrarily complicated benefit functions and decrement tables without knowledge of actuarial mathematics at all. All we need to do is to express a given decrement table as a transition graph and simulate from it. Figure 3 shows the transition graph for a simple decrement table.

To illustrate previous figures I will take you through one particular sample path. The path is purely illustrative.

1. Each period we draw a random number ϕ from a uniform distribution (θ takes on values between 0 and 1 with equal probability). As long as $\theta < p_x = 1 - q_x$ our active employee (initially aged 30) survives for another period. Next period we compare a new draw of θ with p_{x+1} and decide whether the employee continues to live in our model.
2. Suppose that an employee dies at $x = 59$, that is, $p_x < \theta$ for the first time. We now need to simulate his marital status. Again we draw a uniform random number ζ and compare it with $h(x)$, which is 0.83 – that is to say there is an 83% probability that an active employee aged 59 is married in his year of death. If $\zeta < h(x)$, we conclude he is married (in this particular sample path of his life).
3. In this case he leaves on average a 56-year-old wife, who is entitled to a fraction (say 50%) of his retirement benefits earned up

Figure 3 Transition graph for active male employee (simple decrement table)
For each arrow we can specify the respective probability of transition from one state to another. The probability of remaining an active employee equals the probability of not dying. If death occurs, the male employee either dies unmarried or leaves a wife who continues to collect benefits. The retirement branch is connected by a dotted line, as this path is drawn (with probability one) only if the employee arrives at retirement age

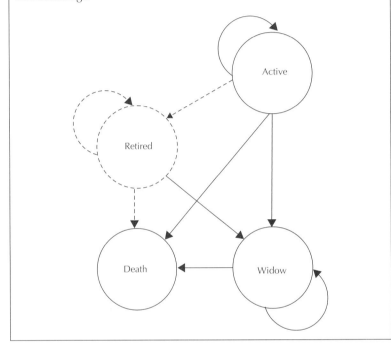

to then. The employee concluded 28 years of service. Each year secured an annual payment of €1,000. This totals €28,000 retirement benefits, from which his widow is entitled to collect 50%, or €14,000, for each year she continues to live. We continue to simulate the widow's life. Again, we draw uniform random numbers and compare them with p_y where $y = h(x)$ in the first year. If the widow dies when she is 69 ($\theta > p_{y\,=\,59}$) all payments stop.

Performing this exercise 10,000 times – in other words, simulating a representative life 10,000 times – yields Figures 4 and 5. As death benefits we assumed that the surviving wife is entitled to 50% of

Figure 4 Expected cashflows for 30-year-old male (with death and retirement benefits).
While annual payments for retired workers amount to €30,000, the expected payouts in every period are considerably less as employees die on their way to retirement. After 30 years we see a massive jump in liability payments due to retirement at 60

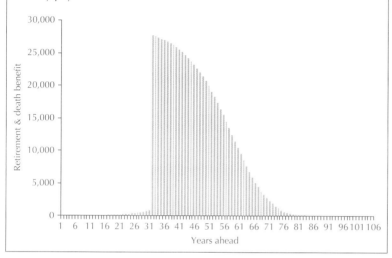

Figure 5 Expected cashflows for 30-year-old male (without death benefits). Without retirement benefits paid to surviving wives, liability duration is considerably lower

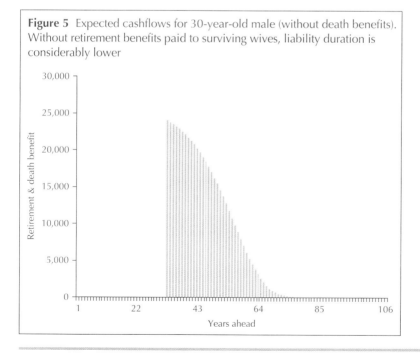

accumulated pension claims. In Figure 4 we see expected cashflows $\left(l_{t_1}, l_{t_2}, \ldots, l_{t_n}\right)$ with death benefit.

While retirement starts in 30 years' time, some employees die earlier. In this case pension payments also start earlier. In most of the paths our representative employee retires as a 60-year-old. However, as he died before retirement in some paths, the expected payment at retirement age is less than €30,000 (30 years of service with a fixed benefit of €1,000 each). Furthermore cashflows stretch out much further than without death benefits in Figure 5. This is because surviving widows are on average younger and live longer than their diseased partners.

ACTUARY VERSUS FINANCIAL ECONOMIST: WHAT DISCOUNT RATES SHOULD WE USE?

The problem with pension mathematics is threefold. *First*, actuarial pension mathematics assumes flat yield curves, ie, discount rates do not change with maturity. This allows the convenient use of tabulated commutation functions as they can be found in actuarial textbooks. However this is comes at a price. It is inconsistent with observed market prices. Yield curves are in general not flat and they change shape as well a level all the time. At a bare minimum it is required to use $d(0, t_i) = \left(\frac{1}{1 + s_{t_i}}\right)^{t_i}$ instead of $d_i = \left(\frac{1}{1 + s_{actuarial}}\right)^{t_i}$ in (1.23). A valuation technology that uses different discount rates for the same cash flows, dependent on whether they are labelled assets or liabilities is inconsistent and ultimately flawed. We will deal with non flat yield curves in the first section of Chapter 2.

While it is straightforward to fix the first problem a second more conceptional problem exists. Suppose we analyse a fully funded (assets equal liabilities at market value) pension plan. Actuarial analysis would not be able to calculate the value of the pension funds conditional claim against the assets of the plan sponsor. The risk that plan assets fall below pension liabilities (for example due to changes in interest rates) represents a contingent liability. The likelihood of this to happen depends on the asset liability relative risk. A 100% funded plan that is invested into matching fixed income is obviously the least risky investment in terms of conditional liabilities, while an investment into 100% cash would indeed expose the plan sponsor to much more risk. How much this risk is worth in terms of how much would it cost to insure against it, can only be answered within a financial economics framework. The *third* problem that arises with actuarial discounting is the treatment of credit risk in the calculation of pension liabilities. Suppose an actuary dropped the assumption of flat yield curves and employs instead

$$l = \sum_i prob\left(C_{t_i}\right) \cdot C_{t_i} \cdot d^{Credit}\left(0, t_i\right) \qquad (1.24)$$

where $d^{Credit}(0, t_i)$ denotes the appropriate discount factor that fully reflects the credit risk inherent in any given pension plan. But where does he find this discount factor from and how could he possibly know it is correct? The financial economist would model all conditional cash flows under the risk neutral distribution and discount them at the risk free rate. He would for example model the possibility that the plan sponsor defaults at the same time than the pension fund is not sufficiently funded allowing for the exact split of claims between the pension claimants and other holders of corporate debt on the plan sponsors assets. This will directly price l. After the liability value has been established we can indirectly infer $d^{Impl}(0, t_i)$ from (1.24). The actuarial approach is different. An actuary would start with an estimate of the implied credit risk for a given liability cash flows. Suppose he ranks a credit as single A plus. He would then ask how the market prices other A+ credits and discount the promised cash flows at $d^{A+}(0, t_i)$ ignoring all conditional payments. The actuarial way will only by accident be correct. In general we will find, that

$$d^{Credit}\left(0, t_i\right) \neq d^{Impl}\left(0, t_i\right) \qquad (1.25)$$

The key difference between actuaries and financial economists is the pricing of conditional cash flows. Financial economists apply Nobel-price winning option pricing technology, that is they calculate the value of contingent claims (like the corporate guarantee to fill pension fund gaps, the pension guarantee by the pension benefit guarantee company, the plan sponsors default put, ...) under the risk neutral distribution. Actuaries instead use a discounting framework, where they have to supply the appropriate risk premium, ie, they work with the real probability distribution. This makes their work subjective and generally not arbitrage free. The last line of actuarial defence is that we can not apply contingent claim analysis as markets are not complete. What is meant by that is that we can neither readily buy and sell pension liabilities nor perfectly replicate cash flows. They are an untraded asset. Not only does this seem like a very purist shift to financial economics, it also offers no alternative. Actuarial discounting as such can not even help us at pricing traded assets. It remains therefore unclear why we should rely on it, when it comes to pricing untraded assets. If markets are incomplete we need to default to utility based pricing, with all its arbitrariness and the ultimate challenge: whose utility function do we take?

PRICING AND HEDGING OF ACTUARIAL RISK

We start with providing two examples of how actuarial risk enters corporate pension plans. Essentially, retirement benefits within a defined benefit plan equals a survivor bond. Survivor bonds continue to pay coupons as long as an individual is alive. While the coupon (c) is fixed, its maturity is not. We assume as a starting point that the issuer of a survivor bond requires no risk premium for taking on mortality risk. The price for this bond will equate the survival probability weighted cashflows discounted at the relevant yields for the respective horizon date.

$$P = \sum_{i=1}^{Z} c \cdot {}_i p_x \cdot d\left(0, t_{x+i}\right) \tag{1.26}$$

If the government were to issue this type of bond, where the actual coupon paid varies with the number of survivors, this could help reduce the problem of hedging longevity risk. However, the government faces similar risks in the first pillar of pension finance and is unlikely to double its bets. If every plan member dies exactly in line with the respective mortality table, cashflows can be replicated by buying an ordinary bond with coupon $\bar{c} = {}_i p_x \cdot c$. A variation of this theme is a defined benefit plan, where each plan member is promised to receive at least his nominal contributions in the year he finally dies. What is the value of this guarantee? How does it depend on the chosen asset allocation? Intuitively we can price this guarantee as a portfolio of put options, where option maturities correspond with all possible years of death, while weights are given by the probabilities of dying within each specific year. We assume a defined contribution plan for 100 active employees aged 40. The plan invests into an asset allocation with volatility $\sigma = 20\%$.

Interest rates are given by $r = 2\%$. At retirement age $z = 65$ the guarantee ends. As the perfect hedge (ignoring actuarial risk) for this guarantee is provided by a portfolio of put options we can calculate its value from

$$\sum_{i=1}^{z-x} {}_iP_x q_{x+i} P_{B\&S}\left(\sigma, r, X, i\right) = \sum_{i=1}^{65-40} {}_iP_x q_{x+i} P_{B\&S}\left(\sigma = 20\%,\right.$$
$$r = 2\%, X = 1, i\left.\right)$$
$$= 99.85\% \cdot 0.15\% \cdot 6.94 + \cdots$$
$$+ 98.54\% \cdot 1.64\% \cdot 14.33$$
$$= 2.09$$

$$(1.27)$$

A replicating portfolio for the nominal contribution guarantee conditional upon death would cost 2.09% for the contribution of a life aged 40. Apart from mortality, we find that volatility, as well as interest rates, has an impact on the value of this guarantee. Interestingly the value of this guarantee decreases if employees live longer than life tables predict. Trivially living longer means dying later. However as the value of short dated puts is higher than the value of long dated puts, total value decreases as more weight (probability) is given to longer dated puts. Products of this kind might hence serve as a hedge against (systemic) longevity risk. The impact of volatility is given in Table 3.

For risky allocations, the value of the implicitly provided guarantee is well above 1%. So far we did not conceptualise that the number of actual deaths differs from the planned numbers.

What if employees do not die according to plan? We can visualise actuarial risk inherent in defined benefit and defined contribution plans (with contribution guarantee upon death) by simulating the difference between the expected and realised number of deaths within pension plans of different size (number of plan members).

Suppose we look at the pension plans of three companies that differ in size. The smallest company has 10 employees aged 40, while the two larger companies employ 100 and 1,000 employees of this

Table 3 Asset allocation risk and conditional contribution guarantee
As volatility falls so does the required insurance premium

Volatility	20%	18%	16%	14%	12%	10%	8%	6%	4%
Premium	2.09	1.76	1.44	1.12	0.82	0.54	0.30	0.12	0.02

Figure 6 Actuarial risks.
It is expected that 85% of current employees aged 40 will reach the retirement age of 65. The uncertainty around this fraction depends on the number of employees. Assuming that individual mortality is uncorrelated among employees (independent draw), the uncertainty around the expected percentage decreases with the number of employees (number of independent draws)

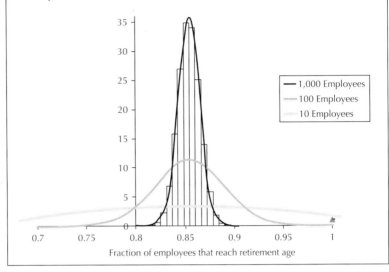

Fraction of employees that reach retirement age

age. The probability that a 40-year-old will reach retirement is about 85%. The distribution of the actual number of employees dying between 40 and 65 is summarised in Figure 6. Clearly, the estimation error becomes small for a large number of homogeneous employees. This is simply the law of large numbers, but what do we mean by homogeneous? Even if the number of employees were large, but they dramatically differed in rewarded benefits, this could well undermine the law of large numbers above, meaning that the uncertainty about the death of the 40-year-old CIO is likely to have a 20-times-higher impact than for someone working on the assembly line.

How should actuarial risks be priced? Can we discount cash-flows subject to actuarial (mortality) risks by applying a risk-free rate, or do we need to build in a risk premium as we would require in the case of credit risks? We start with the observation that economy-wide risks are generally orthogonal to mortality risks (with the exception of war, major diseases killing half of the population, and so on). Virtually all asset-pricing frameworks in financial economics relate the pricing of risks to the covariation with systematic risk factors that cannot be diversified away. The most popular model still is the capital asset pricing model (CAPM) given below:

$$E\left(r_i\right)-r_f = \frac{\text{cov}(r_i,r_m)}{\text{var}(r_m)}\left(E\left(r_m\right)-r_f\right) \tag{1.28}$$

The expected risk premium required for a given asset i denoted by $E(r_i) - r_f$ depends positively on both the covariation of type-i returns with market-wide returns (given by $\text{cov}(r_i, r_m)/\text{var}(r_m)$) and the risk premium for taking on economy-wide risk in general (denoted by $E(r_m) - r_f$). Risks that show no covariation with market risks, ie, $\text{cov}(r_i, r_m) = 0$, require no risk premium above the risk-free rate. Investors cannot require a risk premium for risks that can be diversified away. While the CAPM is essentially a one-period model, there is no limit on the length of this period. In other words: 10-year zero bonds are the zero beta asset if the time horizon is 10 years. If long-term actuarial risks are uncorrelated with market risks, we can simply discount them with the appropriate (equivalent maturity) risk-free rate. However, it is one thing to state that actuarial risks are uncorrelated with market factors and should hence require no risk premium, but what happens to these risks? Even if risks are orthogonal to market risks this does not mean that we can necessarily ignore them. The question we need to ask is whether actuarial risks require a capital reserve? To put it differently: under what circumstances can actuarial risks be completely diversified? We need to distinguish between individual mortality risk (risk that an *individual* plan member dies sooner or later than expected) and collective mortality risk (risk that *all* plan members live longer or shorter than expected). The first risk can be diversified away among many homogeneous plan members. However, for small inhomogeneous pension plans, retirement plans might well expose these firms to large risks that have nothing to do with its core business. In this case diversification among a large pool of pension claimants (self-insurance) does not work. Plan sponsors should in this instance reinsure actuarial risks as they otherwise need to build a capital buffer (risk capital) to deal with unexpectedly large pension claims. This risk capital, however, cannot be used in the plan sponsor's core business. As long as the required insurance premium is fair (equals expected claims) it is value-detracting not to reinsure actuarial risks. Systemic risk, on the other hand, cannot be diversified away by pooling a large number of contracts. The most obvious risk of these systematic risks is longevity risk. It is largely uncorrelated with capital market risk (apart from pharmaceutical companies, which benefit from rising treatment costs and increased numbers of prescriptions), but affects all pension claimants at the same time and can have substantial impact on liability calculations. As it cannot be diversified and its impact is severe, corporations need to hold risk capital, which in turn would crowd out positive-NPV (net present value) projects. Corporations should always hedge out actuarial risks in case they are substantial and cannot be diversified away. The corporate finance rationale for this is well studied and can range from risk shifting to a reduction of agency costs (see Mayers and Smith, 1982) as well as lowered costs of financial distress (see MacMinn and Han, 1990). This is more or less obvious in case the insurance premium is fair and risk can be swapped at its expected value. Reducing excess volatility will increase corporate value as it lessens the option-like claims of corporate outsiders (tax option, distress costs) as well as reducing liquidity costs. While this is obvious, the question remains what to do if insurance is unfairly priced? Even in this case it has been shown that insurance demand has a strategic effect on the product market. Insurance makes firms more aggressive due to limited risk costs and moves it into the "as if Stackelberg leader" position.[4] The indirect gains in the product market compensate the direct insurance costs.

A TYPICAL PENSION PLAN

I will conclude this chapter with a typical pension plan for a DAX 30 corporate. Projected cashflows (normalised to a first payment of one monetary unit) up to the next 50 years are given in Figure 7.

The shape reminds one of a smoothed version of Figures 4 and 5. The worrying detail in Figure 7 is the massive cashflow difference between the standard actuarial life tables (official tables that are well known to overstate mortality) and proprietary mortality tables used by insurance companies that have been much quicker in picking up the trend in increasing life expectancy. Even though companies are forced to report pension liabilities under standard

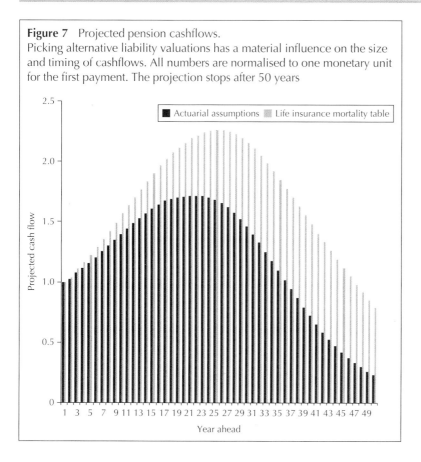

Figure 7   Projected pension cashflows.
Picking alternative liability valuations has a material influence on the size and timing of cashflows. All numbers are normalised to one monetary unit for the first payment. The projection stops after 50 years

actuarial assumptions, it seems very critical to hide these differences from investors. To put a perspective on the size of hidden debt, we calculate the present value of both cashflow streams. At a 3.5% discount rate standard mortality tables yield a liability valuation of 30.17. More realistic mortality assumptions, however, arrive at a valuation of 39.29. There is a valuation gap of 30.23% hidden to investors. Suppose a company runs a pension plan valued at 6 billion under standard acturarial tables. This could overstate the value of equity by 1.8 billion and disguise 1.8 billion of debt. To the extent a company knows the true values, this is a serious breach of investors trust, possibly more.

What other consequences arise from the use of different mortality tables? Expected liability cashflows will not only be higher at

Table 4 Liability sensitivities.
An increase in real interest rates leads to a 15.3% fall the present value of liability cashflows for standard actuarial calculations, while the liability falls by 17.5% for the more up-to-date mortality tables. The difference in inflation sensitivity (inflation duration) is much less pronounced

	Inflation duration	Real rate duration
Actuarial mortality	−5.83	−15.29
Life insurance mortality	−5.87	−17.49

every maturity, but also stretch out far longer. This will increase both duration and convexity of liability cashflows.

If duration hedging activities were based on numbers in Table 4, investors are likely to underhedge their true economic exposure as the expected increases in life expectancy should already change current valuations. Pension plans that seem to be funded on the basis of accounting figures carry in reality an economic deficit. In Germany this applies to most pension plans. We see that pension liabilities are not transparent to outside investors. Note, however, that external funding will not increase transparency. The above valuation problem will remain.

SUMMARY

This chapter has shown that pension liabilities can be regarded as a series of future cashflows. At the same time I have sketched the deficits in actuarial valuation. The use of flat discount rates that adjust for neither maturity nor credit risk will result in valuations inconsistent with market prices. Additionally, corporate guarantees cannot be priced within a framework of fixed discount factors. We will see in Chapters 2, 5 and 6 how important contingent claims analysis will become in a corporate finance rather than an actuarial context. The next chapter will introduce modern valuation principles and apply them to pension liabilities.

1   We ignored the probability of becoming disabled because it would not increase the insight into actuarial calculations, while at the same time increasing the complexity of the covered material. The objective of this section is to get an intuitive understanding of what is maybe unique to actuarial mathematics.

2   This section follows Kussmaul and Schwinger (2003). A very good treatment of actuarial mathematics is Gerber (1997).
3   Winklevoss (1977) provides a very good overview about traditional actuarial pension mathematics.
4   On the strategic aspects of insurance demand see Seog (2004).

REFERENCES

Gerber, H., 1997, *Life Insurance Mathematics*, 3rd edn (Zurich: Springer).

Kussmaul, A. and R. Schwinger, 2003, "Pension Mathematics in Actuarial Science", in B. Scherer, *Asset and Liability Management Tools* (London: Risk Books).

MacMinn, R. and L. Han, 1990, "Limited Liability Corporate Value and the Demand for Liability Insurance", *Journal of Risk and Insurance,* **57**, pp 581–607.

Mayers, D. and C. Smith, 1982, "On the Corporate Demand for Insurance", *Journal of Business,* **52**, pp 281–96.

Seog, H., 2004, "Strategic Demand for Insurance", Working Paper, Graduate School of Management, Seoul.

Winklevoss, H., 1977, *Pension Mathematics with Numerical Illustrations*, 2nd edn, (Pennsylvania: University of Pennsylvania Press).

2

Valuation of Pension Claims

In this chapter, I will introduce the reader to key valuation principles in financial economics as they apply to pension liabilities. The basic idea is simple. Each time we need to price a given set of (liability) cashflows, we do not need to begin with a complicated valuation exercise from scratch, again and again. All we need to do is to price these cashflows from existing fixed-income securities. Market prices (prices of traded assets) reflect the best possible guess of economic value. This guess does not need an adjustment for the long run. To say that millions of market participants got it wrong and that the valuing actuary has a better insight into long-term valuation not only is arrogant and will on average lead to valuation errors, but it will also yield to differing valuations depending on the actuaries involved. Market-based valuations on the contrary do not require subjective inputs, since they can be derived from a pricing framework that is independent of the estimation of risk premiums.

Note that actuarial techniques that use a flat yield curve (discount rate does not change with maturity) are in general not consistent with observed market prices. Yield curves are in general not flat and they change shape as well as level all the time. The application of tabulated commutation functions as they can be found in actuarial textbooks is seriously flawed. It must be quite interesting for students to visit a financial engineering class after they have attended a lecture in pension mathematics. If actuarial discounting cannot help us at pricing even traded assets, it is not clear why we should rely on it, when it comes to pricing untraded assets. This becomes obvious when we think about assessing the potential market price for a takeover candidate with substantial pension liabilities. No reasonable corporate bidder would rely on actuarial values. Interestingly enough, the most oft-heard criticism against market valuation (or market-value-oriented accounting such as IFRS) is that valuations based on traded securities are too volatile. Actuarial valuations in contrast exhibit less volatility – mostly because actuaries don't like volatility themselves and regard a large change in valuation one year down the road as evidence that last year's valuation has been wrong. Economists don't have these fears. After all, the world is how it is. If interest rates fall and bond prices rise, it is not understandable that liability values remain largely unaffected. This would also mean that the same cashflows get different values assigned, depending on whether they are corporate liabilities or trade bonds. To refuse to look out of the window does not change the weather. Plans' sponsors need to decide whether they prefer valuations to be volatile, or always wrong.

DETERMINISTIC DISCOUNT FACTORS

The previous chapter has shown that a corporate pension promise can be summarised as a series of future cashflows. We can therefore calculate the market value of pension liabilities by discounting each cashflow with an appropriate discount rate that reflects both maturity and credit risk. There is no difference from valuing other forms of corporate debt. The relevant valuation tools are readily available from the financial analysts toolbox.

Suppose discrete liability cashflows $l_{t_1}, l_{t_2}, \ldots, l_{t_n}$ occur at times $t_1, t_2, \ldots, t_n$. The present value of pension liabilities (l) is given by

$$l = d(0, t_1) l_{t_1} + d(0, t_2) l_{t_2} + \cdots + d(0, t_n) l_{t_n} \qquad (2.1)$$

where $d(0, t_n) = (1 + s_{t_n})^{-t_n}$ denotes the discount factor (between zero and one) for maturity t_n, and s_{t_n} reflects the corresponding yield on a zero coupon bond. For example if $s_{t_n} = 0.05$ and $t_n = 30$ we need to multiply any payment in 30 years by 0.23. But where do we get the unobservable discount factors from? Suppose we are given AA swap rates from the market as provided in Table 2. For illustrative purposes as well as data availability we assume the credit risk of a given pension promise is equivalent to credit risk captured in AA swap rates.

While there are many procedures to extract discount rates (zero coupon bonds) from a given coupon structure, we will focus on the Nelson–Siegel (1987) model of the yield curve, as it has many advantages over more complicated alternatives. For a start, it is a so-called parsimonious model, which means there are only a few parameters to estimate. Second, as it presumes a given functional form that guarantees smoothly behaved forward rates, we will avoid unreasonable spikes in the forward curve. The most signifi-cant advantage, however, is that many empirical studies suggest the superior performance of Nelson–Siegel relative to rival methods.[1] The model postulates that

$$s_n\left(\theta, t_n\right) = b_0 + b_1\left(\frac{1-e^{-t_n/\tau}}{t_n/\tau}\right) + b_2\left(\frac{1-e^{-t_n/\tau}}{t_n/\tau} - e^{-t_n/\tau}\right) \quad (2.2)$$

using four parameters $\theta = \{b_0, b_1, b_2, \tau\}$. Each parameter can also be given an intuitive meaning.

❑ The level of a given term structure (long-term interest rate) is captured in b_0. It is the only expression left for $t_n \to \infty$.
❑ For $t_n \to \infty$ the expression $\frac{1-e^{-t_n/\tau}}{t_n/\tau}$ converges to one. We can there-fore interpret b_1 as the term structure spread, while b_2 measures its curvature.

To see the mechanics in (2.2) we fit the Nelson–Siegel model to a particular dataset of zero bonds. In this case we need to minimise the squared difference between actual prices and model prices.

$$\min_{b_0, b_1, b_2, \tau} \sum_i \left(d_i - \sum_i \frac{1}{\left(b_0 + b_1\left(\frac{1-e^{-t_i/\tau}}{t_i/\tau}\right) + b_2\left(\frac{1-e^{-t_i/\tau}}{t_i/\tau} - e^{-t_i/\tau}\right)\right)^i}\right)^2 \quad (2.3)$$

where d_i is the market price of the i-th zero bond. Solving the above problem results in Figure 1 for discount factors and Figure 2 for yields. Table 1 summarises end values for that result from (2.3)

The interested reader can also try a more complex version of the above model, suggested by Svenson (1995).

$$s_n = b_0 + b_1\left(\frac{1-e^{-t_n/\tau}}{t_n/\tau}\right) + b_2\left(\frac{1-e^{-t_n/\tau}}{t_n/\tau} - e^{-t_n/\tau}\right) + b_3\left(\frac{1-e^{-t_n/\zeta}}{t_n/\zeta} - e^{-t_n/s}\right) \quad (2.4)$$

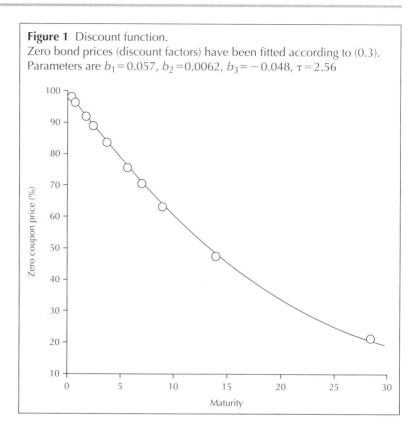

Figure 1 Discount function.
Zero bond prices (discount factors) have been fitted according to (0.3). Parameters are $b_1 = 0.057$, $b_2 = 0.0062$, $b_3 = -0.048$, $\tau = 2.56$

The above specification introduces a second inflection point (ζ) and a second curvature measure (b_3).

Above we fitted the Nelson–Siegel model to zero coupon yields. However, how do we proceed if we need to fit a zero coupon curve to coupon bond data. Fitting the Nelson–Siegel model to prices on coupon bearing bonds, we proceed as follows.

1. Begin with some starting values for b_0, b_1, b_2, τ.
2. Calculate the resulting spot rates and price all available coupon bonds (in the above example the price is 100 as swap rates are essentially par bond rates) from this spot curve.
3. Measure the squared difference between model prices and market prices for all bonds in your universe.
4. Repeat this procedure until the sum of squared differences becomes zero.

Figure 2 Fitted yields.
Market yields and model yields as provided by the best fitting
parameterisation of $s_n\left(\theta, t_n\right) = b_0 + b_1\left(\frac{1-e^{-t_n/\tau}}{t_n/\tau}\right) + b_2\left(\frac{1-e^{-t_n/\tau}}{t_n/\tau} - e^{-t_n/\tau}\right)$.
Parameters are $b_1 = 0.057$, $b_2 = 0.0062$, $b_3 = -0.048$, $\tau = 2.56$

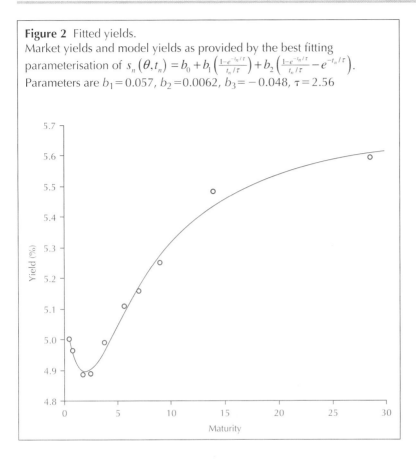

Table 1 Fitting process.
For each maturity, we have fitted a model price. Parameters θ
are varied until the sum of squared difference converges to a
minimum

t_i	$d(0, t_i)(\%)$	$\hat{d}(0, t_i)(\%)$	$[d(0, t_i) - \hat{d}(0, t_i)]^2$
0.455	97.81	97.79	1.0278E-08
0.789	96.25	96.25	1.8505E-11
1.789	91.82	91.81	1.1634E-08
2.496	88.77	88.75	6.1219E-08
3.751	83.31	83.39	5.7612E-07
5.666	75.41	75.47	3.3097E-07
7.003	70.32	70.22	8.9026E-07
9.005	63.07	62.91	2.6069E-06
14.008	47.34	47.59	6.1248E-06
28.515	21.19	21.08	1.2653E-06

Essentially, the problem becomes a variant of (2.3). This time, however, we need to distinguish between individual bonds $j = 1, ..., J$ and individual spot rates $i = 1, ..., I$. The new problem becomes

$$\min_{b_0, b_1, b_2, \tau} \sum_j \left(p_j - \sum_i \frac{c_{ij}}{\left(b_0 + b_1 \left(\frac{1 - e^{-t_i/\tau}}{t_i/\tau} \right) + b_2 \left(\frac{1 - e^{-t_i/\tau}}{t_i/\tau} - e^{-t_i/\tau} \right) \right)^i} \right)^2 \tag{2.5}$$

where p_j is the market price of the j-th coupon bond and c_{ij} is the respective cashflow for time t_i. The corresponding results are summarised in Table 2. A historical perspective on the level of yields as well as on yield changes can be found in Figure 3.

In contrast to the actuarial approach we are given a complete set of discount factors reaching over the whole possible life span of an individual, where $d(0, t_i) = \left(\frac{1}{1 + St_i} \right)^t$. Note that we can use the resulting discount factors to calculate forward discount factors.

$$d(t_{n-i}, t_n) = \frac{d(0, t_n)}{d(0, t_{n-i})} \tag{2.6}$$

The corresponding forward rate is then found by

$$f(t_{n-i}, t_n) = \left(\frac{1}{d(t_{n-i}, t_n)} \right)^{1/i} - 1 \tag{2.7}$$

The use of AA swap rates under accounting rules (US GAAP) should not be confused with economic realities. In principle we can evaluate pension liabilities by using an appropriate discount rate. If the pension promise is similar in seniority to a BBB bond we should use BBB discount rates to calculate the economic value of a pension promise. BBB discount curves can in turn be found from BBB corporate bonds.

However, it is often difficult to find the appropriate discount rate. For example, what is the value of pension liabilities of a single-A corporate sponsor that runs an overfunded pension plan, mainly invested into Indian private equity? While the rating of the sponsor company is only single A, the employees claim is overcollateralised. On the other hand, the collateral has a fairly low quality. How

Table 2 Swap data and discount factors.
Market swap rates are denoted by y_{swap}. The gaps in market rates are filled with fitted swap rates $\hat{y}_{swap}$. The corresponding discount factors and spot rates are given by $d(0, t_n)$ and s_n. The last column shows the evolution of term-structure-implied one-period forward rates. The forward rate that can be contracted today for investing in Period 2 for one year (that is, to Period 3) is $f(2, 3) = 3.17$

n	y_{swap}	$\hat{y}_{swap}$	$d(0, t_n)$	s_n	$f(t_{n-1}, t_n)$
1	2.26	2.20	0.98	2.20	–
2	2.46	2.47	0.95	2.47	2.74
3	2.66	2.69	0.92	2.70	3.17
4	2.85	2.89	0.89	2.91	3.53
5	3.03	3.06	0.86	3.09	3.82
6	3.19	3.22	0.83	3.25	4.05
7	3.34	3.35	0.79	3.39	4.25
8	3.47	3.46	0.76	3.52	4.41
9	3.59	3.56	0.73	3.63	4.54
10	3.69	3.65	0.69	3.73	4.65
11		3.73	0.66	3.82	4.75
12	3.83	3.80	0.63	3.91	4.82
13		3.87	0.60	3.98	4.89
14		3.92	0.57	4.05	4.94
15	4.00	3.98	0.55	4.11	4.99
16		4.02	0.52	4.17	5.03
17		4.06	0.50	4.22	5.07
18		4.10	0.47	4.27	5.10
19		4.14	0.45	4.32	5.12
20	4.2	4.17	0.43	4.36	5.15
21		4.20	0.41	4.40	5.17
22		4.22	0.39	4.43	5.19
23		4.25	0.37	4.47	5.21
24		4.27	0.35	4.50	5.23
25	4.28	4.29	0.33	4.53	5.25
26		4.31	0.31	4.56	5.26
27		4.33	0.30	4.58	5.28
28		4.34	0.28	4.61	5.29
29		4.36	0.27	4.63	5.31
30	4.31	4.37	0.26	4.65	5.33

should we proceed? The only way to calculate the fair value of pension liabilities in the above example is to evaluate all contingent claims under a risk-neutral distribution. This means to evaluate the sponsors ability to cover pension fund deficits in case the collateral fell by more than the overcollateralisation, figuring in the correlation

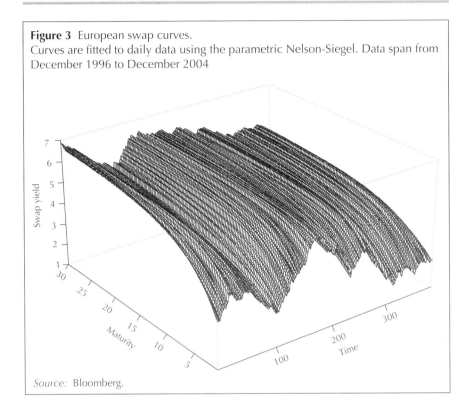

Figure 3 European swap curves.
Curves are fitted to daily data using the parametric Nelson-Siegel. Data span from
December 1996 to December 2004

Source: Bloomberg.

between pension assets and operative revenues. After we have
found the respective values we can work backwards to arrive at the
appropriate risk-adjusted discount rates. Guessing discount rates
will only accidentally yield correct answers. This is another important difference to the actuarial approach. We will elaborate on this
approach in Chapter 6.

INFLATION INDEXATION: REAL YIELD CURVE ESTIMATION

Suppose we are given a set of indexed, ie, real cashflows. Real cashflows need to be discounted at real rates. How can we derive prices
for real zero coupon bonds? Principally we can either strip out real
zero bond prices from inflation-linked government bonds or use the
inflation swap market. Let us start with the latter. The inflation
swap market is an over-the-counter (OTC) market that derives its
attractiveness from its flexibility. Swaps are customisable with
respect to the specification of the relevant inflation index as well as

maturity structure. There is liquidity up to 50 years (little liquidity above 40 years). However, liquidity is driven by the corporate bond market and there are not too many natural payers of inflation. Large transactions (>100 millions) are still best dealt with using only one counterparty (don't call everyone to announce that a deal is coming). The mid-offer price for a €30 million 20-year swap transaction is about 2 bps per annum in terms of yield. While inflation swaps come in many forms (zero coupon swaps, revenue inflation swap, year-on-year inflation swaps) we will focus on zero coupon inflation swaps. At maturity t_n the fixed-rate payer pays the fixed amount

$$N\left[(1+K)^{t_n}-1\right]$$
(2.8)

where N denotes the contract nominal and K reflects the fixed swap rate. In exchange the party receives a floating amount of

$$N\left(\frac{I_{t_n}}{I_{t_0}}-1\right)$$
(2.9)

where I_{t_n} and I_{t_0} stand for the CPI (consumer price index) levels at dates t_n and t_0. Note that (2.8) and (2.9) imply that no principal is being exchanged at maturity and no cashflows occur in between $t_0, \ldots, t_n$. The market for zero coupon inflation swaps quotes fixed payments as a function of swap maturity K_{t_i}. At the time when both parties enter the swap it has a market value of zero, ie, floating and fixed side are equally valuable. The difference in price between a real bond $b(0, t_i)$ and a nominal bond $d(0, t_i)$ must reflect cumulative inflation and hence the value of the floating leg, while the fixed leg consists of the known fixed (nominal) payment at t_i discounted by the appropriate discount rate. We therefore get

$$\underbrace{N\cdot\left[b\left(0,t_i\right)-d\left(0,t_i\right)\right]}_{\text{floating leg}}=\underbrace{d\left(0,t_i\right)\cdot N\cdot\left[\left(1+K_{t_i}\right)^{t_i}-1\right]}_{\text{fixed leg}}$$
(2.10)

Equation (2.10) is derived simply by arbitrage arguments and will hold under any term structure or inflation model. We can therefore strip out the prices for real bonds by solving for $b(0, t_i)$.

$$b\left(0,t_i\right)=d\left(0,t_i\right)\cdot\left(1+K_{t_i}\right)^{t_i}$$
(2.11)

Figure 4 Deriving real zero bonds.
Swap rates K from zero-inflation break-even swaps quoted by Deutsche
Bank on Reuters at 10 December 2004

n	y_{swap}	$\hat{y}_{swap}$	K	$\hat{K}$	$b(0, t_n)$
1	2.26	2.20			
2	2.46	2.47	2.24	2.25	0.99
3	2.66	2.69	2.26	2.26	0.99
4	2.85	2.89	2.28	2.27	0.98
5	3.03	3.06	2.29	2.28	0.96
6	3.19	3.22		2.29	0.95
7	3.34	3.35	2.30	2.30	0.93
8	3.47	3.46		2.32	0.91
9	3.59	3.56		2.33	0.89
10	3.69	3.65	2.33	2.34	0.87
11		3.73		2.35	0.85
12	3.83	3.80	2.36	2.36	0.84
13		3.87		2.37	0.82
14		3.92		2.38	0.80
15	4.00	3.98	2.39	2.39	0.78
16		4.02		2.40	0.76
17		4.06		2.41	0.74
18		4.10		2.42	0.72
19		4.14		2.43	0.71
20	4.2	4.17	2.45	2.44	0.69
21		4.20		2.45	0.67
22		4.22		2.46	0.66
23		4.25		2.47	0.64
24		4.27		2.48	0.63
25	4.28	4.29		2.49	0.61
26		4.31		2.50	0.60
27		4.33		2.51	0.58
28		4.34		2.52	0.57
29		4.36		2.53	0.56
30	4.31	4.37	2.54	2.54	0.54

The result of this exercise is summarised in Figure 4. Missing swap rates are fitted (interpolated) using the Nelson–Siegel methodology.

Apart from deriving real discount rates, what else can we use inflation swaps for? While inflation-linked corporate bonds come very close to the economic nature of inflation-indexed liabilities, there is limited supply in the corporate sector. Natural issuers would ideally receive inflation-linked revenues combined with fixed liabilities (utilities). Most inflation-linked bonds are essentially government bonds with the accompanying lower yields due to a lack of credit risks. Investors who are interested in a liability-matching position would be better advised to invest into a diversified portfolio of higher-yielding corporate bonds (to reflect the respective credit risk of a given set of pension liabilities) and overlay their structure with inflation swaps. The required position is to pay a fixed K (today's expected inflation) and receive floating, ie, future-realised, inflation. Future (fixed) cashflows generated from the corporate bond portfolio are exchanged in return for yet unknown inflation payments. Yields on these overlay structures are generally higher than yields on equivalent inflation-linked bonds (ILBs), due to several sources of extra risks. In general there is credit risk (one or several corporate bonds default), counterparty risk (investment bank defaults on swap payments) and liquidity risk (risk to borrow additional funds at unfortunate terms).

ILBs provide an alternative way to back the prices for real zero bonds, which in turn help to derive inflation expectations. We start with the theoretical case of perfect inflation indexation. An ILB pays a real coupon C_R at times $t_1, t_2, \ldots, t_n$. Each coupon payment is adjusted to reflect realised inflation. If we denote π_{t_i} as the inflation between time t_{i-1} and t_i, we calculate the nominal coupon payment at time t_4

$$C_R \prod_{i=1}^{4} (1+\pi_i) \qquad (2.12)$$

From (2.11) we know that the linkage between nominal and real discount factor can be expressed as

$$d(0, t_4) = \frac{b(0, t_4)}{\prod_{i=1}^{4} (1+\pi_i)} \qquad (2.13)$$

Hence discounting (2.12) with (2.13) yields

$$d(0, t_4) C_R \prod_{i=1}^{4} (1+\pi_i) = \frac{b(0, t_4)}{\prod_{i=1}^{4} (1+\pi_i)} C_R \prod_{i=1}^{4} (1+\pi_i)$$
$$= b(0, t_4) C_R \qquad (2.14)$$

Real cashflows are discounted with real rates. We can now write down the pricing equation for ILBs as

$$p_r = \sum_{i=1}^{n} b(0, t_i) C_R + b(0, t_n) \qquad (2.15)$$

We could estimate real discount factors along the lines of section 0. However, perfect indexation is practically impossible as indexation lags occur due to the publication lag of measured inflation. Suppose inflation adjustments are lagged by one period.[2] In this case coupon payments at time t_4 are accumulated with inflation ranging from t_0 to t_3. Instead of (2.12) we arrive at

$$C_R \prod_{i=0}^{3} \left(1 + \pi_i\right) \tag{2.16}$$

The difference between full indexation in (2.12) and lagged indexation in (2.16) can be expressed as

$$\frac{\prod_{i=0}^{3} \left(1 + \pi_i\right)}{\prod_{i=1}^{4} \left(1 + \pi_i\right)} = \frac{\left(1 + \pi_0\right)}{\left(1 + \pi_4\right)}$$

More generally we need to change (2.15) into

$$p_r = \sum_{i=1}^{n} b\left(0, t_i\right) \frac{\left(1 + \pi_0\right)}{\left(1 + \pi_{t_i}\right)} C_R + b\left(0, t_n\right) \frac{\left(1 + \pi_0\right)}{\left(1 + \pi_{t_n}\right)} \tag{2.17}$$

as the discount factor is not affected by the indexation lag. In order to back out real bond yields, we need to make assumptions on the path of future inflation. It is therefore highly recommended to use the inflation swap market instead of backing out real zero bond prices.

LIMITED INFLATION INDEXATION

Inflation indexation protects the real spending power of pension claims. The previous section introduced instruments that exposed investors to positive as well as negative inflation. However, indexation is not necessarily symmetric.

Generically, existing pension plans face two sorts of asymmetries:

❑ *Capped indexation.* Pension claims rise by the maximum of actual inflation and an upper limit. Essentially, this places an upper limit on inflation indexation.
❑ *Floored indexation.* Pension claims do not fall if inflation becomes negative (ratchet effect). This is equal to no-deflation participation.
❑ *Contingent indexation.* Sometimes indexation depends on how well a pension fund (or alternatively how well the sponsoring company) does. An example is the Dutch system, where indexation depends on the pension funds funding ratio. If the assets

perform well relative to liabilities and funding is for example above a threshold of 110, all liability cash flows rise with a specified fraction of inflation (this depends on what is called the pension deal) for that very year. If funding drops below 110 next year, there will be no indexation next year, but past indexation remains guaranteed.[3]

We start with the assumption that the level of consumer price inflation (I_{t_i}) follows a geometric Brownian motion. Note that units are chosen such that $I_{t_0} = 1$. The process is described below

$$\left(I_{t_i} - I_{t_{i-1}}\right) = I_{t_{i-1}}\left(\alpha dt + \sigma dz\right) \tag{2.18}$$

where α and σ denote (instantaneous) mean and standard deviation of inflation and $E(dz) = 0, E(dz^2) = 1$. A European call option on inflation pays the difference between realised inflation and a prespecified inflation hurdle $(1+\kappa)^{t_n}$ also called strike in option terms.

$$\max\left(\frac{I_{t_n}}{I_0} - (1+\kappa)^{t_n}, 0\right) \tag{2.19}$$

where

$$\frac{I_{t_n}}{I_0} = \prod_{i=1}^{n}\left(1+\pi_{t_i}\right) \tag{2.20}$$

Under the assumption of horizontal term structures for both nominal and real rates we can price this option as

$$C(0, t_n) = N(z_1)b(0, t_n) - N(z_2)d(0, t_n)(1+\kappa)^{t_n} \tag{2.21}$$

where

$$z_1 = \frac{\ln\left(\frac{b(0, t_n)(1+\kappa)^{-t_n}}{d(0, t_n)}\right) + \frac{1}{2}\sigma^2 t_n^2}{\sigma\sqrt{t_n}}, z_2 = z_1 - \sigma\sqrt{t_n} \tag{2.22}$$

To illustrate the above equation we set $\kappa = 0$ to arrive at

$$C(0, t_n) = N(z_1)b(0, t_n) - N(z_2)d(0, t_n) \tag{2.23}$$

$$z_1 = \frac{\ln\left[\frac{b(0,t_n)}{d(0,t_n)}\right] + \frac{1}{2}\sigma^2 t_n}{\sigma\sqrt{t_n}} \quad , \quad z_2 = z_1 - \sigma\sqrt{t_n} \qquad (2.24)$$

Note that a call on inflation equals the payment of positive cumulative inflation. We can compare (2.23) with the floating leg of an inflation swap in (2.10). The replicating (hedging) portfolio consists of $N(z_1)$ real bonds and $N(z_2)$ nominal bonds. Assume the above call on cumulative inflation is deeply in the money. In this case owning this call is very close to receiving floating inflation. In terms of (2.24) "deep in the money" means that nominal interest rates are substantially above real rates, ie, there is a large implied inflation growth. Mathematically, the expression $b(0, t_n)/d(0, t_n)$ becomes large. Suppose 10-year nominal zero bonds trade at $d(0, 10) = 0.65$ (5% continuously compounded nominal rate) while real bonds with the same maturity trade at $b(0, 10) = 0.9045$ (1% continuously compounded rate). Further, assume inflation volatility to be around 2%. In this situation the replicating portfolio consists of 100% long real bonds and short 100% nominal bonds,

$$N(z_1) = \frac{\ln\left[\frac{0.90}{0.65}\right] + \frac{1}{2}\cdot 0.02^2 \cdot 10}{0.02\cdot\sqrt{10}} = N(5.26) = 1, N(z_2) = N\left(z_1 - \sigma\sqrt{10}\right) = 1$$

which is synthetically long cumulative inflation. This is exactly what we intuitively expect. From here it is easy to engineer the hedging portfolio for capped inflation indexation. The price for capped inflation insurance equals a long position in an ordinary CPI call (with strike of 1) and a short position in a CPI call with strike equal to the level of inflation cap (κ).

$$\max\left[0, \frac{I_{t_n}}{I_0} - 1\right] - \max\left[0, \frac{I_{t_n}}{I_0} - (1+\kappa)^{t_n}\right] \qquad (2.25)$$

This resembles an option spread strategy, where a low strike is bought while a higher strike is sold.

STOCHASTIC DISCOUNT FACTORS

So far we have been looking at the valuation of fixed cashflows using perfect replication, that is, we valued a liability stream as a portfolio of zero coupon bonds. This is the traditional method for pricing lia-bilities. Although it works perfectly well with fixed cashflows, it is of no use at all when we are confronted with interest-rate-sensitive cash-flows, that is, when cashflows are dependent on the level of interest rates. In this case we need to be able to model the evolution of interest rates in order capture the conditional element of pension liabilities. There are many applications for this kind in modern asset liability management. We need to be able to evaluate the value of a fixed-rate guarantee (defined benefit payment) for a given asset (bond) alloca-tion. A plan sponsor might invest in a portfolio of shorter duration than his pension liabilities in order to benefit from rising rates. What is the value of the implicit guarantee given by the plan sponsor if his interest rate view turns out to be incorrect? Also, we might want to be consistent and value our pension liabilities within the same frame-work we price fixed-income derivatives for hedging purposes (like swap options and constant maturity swaps, for instance). It will turn out that, rather than apply a fixed discount rate to a fixed cashflow at date t (deterministic discount factor), we now apply varying dis-count factors to different states of the world (stochastic discount fac-tors). The principle of "multiply and add" will however remain. Essentially, this is the death of the actuarial mathematics. The use of a fixed actuarial rate is unable to deal with any kind of contingencies and will not be useful for solving real world problems.

Any analysis involving term-structure dynamics (evolution of interest rate curves over time) will start with an assumption on the interest rate process. There is an almost infinite number of term-structure models.[4] I will focus on a simplified version of the Black–Derman–Toy (BDT) model to build our intuition and develop a generic framework. What I mean by a particular model is that each model implies a different behaviour of interest rates. Note that differ-ent interest rate models will leave the value of fixed liabilities unchanged (as long as they are calibrated to the same term structure) but will put different values on interest rate optionalities (which must depend on the chosen rate process). The evolution of short-term inter-est rates is modelled within a binomial tree. There are $t_i = 1, \ldots, t$ time steps. The probability of moving from state (t_i, j) to either an up state $(t_{i+1}, j + 1)$ or a down state $(t_{i+1}, j - 1)$ is assumed to be 50% each.

Looking at the tree structure it is easy to see the labelling system (in bold). This will be of great use when actually programming the solution. It is also an intuitive name to name alternative states of the world. Note that we assumed the tree to be recombining, ie, moving up first and down second, which is equivalent to moving first down and then up. What are the probabilities of reaching a particular node within the tree? Suppose we want to calculate the probabilities for every node in Period 10. First we note that as the probability of a down move is the same as for an up move, each particular path is equally likely. To move up along the first five time steps and then move down every single period thereafter is as unlikely as to move up ten times in a row. However, while only one path can end in a node (10, 10), there will be a total of 252 possible paths (out of $2^{10} = 1024$) that end in the state (10, 5). Hence the probability of ending in this particular state is $252/1024 = 24.6\%$. In general the probability of arriving at a single state is given by

$$prob\left(knod\left(t,n\right)\right) = \binom{t}{n} \bigg/ \sum_{i=1}^{t}\binom{t}{i} \qquad (2.26)$$

In principle we could use a tree also for Monte Carlo simulation. All we need is to branch through the tree, drawing a uniform random number $\tilde{u}$ at each node to decide whether the process moves up ($\tilde{u}>0$) or down ($\tilde{u}<0$). The particular process for the BDT model with constant volatility is given by the following relationship between the current short rate s, a set of time-varying drift factors a_t used later for calibrating the model to actual market prices and interest rate volatility σ.

$$s\left(t_i,j\right) = s\left(0,0\right)e^{\left(\sum_{t=1}^{t_i} a_t\right)dt + j\sigma\sqrt{dt}} \qquad (2.27)$$

For a particular node and assuming $dt = 1$, we can write this for example as

$$s\left(3,-3\right) = s\left(0,0\right)e^{\left(\sum_{t=1}^{3} a_t\right)-3\sigma} \qquad (2.28)$$

Generically, the interest rate tree looks like as in Figure 6. With regard to the nodes we see the same pattern as in Figure 5.

Note that $s(t_i, j)$ is the short-term rate known at the start of period t_i in state j (but not today), while s is known with certainty from today. How can we interpret the volatility parameter? Is it absolute or percentage volatility? We know that $e^x \approx 1 + x$ for small x. For

Figure 5 Generic binomial tree.
Each individual node is characterised by two entries. The first entry labels the time period starting from 0 (today). For each time period we observe different states (always one state more than the respective time period). The state number reflects the number of cumulative up movements. State (3,1) is a state in 3 periods (for example years) from now, where the interest rate process went two time up and one time down

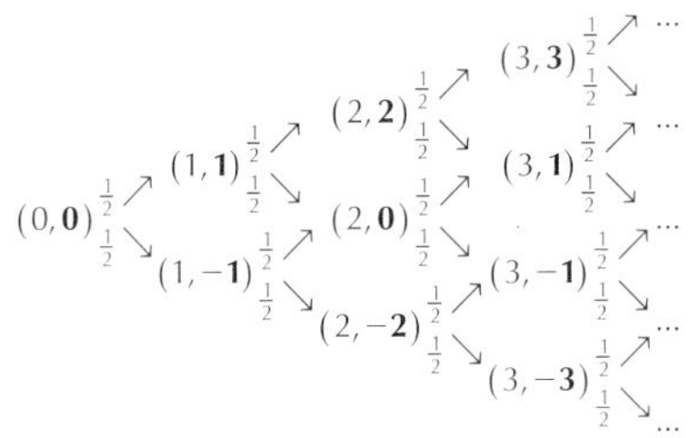

Figure 6 Binomial tree for Black–Derman–Toy () model with constant volatility.
The interest rate process for the short rate evolves according to (2.27). Each branching occurs with equal probability. Interest rate volatility is assumed to be constant throughout the tree

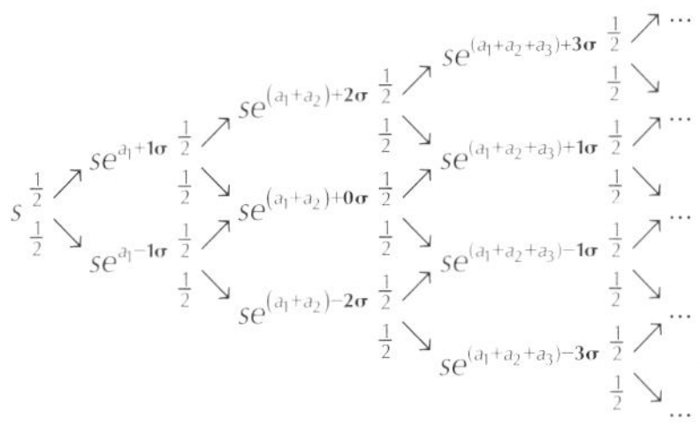

$dt = 1$ and $a_1 = 0$ we can write $s = se^{\sigma} \approx s(1 + \sigma)$. Hence we know that σ has a percentage interpretation. For example $\sigma = 10\%$ implies that the current one-year rate of 2.5% can rise and fall approximately by 25 basis points.

So far we set up an interest tree for short-term rates. But how can we price bonds of arbitrary maturity as well as options on bonds, swaps, and so forth from a given tree? How can we make sure that a given tree will correspond to market reality? I will explain the

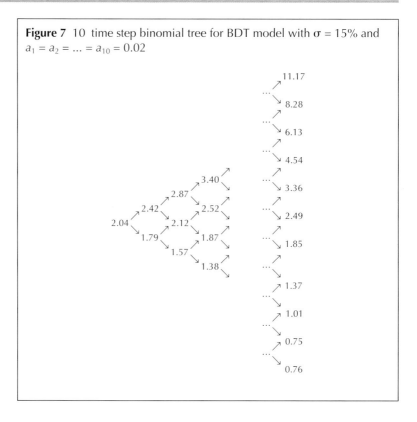

Figure 7 10 time step binomial tree for BDT model with σ = 15% and $a_1 = a_2 = \dots = a_{10} = 0.02$

different concepts by working through an example. Suppose we start with a given tree and assume σ = 15% and $a_1 = a_2 = \dots = a_{10} = 0.02$. The corresponding tree can be found in Figure 7.

You will notice a valuable feature of the chosen model. Even though we modelled a binomial tree with equally likely up and down moves in rates, short-term interest rates remain positive across all states of the world. The reason for this property is the log normality assumption for rates inherent in the rate process. We can see this by plotting the one-year spot rates in Year 10 (last column in Figure 7) against the respective probabilities calculated from (2.26). The distribution of short-term rates (Figure 8) is lognormal.

We come back to our question how to price bonds for different maturities on a tree that provides only short rates. In order to do this we will introduce the building blocks of modern finance: state price securities (also called Arrow–Debreu, or primitive securities).

Figure 8 Lognormal distribution of short rates.
In a simple binomial branching (one split every year) we arrive at 11 nodes in Year 10 (always on node more than years). The x-axis shows the value of the one-year interest rate that each node carries, while the y-axis reflects the probability of arriving at a particular node according to equation (2.26)

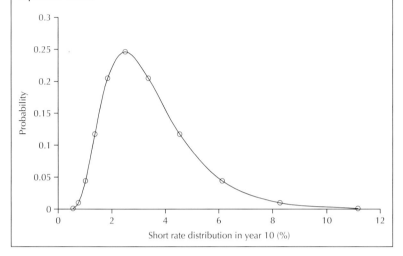

Short rate distribution in year 10 (%)

A state price is the price of an asset that pays 1 monetary unit in one particular state of the world only, and nothing in all other states. It is like a lottery ticket that pays 1 if a particular state occurs and nothing else. If we knew the prices for such securities we could price any interest rate optionality. Modern finance is mainly about arbitrage and replication. We will therefore try to model the price of these securities. Suppose for a moment we knew the price for one- and two-year securities to be 98 and 95.8. Note that a two-year bond today will be a one-year bond in one year. In one year ahead rates are either 2.42% or 1.018%. Hence bond prices are either 97.63 (after an up move in rates) or 98.24 (if rates move down). We also know that a one-year bond will pay 100 in one year. Can we find a portfolio of one- and two-year bonds that pays 1 in the up state and 0 in the down state? The condition for this is

$$\theta_{1Year}\,100 + \theta_{2Year}\,97.63 = 1$$
$$\theta_{1Year}\,100 + \theta_{2Year}\,98.24 = 0$$

There are two unknowns in two equations. Solving for θ_{1Year} and θ_{2Year} yields -1.66 and 1.63. The price for AD_u (Arrow–Debreu security up) amounts to $AD_u = -1.66 \cdot 95.8+1.63 \cdot 98 = 0.49$. Repeating this for

$$\theta_{1Year} 100 + \theta_{2Year} 97.63 = 0$$
$$\theta_{1Year} 100 + \theta_{2Year} 98.24 = 1$$

yields $AD_d = 1.66 \cdot 95.98-1.62 \cdot 98 = 0.49$. If we buy both AD_d (down) and AD_u, we hold a portfolio of securities that pay 1 in all possible states of the world. This is by definition a riskless security. In fact the value of a one-period bond is exactly $AD_u + AD_d = 1/(1+r)$ or $(0.49 + 0.49) = 0.98$. If we denote values in up and down states by C_u and C_d we can write more generally

$$V = AD_u C_u + AD_d C_d \qquad (2.29)$$

Note that (2.29) can be applied to find the value (V) for any security. This means that (2.29) unifies derivative pricing as well as asset pricing. All we need to know are the payoffs in different states as well as the respective state prices. Reformulating (2.29) yields the risk neutral valuation principle.

$$V = \frac{1}{1+r}\left(\frac{AD_u}{\frac{1}{1+r}} C_u + \frac{AD_d}{\frac{1}{1+r}} C_d \right) = \frac{1}{1+r}\left(p_u C_u + p_d C_d \right) \qquad (2.30)$$

where p_u and p_d are called risk-neutral probabilities. Equation (2.30) calculates the expected value (under the risk-neutral distribution). Note that (2.30) is equivalent to (2.29). We can now use (2.30) to price securities along any node of a given interest rate tree. All securities are expected to grow at the risk-free rate $V(1+r) = p_u C_u + p_d C_d$. Let us exemplify this first we price a two-year zero bond with the use of (2.30) as described in Figure 9. After one year, the two-year zero bond becomes a one-year zero bond. Once the state of the world is revealed there is no uncertainty left. The respective payments become 97.63 in the up state and 98.24 in the down state. The value of 95.98 or alternatively $d(0, 2)$ is the expected value in one year discounted with the risk-free rate. The method is called backward induction, since we work through the tree from the back. So far we assumed risk-neutral probabilities to be of equal value. This seems at odds with (2.30). Risk-neutral rates have been endogenous, but when we derived state prices we used

Figure 9 Calculation of $d(0, 2)$ using backward induction.
At each individual node we apply risk neutral valuation, that is, we calculate the expected payoff under the risk-neutral distribution (assuming equal probability of branching in either direction) and discount it with the state-specific risk-free rate according to (2.30)

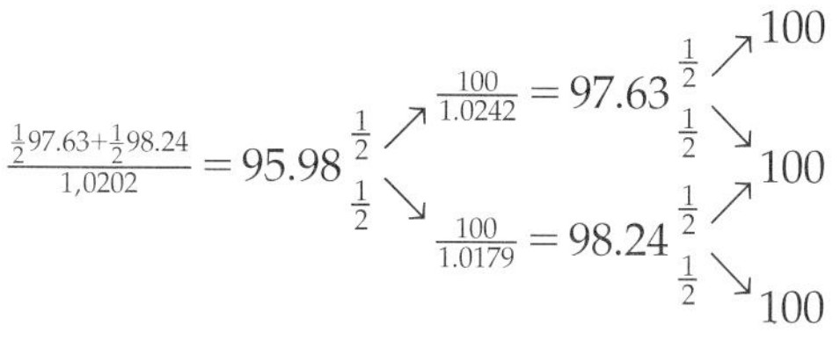

$$\frac{\frac{1}{2}97.63+\frac{1}{2}98.24}{1,0202}=95.98 \quad \frac{\frac{1}{2}}{\frac{1}{2}} \nearrow \frac{100}{1.0242}=97.63 \quad \frac{\frac{1}{2}}{\frac{1}{2}} \nearrow 100 \quad \searrow 100$$

$$\searrow \frac{100}{1.0179}=98.24 \quad \frac{\frac{1}{2}}{\frac{1}{2}} \nearrow 100 \quad \searrow 100$$

Figure 10 Calculation of $d(0, 4)$ using backward induction.
Each node represents a binomial subtree. Pricing securities on a given tree equals repeated expected value calculations and discounting at the prevailing risk-free rate

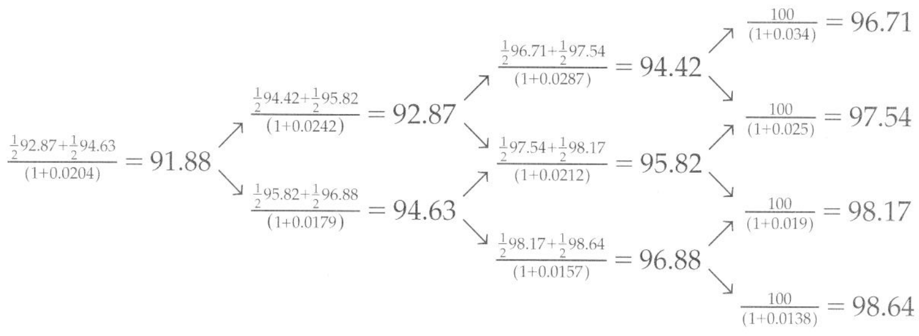

$$\frac{\frac{1}{2}92.87+\frac{1}{2}94.63}{(1+0.0204)}=91.88$$

$$\frac{\frac{1}{2}94.42+\frac{1}{2}95.82}{(1+0.0242)}=92.87$$

$$\frac{\frac{1}{2}95.82+\frac{1}{2}96.88}{(1+0.0179)}=94.63$$

$$\frac{\frac{1}{2}96.71+\frac{1}{2}97.54}{(1+0.0287)}=94.42$$

$$\frac{\frac{1}{2}97.54+\frac{1}{2}98.17}{(1+0.0212)}=95.82$$

$$\frac{\frac{1}{2}98.17+\frac{1}{2}98.64}{(1+0.0157)}=96.88$$

$$\frac{100}{(1+0.034)}=96.71$$

$$\frac{100}{(1+0.025)}=97.54$$

$$\frac{100}{(1+0.019)}=98.17$$

$$\frac{100}{(1+0.0138)}=98.64$$

a given payoff matrix. Building a tree, we can either adjust cash-flows for given risk-neutral probabilities or vice versa. We repeat this example with four-year zero bonds: $d (0, 4)$.

At the end of the third year, a four-year zero bond has only one year left. We can therefore calculate the prices for one-year zero rates for each particular state. At the end of the second year we calculate the expected value of one-year zero bond prices, discounted at the respective one-period rate. Continuing with this process until the starting node will result in a valuation for the four-year zero bond. Repeating this exercise for every single bond (which is tedious and we will shortly introduce a quicker

47

method), we create a whole series of zero bond prices. But how can we rely on these prices? What makes us confident that we built the correct tree?

We can use the term structure of interest rates generated from the one-period short-rate tree, in order to calibrate our yield curve model. Calibrating means using the drift rates (a_{t_i}) to adjust the interest rate tree in such a way that all market prices are exactly recovered. Suppose we want to fit the BDT model to our dataset. We need to write an optimisation routine that will minimise the following objective

$$\sum_{i=1}^{30} \left(d\left(0, t_i\right) - d_{BDT}\left(0, t_i\right) \right)^2$$

with respect to $a_1, \ldots, a_{30}$, where $d_{BDT}\left(0, t_i\right)$ is the discount function arising from the BDT tree. As the number of free parameters equals the number of yield curve points to calibrate, the squared deviations will actually become zero.[5]

The unnerving part which I have described so far is the calculation of $d_{BDT}\left(0, t_i\right)$ by discounting within subtrees of increasing size. Alternatively, we can use the concept of state prices introduced earlier. The idea here is called forward induction, as we work through the tree starting from the first node. The state price for the up state in Period 1 can be calculated from

$$\frac{\frac{1}{2}1 + \frac{1}{2}0}{\left(1 + 0.0204\right)} = 0.49$$

This is the price of a security that pays 1 in the upstate and has an expected return equal to the risk-free rate. For the downstate we must arrive at the same price, because of the perfect symmetry within the first period.

We arrived at the state prices for state (1, 1) and (1, −1) as we labelled states in Figure 11. What is the state price for a payment of

Figure 11 Forward induction.
Working through the state tree from the start is called forward induction. Repeatedly buying state price securities guarantees to cover every payoff along the path

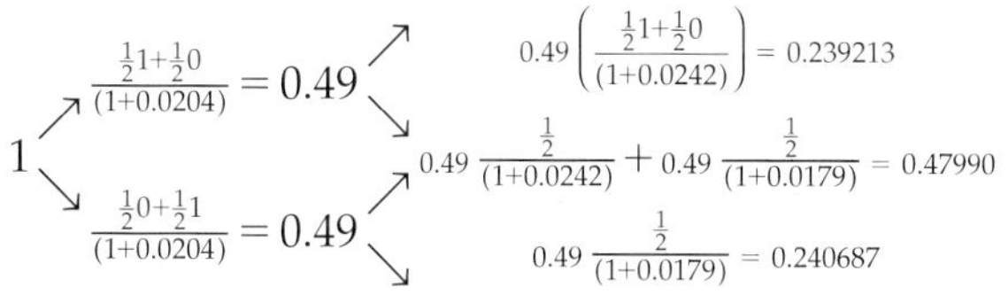

1 in state (2, 2) from the perspective of state (0, 0)? The state price from the perspective of state (1, 1) follows the same logic as for (0, 0). It is given by

$$\frac{\frac{1}{2}1+\frac{1}{2}0}{(1+0.0242)} = 0.488$$

However, in order to end up with a payment in (2, 2) we need to pass through (1, 1). Consequentially, the state price for (2, 2) is given by

$$0.49\left(\frac{\frac{1}{2}1+\frac{1}{2}0}{(1+0.0242)}\right) = 0.2391$$

State (2, 0) can be reached via two alternative paths. In order to replicate a claim that pays in (2, 0) we need to buy securities that pay off in all states that lead to (2, 0), so that we can reinvest the money received (at the end of Period 1) into another state price security that pays off in (2, 0). Replication means that we buy securities that pay off along all possible paths to a certain node, so that we can reinvest the money received in another state price security that guarantees to pay if the respective path is taken.

How can we check that state prices are correct? Buying all Period 2 state securities at their respective state price guarantees the same payoffs as a riskless two-period zero bond. They must therefore be equally priced.

Figure 12 Fitted state price tree.

In the fitted tree model prices equal market prices. The assumption of equal risk-neutral probability is not critical to this. Instead we could have changed the probabilities to any arbitrary number (apart from 1, as this generates arbitrage). A different short-term interest rate tree would have been generated to reflect this. Note that we need as many calibration parameters (specifying the interest rate process) as we have instruments that need pricing

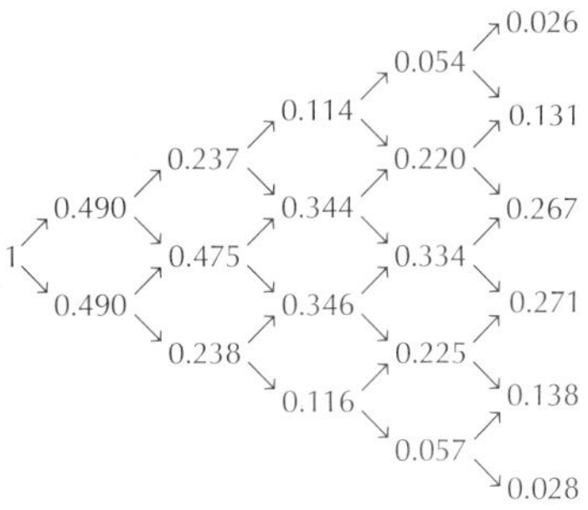

$$d_{BDT}(0,2) = AD(2,2) + AD(2,0) + AD(2,-2)$$
$$= 0.23921 + 0.47990 + 0.24068$$
$$= 0.95980$$
$$= d(0,2)$$

Forward induction is a computationally much more efficient way to fit a binomial tree to a given term structure of interest rates. The state price tree (for the first five periods) corresponding to our dataset in Table 2 is provided in Figure 12.[6]

Again, we can easily check the results. Adding up the state prices for Period 5, we arrive exactly at the price of a five-year zero bond on 13 December 2004.

$$d_{BDT}(0,5) = AD(5,5) + AD(5,3) + AD(5,1) + AD(5,-1)$$
$$+ AD(5,-3) + AD(5,-5)$$
$$= 0.026 + 0.131 + \cdots + 0.028$$
$$= 0.86$$
$$= d(0,5)$$

Fixed cashflows are now exactly priced in the same way as under traditional discounting. In addition, we can now also price the value of payments conditional on the level of interest rates. This will prove to be useful in pricing the value of implicit guarantees by the sponsoring company or in a consistent pricing of hedging instruments.

PRICING OF ULTRA-LONG LIABILITY CASHFLOWS

Pension liabilities are similar to very long dated bonds. Given this fact that expected liability payments stretch out to 70 years and more, we need to look at the principles at which capital markets (should) price long-term bonds (see Pearson, 2000).

For simplicity we assume a flat term structure where 40-year par bonds traded at face value (ie, the coupon equals its yield) carry a 5% coupon.

$$d(0, t_i) = \left(\tfrac{1}{1+s}\right)^{t_i}, i = 1, \ldots, 40 \qquad (2.31)$$

Suppose we need to calculate the yield of a 100-year par bond from this, while we do not know discount factors after Year 40. Could we expect this bond to trade at 5.6%, ie, a 60 bps risk premium per annum for extending maturity by 60 years? Rather than real pricing we can perform a plausibility test. Assume that the term structure of forward rates for all payments between Year 40 and Year 100 is also flat:

$$d(t_{n-1}, t_n) = \tfrac{1}{1+f}, n = 41, \ldots, 100 \qquad (2.32)$$

What forward rate (f) would be required to value a 5.75% coupon bond at par? We need to solve the bond-pricing equation

$$\sum_{i=1}^{40} (C+h) d(0, t_i) + d(0, 40) \left(\sum_{i=1}^{60} (C+h) \left(\tfrac{1}{1+f}\right)^i \right)$$
$$+ d(0, 40) \left(\tfrac{1}{1+f}\right)^{100} = 1 \qquad (2.33)$$

for f. The first part in (2.33) prices coupon payments up to Year 40 at the known term structure, while the second term values all remaining coupons at the yet unknown forward rate. Coupon payments are the sum of the known coupon for a 40-year par bond (5% in the above case) and a term premium h. Trivially the last term does the same for the principal payment. In this example the implied forward rate equals $f = 20.35\%$.

Figure 13 Term premium versus forward rate.
For each term premium we calculate the corresponding forward rate f from (0.33). Unless investors believe that forward rates of 20% are reasonable, it is difficult to argue that the term premium should exceed 60 basis points

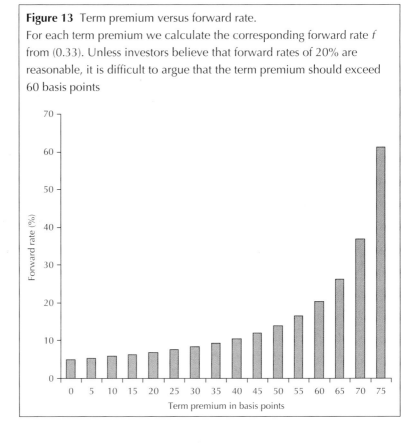

We can repeat this exercise for varying term premium to arrive at Figure 13. An increase in term premium is followed by an exponentially rising implied forward rate. While the previous analysis does not help us in selecting a term premium for longer-dated bond yields, it provides us with a range of reasonable outcomes. Given Figure 13, most readers would regard a term premium of more than 50 basis as questionable. What is the basis of this intuitive assessment?

We know from our binomial tree analysis that we can calculate the price of a zero bond as the expected present value of a payment at maturity evaluated at all possible interest rate paths under a risk-neutral probability measure. We can therefore write

$$d(0,T) = E_Q \exp\left(-\int_0^T r_s ds\right) \tag{2.34}$$

where now r_s describes the path of instantaneous spot interest rates from time 0 to T. The instantaneous forward rate quoted in time 0 for time T is defined as

$$f(0,T) = \frac{\delta \ln d(0,T)}{\delta T}$$

$$= -\frac{1}{d(0,T)} \frac{\delta d(0,T)}{\delta T} = \frac{E_Q\left(r_T \exp\left(-\int_0^T r_s ds\right)\right)}{E_Q\left(\exp\left(-\int_0^T r_s ds\right)\right)} \qquad (2.35)$$

Equation (2.35) describes the forward rate as the value of the time T short rate under all possible interest rate paths. The weight given to an individual spot rate is given by $\exp\left(-\int_0^T r_s ds\right) E_Q\left(\exp\left(\int_0^T r_s ds\right)\right)$. All possible realisations of r_T are weighted by the respective scenario probabilities as well as the scenario-dependent discount factors. Weighting by discount factors increases the importance of paths ending at lower rates, simply because the discount factor $\exp\left(-\int_0^T r_s ds\right)$ is higher. This effect becomes increasingly dominant with an increase in T. The power of compounding increases the difference in discount factors for high- and low-yield environments. Figure 13

We can draw two conclusions from the above analysis of forward rates. First we see that forward rates are below expected spot rates:

$$E_Q(r_T) > \frac{E_Q\left(r_T \exp\left(-\int_0^T r_s ds\right)\right)}{E_Q\left(\exp\left(-\int_0^T r_s ds\right)\right)} \qquad (2.36)$$

This is true, because discount factors tend to be small (large weight) if rates are low and vice versa. A closer inspection of this result will lead us to our second conclusion. For very long time horizons T, instantaneous forward rates are more and more influenced by the most bullish interest rate scenario as $\exp\left(-\int_0^T r_s ds\right)$ approaches one for very low rates (see Dybvig and Marshall, 1996).

Figure 14 Convexity and local return hypothesis.
Forward rates (one-year roll-down returns) fall with maturity. Spot rates
(calculated from forward rates) also decrease with maturity. The difference
between local returns (essentially current flat-term structure) and forward
rates can be regarded as convexity bias. Any risk premium must be at least
as large as the convexity bias in order to make rising forward rates plausible

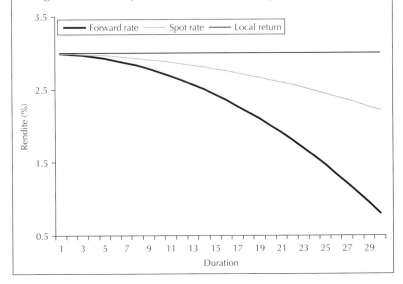

Forward rates are not an unbiased average of future interest rates,
but are rather pulled to the most bullish interest rate scenario. This
provides an additional argument against a large term premium in
Figure 13. Large forward rates for long maturities are simply not
possible, given the inherent pull to the very extreme low-interest-
rate scenarios.

The above shown tendency of forward rates to decline with
increasing maturity is virtually the same as the well-known convexity bias. Can we put a number on the convexity bias and how
does it affect the pricing of longer-maturity bonds?

We know from a second-order Taylor approximation that the
expected total return of a particular zero bond equals roll-down
plus convexity gain. The convexity C_{gain} gain is

$$C_{gain} \approx \frac{1}{2} C \sigma_{\Delta y} \qquad (2.37)$$

where C measures the zero bond convexity and $\sigma_{\Delta y}$ equals the volatility of yield changes. A zero bond with convexity of 2 and yield volatility of 100 bps will experience a 1% convexity gain. A 100-basis-point drop in yields will lead to an absolute price change that is considerably larger than the absolute price change for a 100 bps increase in yields. While the expected value of yield changes is zero (assuming equal probabilities) the expected total return is positive. Under the local return hypothesis, the holding period return is equal across all maturities. Bonds that offer high-convexity gains will not need to offer large returns from roll-down. Note that one-period returns essentially equal one-period forward rates (under the assumption that the yield curve remains unchanged). Putting this all together yields Figure 14. Forward rates fall with maturity. For forward rates to considerably rise – as it was required in (2.33) – we require unusually large risk premiums to overcompensate the convexity gain.

INTEREST RATE TREES: PRICING OF PENSION FUND GUARANTEES

Earlier, I described how to fit term structure models to real market data. I used a simplified version of the BDT model, but the procedure will be similar for other models. Now I will apply the fitted binomial tree to price the value of a pension fund guarantee.[7]

Suppose a plan sponsor is fully funded with assets and liabilities at 100 each. Liabilities are equal to 116.239 zero bonds paying 1 at maturity ($116.239 \cdot d(0, 5) = 116.239 \cdot 0.86 = 100$). Assets consist of 105.045 two-year zero bonds. The balance sheet is given in Figure 15.

Figure 15 Pension fund balance sheet.
Hypothetical balance sheet with short-duration assets and long-duration bonds. Assets and liabilities are summarised as cashflows

	t_1	t_2	t_3	t_4	t_5
a_{t_i}	0.0	105.4	0.0	0.0	0.0
$a_{t_i} B(0, t_i)$	0.0	100.0	0.0	0.0	0.0
l_{t_i}	0.0	0.0	0.0	0.0	116.2
$l_{t_i} B(0, t_i)$	0.0	0.0	0.0	0.0	100.0

Figure 16 Fitted short-term rate tree.
The above tree has been calibrated to market data. It can now be used to price any asset using risk-neutral valuation at every node of the tree

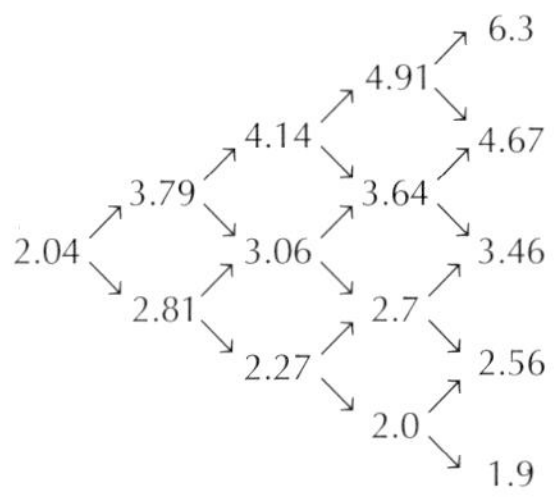

```
                                          6.3
                                   4.91
                            4.14          4.67
                     3.79          3.64
              2.04          3.06          3.46
                     2.81          2.7
                            2.27          2.56
                                   2.0
                                          1.9
```

After the end of the year, it is company policy to fund any pension fund shortfall. How valuable is the pension guarantee? The sponsor does not invest in equities as he is convinced that equity investing will not be appreciated by his shareholders. However, the investor runs a mismatch of cashflows. If cashflows were identical across all time periods no mismatch would appear. Note that a cashflow mismatch is not necessarily the same as a duration mismatch (even though it is in this example). Investors could be duration-matched and still have a cashflow mismatch. Cashflow mismatch is a more general indication of reinvestment risk. Investing in short bonds versus a long-term liability essentially aims to benefit from an anticipated rate rise. This is indicative on how most pension funds have been positioned during 2003 to 2005.

Effectively, we price a put option on the pension fund surplus, given by the difference in value of five- and two-year zero bonds one year ahead. Let us start with the fitted tree of one-year rates in Figure 16. Assets and liabilities are priced from the same tree.

We start with pricing both zero bonds along the binomial tree. Note that under risk-neutral valuation the price of any fixed-income instrument derived from the tree in state (t_i, j) can be calculated by discounting the expected price across states $(t_i, j + 1)$ and $(t_i, j - 1)$ with the short rate prevailing at (t_i, j). The result is shown in Figure 17.

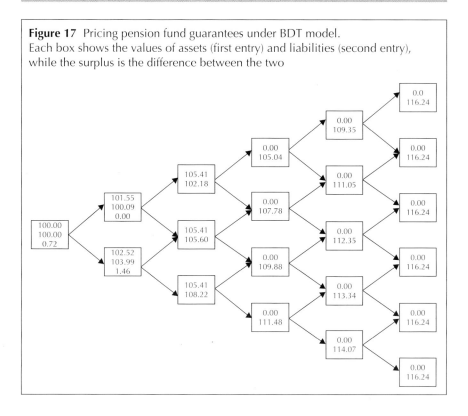

Figure 17 Pricing pension fund guarantees under BDT model.
Each box shows the values of assets (first entry) and liabilities (second entry),
while the surplus is the difference between the two

The first element in each box is the asset value. Note that for the last three periods this value is zero as cashflows for a two-period zero occur in Year 2. The value of a portfolio of five-year zero bonds is known at maturity to be 116.24. We start working backwards through the tree. Below, a couple of examples are given where $l(t_i, j)$ represents the liability value in the respective scenario

$$l(4,4) = \frac{\frac{1}{2}l(5,5) + \frac{1}{2}l(5,3)}{1+s(4,4)} = \frac{\frac{1}{2}116.24 + \frac{1}{2}116.24}{1+0.063} = 109.35$$

$$l(3,-1) = \frac{\frac{1}{2}l(4,0) + \frac{1}{2}l(4,-2)}{1+s(3,-1)} = \frac{\frac{1}{2}112.35 + \frac{1}{2}113.34}{1+0.027} = 109.88$$

$$l(3,3) = \frac{\frac{1}{2}l(4,4) + \frac{1}{2}l(4,2)}{1+s(3,3)} = \frac{\frac{1}{2}109.35 + \frac{1}{2}111.05}{1+0.0491} = 105.04$$

Liabilities are generally lower for higher interest rates. This is the scenario our pension plan manager is hoping for.

In Period 2 we receive cashflows from our two-year zero bonds. They can be discounted very much the same way. This results in Period 1 prices (for a zero bond with one year of life left) of 101.55 and 102.55. Here $a(t_i, j)$ reflects the state-dependent asset values. For example

$$a(1,1) = \frac{\frac{1}{2}a(2,2) + \frac{1}{2}a(2,0)}{1+s(1,1)} = \frac{\frac{1}{2}105.41 + \frac{1}{2}105.41}{1+0.0379} = 101.55 \quad (2.38)$$

Period 1 is also the point in time where the guarantee provided by the plan sponsor will trigger positive cashflows into the pension fund, should any underfunding occur. Cashflows are given by

$$pbg(1, j) = \max(l(1, j) - a(1, j), 0) \quad (2.39)$$

for $j = 1, -1$, which describes the involved optionality. Should rates rise, a short strategy will prove to be successful. However, if rates fall additional, funding will be costly. At time 0 the guarantee value is given by

$$pbg(0,0) = \frac{\frac{1}{2}pbg(1,1) + \frac{1}{2}pbg(1,-1)}{1+s(0,0)} = \frac{\frac{1}{2}0 + \frac{1}{2}1.46}{1+0.0204} = 0.72 \quad (2.40)$$

Note that we could have used state prices to evaluate the provided pension guarantee.

$$pbg(0,0) = AD(1,1)pbg(1,1) + AD(1,-1)pbg(1,-1)$$
$$= 0.49 \cdot 0 + 0.49 \cdot 1.46$$
$$= 0.72$$

Again, both technologies must provide us with the same result. The value of 0.72% comes directly out of the shareholders' pockets. Depending on the size of the pension fund relative to the sponsoring company, this can be substantial.

OPTION PRICING AND SURPLUS RISK

Corporate sponsors effectively guarantee to fund any pension fund deficit. What is the value of such a guarantee? How does it depend on the chosen asset allocation? This section uses a simple option pricing model, where we assumed no credit risk on the plan sponsor's side.

Suppose both assets and liabilities are stochastic and both follow Brownian motions as described below. Assets and liabilities evolve according to

$$da = \mu_a dt + \sigma_a dz_a \qquad (2.41)$$

$$dl = \mu_l dt + \sigma_l dz_l \qquad (2.42)$$

On the assets side μ_a and σ_a denote instantaneous expected return and risk (both parameters depend on the underlying asset allocation), while μ_l and σ_l carry the same meaning on the liability side. Let the correlation between assets and liabilities be ρ. The instantaneous covariance is then given by $\sigma_{al} = \rho\sigma_a\sigma_l$. To guarantee end-of-year pension deficits ($\tilde{l} - \tilde{a} > 0$, ie, liabilities exceeding assets) across all scenarios, amounts to calculating

$$E^Q \max\left[\tilde{l} - \tilde{a}, 0\right] \qquad (2.43)$$

where E^Q denotes the expected value in a risk-neutral world. Note that under the probability measure Q all assets earn the risk-free rate. Also note that (2.43) implicitly assumes that deficits need to be paid in while surpluses cannot be recovered. The funding ratio is defined as $f = a/l$. It implicitly defines the degree to which the corporate guarantee is in the money, ie, what is the funding situation, when we calculate the guarantee value. For $f < 1$ it is in the money while for $f = 1$ it is at the money. One way to evaluate expression (2.43) is to apply the exchange option pricing model by Magrabe (1974) which yields

$$pbg = l \cdot N(d_1) - a \cdot N(d_2) \qquad (2.44)$$

$$d_1 = \frac{\ln\left(\frac{1}{f}\right) + \frac{1}{2}\sigma_s^2 T}{\sigma_s \sqrt{T}}, d_2 = d_1 - \sigma\sqrt{T} \qquad (2.45)$$

$$\sigma_s^2 = \sigma_a^2 + \sigma_l^2 - 2\sigma_{al} \qquad (2.46)$$

Equation (2.44) expresses the option price in terms of delta hedging equivalents, while (2.45) and (2.46) define the respective inputs. We

Figure 18 Pension benefit guarantee cost.
Guarantee costs depend on funding ratio as well as asset volatility. It is
assumed that liabilities show a volatility of 10% (σ_l = 10%), while the
correlation between assets and liabilities amounts to ρ = 0.5

f	σ_a				
	1%	5%	10%	15%	20%
0.50	50.0	50.0	50.0	50.0	50.0
0.60	40.0	40.0	40.0	40.0	40.0
0.70	30.0	30.0	30.0	30.0	30.1
0.80	20.0	20.0	20.0	20.2	20.7
0.90	10.6	10.4	10.7	11.5	12.7
1.00	3.8	3.5	4.0	5.3	6.9
1.10	0.8	0.6	1.0	1.9	3.3
1.20	0.1	0.1	0.1	0.6	1.4
1.30	0.0	0.0	0.0	0.1	0.6
1.40	0.0	0.0	0.0	0.0	0.2
1.50	0.0	0.0	0.0	0.0	0.1

can now calculate (2.44) for alternative parameter constellations.
We are particularly interested how asset allocation changes (risk of
pension assets) affect the guarantee value. Results are summarised
in Figure 18. Increasing asset risk leads, all things being equal
(unchanged correlation), to an increase in the value of pension
benefit guarantees. Assets can now deviate more substantially from
liabilities.

Note that we calculated the value of a plan sponsor's guarantee as
a function of asset risk only. We did not look at credit risk. If the plan
sponsor's operating business is very risky and largely correlated
with asset risk, the value of the guarantee might be substantially less.
We will return to the these issues in Chapter 6.

OPTION PRICING AND THE VALUE OF PENSION CLAIMS
In the previous section we calculated the value of the plan sponsor's
promise to inject additional money if pension fund deficit occurs.
This implicitly assumed, that the there is no credit risk, that the plan
sponsor will always be around to honour its obligation. In reality plan
sponsors can default. How does this affect the pricing of liabilities?

The value of default-free liabilities after one period is denoted by
l^*. Discounted at the risk-free rate it becomes $l = l^*/(1+r)$. However,

Table 3 Liability pay-offs in different states of the world. For each state we can calculate the respective liability payoffs assuming the seniority of pension claims versus all other claims. The only state where pension claimants will receive less than the liability value is when the combined assets fall below the pension claim. Note that $\tilde{a}_p > l^*, \tilde{a}_p + \tilde{a}_c < l^*$ can never happen as long as $\tilde{a}_c > 0$

State	Payoff
$\tilde{a}_p < l^*, \tilde{a}_p + \tilde{a}_c < l^*$	$\tilde{a}_p + \tilde{a}_c$
$\tilde{a}_p > l^*, \tilde{a}_p + \tilde{a}_c > l^*$	l^*
$\tilde{a}_p < l^*, \tilde{a}_p + \tilde{a}_c > l^*$	l^*

the plan sponsor will not always able to meet its obligations. This is expressed in (2.47), where we distinguish between corporate assets $\tilde{a}_c$ invested into real projects and pension assets $\tilde{a}_p$ invested into capital markets.

$$l^* - \max\left[l^* - \max\left(\tilde{a}_p, \tilde{a}_p + \tilde{a}_c \right), 0 \right] \qquad (2.47)$$

In the notation above ~ stands for the random realisation at the end of our one-period model. If pension assets fall below nominal liabilities and the plan sponsor is at the same time not able to fill the resulting deficit, pensioners will receive less than l^*.

Note that equation (2.47) assumes priority of pension claims versus all other external claims. Liability payoffs across different states of the world are provided in Table 3. The expected value of $\max[l^* - \max(\tilde{a}_p, \tilde{a}_p + \tilde{a}_c), 0]$ under the risk-neutral distribution is equivalent to a put on the maximum of two assets (see Steenkamp, 1998):

$$l = \frac{l^*}{1+r} - p^{\max}\left(a_p, a_p + a_c, l^*, \ldots \right) \qquad (2.48)$$

The size of the pension fund is described by a_p, while the size of the plan sponsor can be measured by a_c. This allows us to identify the three key drivers to pension put valuation. What is their impact on the fair pricing of pension liabilities?

❏ *Relative size between pension fund and plan sponsor.* Large pension funds can easily bring down the plan sponsor. The larger the pension the less valuable is the plan sponsor's guarantee, ie, we approach a situation where the pension fund is very similar to a standalone entity.

❏ *Correlation between corporate assets and pension assets.* Low correlations imply a high degree of diversification. By correlation between pension assets and corporate assets we mean $\rho\left(\tilde{a}_p, \tilde{a}_c\right)$ and not $\rho(\tilde{a}_p, \tilde{a}_p + \tilde{a}_c)$. The latter is the term required as an input into pricing $p^{\max}(a_p, a_p + a_c, l^*)$ and can be calculated from

$$\rho\left(\tilde{a}_p, \tilde{a}_p + \tilde{a}_c\right) = \frac{Cov\left(\tilde{a}_p, \tilde{a}_p + \tilde{a}_c\right)}{\sqrt{Var\left(\tilde{a}_p\right)}\sqrt{Var\left(\tilde{a}_p + \tilde{a}_c\right)}}$$

$$= \frac{a_p^2 \sigma_{a_p}^2 + a_p a_c \sigma_{a_p} \sigma_{a_c} \rho\left(a_p, a_c\right)}{\sqrt{a_p^2 \sigma_{a_p}^2}\sqrt{a_p^2 \sigma_{a_p}^2 + a_c^2 \sigma_{a_c}^2 + 2a_p a_c \rho \sigma_{a_p} \sigma_{a_c}}} \quad (2.49)$$

Low correlation between pension assets and operating assets will be beneficial to pension claimants.

❏ *Volatility of pension assets and corporate assets.* In a one-period model the liability hedging solution is to invest into one-period bonds, which carry no uncertainty about the end-of-period payoff. The degree of hedging is characterised by the volatility of the pension asset.

With the above adjustments we can use the standard formula for pricing a put on the maximum of two assets. Changes in the above inputs (size of pension plan relative to plan sponsor, correlation between pension assets and corporate assets) will have a direct effect on $p^{\max}(a_p, a_p + a_c, l^*, ...)$. This in turn will affect the implicit liability discount rate:

$$y = \frac{l^*}{\dfrac{l^*}{1+r} - p^{\max}\left(a_p, a_p + a_c, l^*, ...\right)} - 1 \quad (2.50)$$

In case $p^{\max}(a_p, a_p + a_c, l^*, ...) = 0$, liabilities are without credit risk and hence $y = r$. In all other cases we will see $y > r$. Participants in defined benefit plans have little interest (actually no interest at all) in risky investment strategies. They hold no stake in a potential

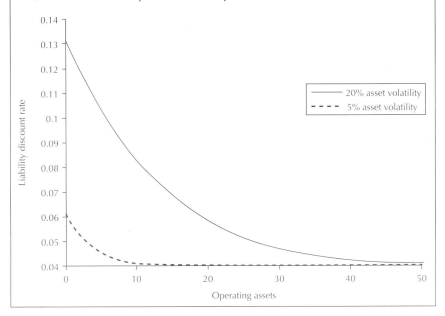

Figure 19 Endogenous liability discount rate.
The fair-value discount rate decreases with the size of the plan sponsor (market value of operating assets). Liability-oriented pension plans, ie, those that invest close to the one-period riskless security (liability matching solution in the one-period model), are less sensitive to the fate of the plan sponsor. It has been assumed that the correlation between pension assets and operating assets equals 0.5, the market value of pension assets equals 100 and the risk-free rate is 4%

surplus, while at the same time they face the risk that the plan sponsor will default on its obligation to cover pension fund deficits. If the pension fund is large relative to the sponsoring company, employees anticipate that the earning power of operating assets will likely not generate enough funds to be transferred to the pension fund in case assets fall below liabilities. At the margin the discount rate of pension liabilities is determined as if the pension fund were a standalone company.

The analysis above has shown that liability discount rates cannot be set exogenously but rather need to be endogenously determined. The market value of pension liabilities is dependent on the value and riskiness of operating and pension assets as well as on the amount of diversification. This alone makes an asset liability approach focusing on the pension fund in isolation dangerously worthless. Chapter 6 will make additional use of conditional claim analysis.

1　For a comprehensive treatment, see Anderson *et al* (1996).

2　This section generally describes some key technical features as the ILBs in different countries vary considerably. For a detailed description of alternative convention see Chapter 6 of Deacon, Derry and Mirfendereski (2004).

3　We can model this form of contingent payments as a series of up and in barrier options on inflation, where the barrier is specified in terms of the funding ratio. Note that an aggressive liability mismatch will increase the value of this indexation option (barriers is more likely to be hit) and therefore reduce the level of economic funding. Inflation sensitivities become now a function of the underlying asset allocation. It remains therefore unclear why a plan sponsor would ever want to become 110% funded.

4　For comprehensive reviews, see Rudolf (2000) or Schlag and Branger (2004).

5　All optimisations have been performed using NUOPT for S-Plus.

6　The reader is encouraged to replicate the numbers within a spreadsheet environment using the EXCEL solver.

7　This section replicates the ideas of Rudolf and Zimmermann (2001), but uses the BDT model instead of Ho and Lee.

REFERENCES

Anderson, N., F. Breedon, and M. Deacon, 1996, *Estimating and Interpreting the Yield Curve* (New York: John Wiley & Sons).

Deacon, M., A. Derry, and D. Mirfendereski, 2004, *Inflation-indexed Securities Bonds, Swaps and Other Derivatives* (New York: John Wiley & Sons).

Dybvig, P. and W. Marshall, 1996, "Pricing Long Bonds: Pitfalls and Opportunities", *Financial Analysts Journal*, pp 32–9.

Margrabe, 1974, "The Value of an Option to Exchange the Asset for Another", *Journal of Finance*, **33**, pp 177–186.

Nelson, C. and A. Siegel, 1977, "Parsimonious Modelling of Yield Curves", *Journal of Business*, **60**, pp 473–90.

Pearson, N., 2000, "Fixed Income Subtleties and the Pricing of Long Bonds", in N. Jegadeesh and B. Tuckman, *Advanced Fixed Income Valuation Tools* (New York: John Wiley & Sons).

Rudolf, M., 2000, *Zinstrukturmodelle* (Physica Verlag).

Rudolf, M. and H. Zimermann, 2001, "Term Structure Models and the Pricing of Pension Benefit Guarantees", Working Paper WHU and University of Basel.

Schlag, C. and N. Branger, 2004, *Zinsderivate* (Springer).

Steenkamp, T., 1998, "Contingent Claims Analysis and The Valuation of Pension Liabilities", Vrije Universiteit Amsterdam, Research paper 1999–19.

Svenson, L., 1995, "Estimating and Interpreting Forward Interest Rates: Sweden 1992–1994", IMF Working Paper.

3

Hedging Corporate Liabilities:
In Search for the Liability Asset

The previous chapter has argued that we can find the value of a
given set of liability cashflows by searching for the appropriate
instruments that perfectly replicate these cashflows. Traditional
fixed income indexes (such as J. P. Morgan UK government bonds
and Lehman Euro Aggregate) do not represent the interest rate or
inflation risk inherent in pension plans. In the previous chapter we
therefore calculated the price for a non-traded asset (liability cashflow that is subject to actuarial risk) by replicating the non-traded
cashflows with traded zero bonds. Pricing and hedging are highly
related concepts. The best way to hedge liability cashflows is to use
the replicating assets. However this is sometimes not desired or
feasible.

❏ *Perfect replication.* While this is the most efficient way, it is
 unlikely to be the immediate future. There are too many vested
 interests between consultants, asset managers and clients. After
 all, portfolio replication is a boring business performed by
 equally boring nerds whom only a few clients would want to go
 to lunch with. Investment consultants would have little to consult about, as they do not need to evaluate the investment
 processes of active managers and can demand little for "due
 diligence".
❏ *Liability indexing.* This would rescue the benchmark approach
 many active managers got so used to and still allow an active
 role for consultants and their hunt for the most successful active

managers. However, it also requires a change in the investment process of many asset managers. It also requires (liability benchmark relative) risk management and performance measurement technology, which only a few asset managers can yet provide.

❑ *Duration matching with derivative structures (overlay management).* This allows asset manager to proceed as if nothing had happened, while overlay management reduces the misfit between traditional benchmarks and liabilities. It is the most widespread approach due to its simplicity, but carries substantial liability hedging risks.

The techniques in this chapter will try to find the best possible hedge, knowing that real-life replication is often imperfect and involves the hedging of interest rate exposures.

Reader should for the time being not be worried if they read statements like this "traditional cash flow matching is not likely to be cost efficient as it prevents the plan sponsor from benefiting from high yielding assets". These statements are factually wrong as we will more formally show in Chapter 5.

DEFINING A GOOD HEDGE

Hedging of interest risk is imperfect, as it relies on assumptions of the nature of term structure shifts as well as the stability of historic yield curve movements. While we might have to live with this risk, we should nevertheless still ask: what defines a good hedge?

We can (by definition) decompose the movement in pension liabilities into a part that has been hedged and a part that randomly fluctuates around pension liabilities.

$$\frac{\Delta l_t}{l_t} = \frac{\Delta h_t}{h_t} + \varepsilon_t \tag{3.1}$$

In case liabilities can be fully replicated, deviations from liability movements become zero, ie, $\varepsilon_t = 0$ for all periods t. However, as we discussed above, this seems to be unrealistic in practice. While we cannot expect (3.1) to hold for each time period, we need at least assurance, that the average hedging error is zero.

$$E(\varepsilon_t) = 0 \tag{3.2}$$

Otherwise, our liabilities could outgrow the hedging assets. A typical situation in which (3.2) is violated arises if liabilities are discounted at interest rates that are well beyond market realities. This happens, when plan sponsors use unrealistically high discount rates in order to come up with lower liability valuation and hence less additional funding. We would also expect that our hedge works well in all market environments and is independent from the hedging portfolio itself:

$$Cov\left(\frac{\Delta h_t}{h_t}, \varepsilon_{t-s}\right) = 0 \quad \text{for all } s \qquad (3.3)$$

Sensible hedging also requires that hedging errors be uncorrelated over time:

$$Cov\left(\varepsilon_t, \varepsilon_{t-s}\right) = 0 \quad \text{for all } s \qquad (3.4)$$

If they were not, we could improve the quality of our hedge, by using the information in past hedging errors. A related argument is that we should use all available instruments, ie, the covariance of the hedging error with an alternative set of hedging instruments h* should also equal zero.

$$Cov\left(\varepsilon_t, \frac{\Delta h^*_{t-s}}{h^*_{t-s}}\right) = 0 \quad \text{for all } s \qquad (3.5)$$

While liability hedging activities by banks involve daily profit-and-loss calculations as well as hedge adjustments (need to be traded off against transaction costs), pension liabilities are evaluated once a year. This happens usually two months before annual reports close, so that necessary "adjustment" in forms of additional funding or adjusted discount rates can still enter the books. This is in strong contrast to banking operations. Usually, this sloppy approach is defended with a reference to the long-term nature of pension liabilities. The idea here is that risk washes out over time. Needless to say, it does not as the variance of hedging errors increases with time.

LINEAR PROGRAMMING APPROACH TO IMMUNISATION

We start from the assumption, that for whatever reason (see the introduction to this chapter), we cannot buy a set of cashflow-matching zero bonds. Suppose instead we are given a set of coupon $k = 1 \dots K$ bonds with differing maturities t_i for $i = 1, \dots, n$ and cashflows C_{k, t_i}. These bonds can be purchased in quantities n_1, $n_2, \dots, n_K$ at price B_i. We are also given a set of liability cashflows l_{t_i}, which we want to match as closely as possible. In vector notation we can write this as:

$$\mathbf{B} = (B_1 \ \ B_2 \ \ \ldots \ \ B_K)^T \tag{3.6}$$

$$\mathbf{l} = (l_{t_1} \ \ B_{t_2} \ \ \ldots \ \ l_{t_n})^T \tag{3.7}$$

$$\mathbf{n} = (n_1 \ \ n_2 \ \ \ldots \ \ n_K)^T \tag{3.8}$$

$$\mathbf{C} = \begin{bmatrix} C_{1,t_1} & \cdots & \cdots & C_{1,t_n} \\ \vdots & \ddots & & \vdots \\ \vdots & & & \vdots \\ C_{k,t_1} & \cdots & \cdots & C_{k,t_n} \end{bmatrix} \tag{3.9}$$

Note that many entries in (3.9) will actually be zero. For example Bond 1 might be a two-period bond that delivers two cashflows:

$$C_{1,t_1} = 0.05, \ C_{1,t_2} = 1.05, \text{ while } C_{1,t_3} = C_{1,t_4} = \ldots = C_{1,t_n} = 0 \tag{3.10}$$

For simplicity we assumed that liability cashflows and bond payments coincide on dates t_i. Given that a set of bond holdings allows us to calculate the associated cashflows as well as the corresponding deviation $\mathbf{c}$ from required liability payments

$$\mathbf{c} = \mathbf{C}^T \mathbf{n} - \mathbf{1} \tag{3.11}$$

where $\mathbf{c} = (c_{t_1}, \ c_{t_2}, \ \ldots, \ c_{t_n})$ are the period t_i cashflow deviations. Suppose we can reinvest these cashflows at rates $r_{t_1}, r_{t_2}, \ldots, r_{t_{n-1}}$ we can carry cash balances forward according to

$$ac_{t_{i+1}} = c_{t_{i+1}} + c_{t_i} \left(1 + r_{t_i}\right) \tag{3.12}$$

The accumulated cash balances are stored in $\mathbf{ac} = (ac_1 \ ac_2 \ \ldots \ ac_{t_n})$. Only positive cash balances are allowed, ie, $\mathbf{ac} \geq 0$. Leaving $\mathbf{ac}$ unconstrained would also allow borrowing. For perfect replication we require $\mathbf{c} = 0$. Note that carrying excess cashflows forward (3.14) always allows perfect replication. The question is to what price? If bonds across the maturity structure are missing and we do not earn the forward rates on the excess cash carried forward, we have to buy too many of the remaining bonds to fill the cashflow gaps. This will make the replicating portfolio more costly than the market value of pension liabilities. It is therefore our objective to keep the replication costs as small as possible. Let us finally define the matrix $\mathbf{R}$

$$\mathbf{R} = \begin{pmatrix} -1 & 0 & & & & & 0 \\ 1+r_{t_1} & -1 & 0 & & & & \\ 0 & 1+r_{t_2} & -1 & 0 & & & \\ & & 1+r_{t_3} & \ddots & 0 & & \\ & & & 0 & -1 & 0 & \\ 0 & & & & 1+r_{t_{n-1}} & -1 \end{pmatrix} \qquad (3.13)$$

We can now express the total problem as minimising replication costs under replication and non-negativity constraints.

$$\min_{\mathbf{n},\mathrm{ac}} \mathbf{B}^T \cdot \mathbf{n} \quad \text{subject to} \qquad (3.14)$$

$$\mathbf{C}^T \cdot \mathbf{n} + \mathbf{R} \cdot \mathbf{ac} = \mathbf{1} \qquad (3.15)$$

$$\mathbf{n} \geq 0, \ \mathbf{ac} \geq 0 \qquad (3.16)$$

The objective (3.14) is equivalent to minimising $\sum_{k=1}^{K} n_k B_k$, ie, replication costs. The replication constraint (3.15) states that cashflows from bond investments $(\mathbf{C}^T \cdot \mathbf{n})$ plus cash carried forward $(\mathbf{R} \cdot \mathbf{ac})$. In other words:

$$\sum_{k=1}^{K} n_k C_{k,t_i} + ac_{t_{i-1}}\left(1+r_{t_{i-1}}\right) - ac_{t_i} = 0 \quad \text{for all } t_i \qquad (3.17)$$

Note that for t_1 we have $ac_0 = 0$. Without this possibility the equality in (3.15) cannot be maintained and it becomes $\mathbf{C}^T \cdot \mathbf{n} \geq \mathbf{1}$ instead, in which case $\mathbf{B}^T \cdot \mathbf{n}$ becomes larger than it needs to be.

Let us illustrate (3.14) to (3.16) with a small-scale example. Suppose we are given a set of $K = 10$ par bonds with maturities ranging from t_1 to t_{10}. The data are summarised in the cashflow matrix $\mathbf{C}$ with $\mathbf{B}$ obviously being a $K \times 1$ vector of ones. All par bonds are consistently priced from market rates. That can easily be bootstrapped from $\mathbf{B} = \mathbf{C}\mathbf{d}$, ie, $\mathbf{d} = \mathbf{C}^{-1}\mathbf{B}$, where $\mathbf{d}$ is the vector of zero coupon prices for maturities t_1 to t_n.

$$C = \begin{bmatrix}
1.0220 & 0.0000 & 0.0000 & 0.0000 & 0.0000 & 0.0000 & 0.0000 & 0.0000 & 0.0000 & 0.0000 \\
0.0247 & 1.0247 & 00000 & 0.0000 & 0.0000 & 0.0000 & 0.0000 & 0.0000 & 0.0000 & 0.0000 \\
0.0269 & 0.0269 & 1.0269 & 0.0000 & 0.0000 & 0.0000 & 0.0000 & 0.0000 & 0.0000 & 0.0000 \\
0.0289 & 0.0289 & 0.0289 & 1.0289 & 0.0000 & 0.0000 & 0.0000 & 0.0000 & 0.0000 & 0.0000 \\
0.0306 & 0.0306 & 0.0306 & 0.0306 & 1.0306 & 0.0000 & 0.0000 & 0.0000 & 0.0000 & 0.0000 \\
0.0322 & 0.0322 & 0.0322 & 0.0322 & 0.0322 & 1.0322 & 0.0000 & 0.0000 & 0.0000 & 0.0000 \\
0.0335 & 0.0335 & 0.0335 & 0.0335 & 0.0335 & 0.0335 & 1.0335 & 0.0000 & 0.0000 & 0.0000 \\
0.0346 & 0.0346 & 0.0346 & 0.0346 & 0.0346 & 0.0346 & 0.0346 & 1.0346 & 0.0000 & 0.0000 \\
0.0356 & 0.0356 & 0.0356 & 0.0356 & 0.0356 & 0.0356 & 0.0356 & 0.0356 & 1.0356 & 0.0000 \\
0.0365 & 0.0365 & 0.0365 & 0.0365 & 0.0365 & 0.0365 & 0.0365 & 0.0365 & 0.0365 & 1.0365
\end{bmatrix}$$

$$(3.18)$$

If we use $\mathbf{d}$ to set r_{t_i} equal to the respective forward rates we can create the matrix $\mathbf{R}$, which is consistent with current market valuations.

$$R = \begin{bmatrix}
-1 & 0 & 0 & 0 & 0 & 0 & 0 & 0 & 0 & 0 \\
1.0274 & -1 & 0 & 0 & 0 & 0 & 0 & 0 & 0 & 0 \\
0 & 1.0317 & -1 & 0 & 0 & 0 & 0 & 0 & 0 & 0 \\
0 & 0 & 1.0353 & -1 & 0 & 0 & 0 & 0 & 0 & 0 \\
0 & 0 & 0 & 1.0382 & -1 & 0 & 0 & 0 & 0 & 0 \\
0 & 0 & 0 & 0 & 1.0405 & -1 & 0 & 0 & 0 & 0 \\
0 & 0 & 0 & 0 & 0 & 1.0425 & -1 & 0 & 0 & 0 \\
0 & 0 & 0 & 0 & 0 & 0 & 1.0441 & -1 & 0 & 0 \\
0 & 0 & 0 & 0 & 0 & 0 & 0 & 1.0454 & -1 & 0 \\
0 & 0 & 0 & 0 & 0 & 0 & 0 & 0 & 1.0465 & -1
\end{bmatrix}$$

$$(3.19)$$

Liability cashflows and discount factors are given by

$$\mathbf{l}^T = (1.0000 \quad 1.0236 \quad 1.0798 \quad 1.1160 \quad 1.1579 \quad 1.2005$$
$$1.2537 \quad 1.3002 \quad 1.3482 \quad 1.3988) \tag{3.20}$$

$$\mathbf{d}^T = (0.9785 \quad 0.9524 \quad 0.9231 \quad 0.8917 \quad 0.8589 \quad 0.8254$$
$$0.7918 \quad 0.7584 \quad 0.7254 \quad 0.6931) \tag{3.21}$$

The present value of liabilities is therefore $l = \mathbf{l}^T \mathbf{d} = 9.8571$. We can now go through some examples to strengthen our intuition. We assume that instead of ten par bond we have only nine par bonds available. In our first optimisation the one-year bond is missing; in our second optimisation the two-year bond is missing – and so on. We will run the optimisations with the assumption that cashflows

Table 1 Cashflow matching as linear programme.
The values above represent the replication costs calculated as $\sum_{k=1}^{K} n_k B_k$ under alternative possibilities to carry excess cash forward. If excess cash can be transferred at forward rates we will always be able to bring the replication costs down to the market value of liabilities: all we need is a single investment of 9.8572 in a one-period bond. All other cashflows can be replicated from this. In case we have as many bonds as cashflows (no bond missing), we will also be able to replicate liabilities at minimal cost (9.8572)

Missing bond	Carry forward with $r_{t_i}=0$	No carry forward	Carry forward with $r_{t_i} = \frac{d(0,t_i)}{d(0,t_{i+1})}$
#1	27.5251	27.5251	9.8572
#2	9.8766	28.1402	9.8572
#3	9.8813	29.6265	9.8572
#4	9.8850	30.5910	9.8572
#5	9.8885	30.5838	9.8572
#6	9.8916	32.8721	9.8572
#6	9.8948	34.3204	9.8572
#8	9.8975	35.5879	9.8572
#9	9.9000	36.9022	9.8572
#10	9.9023	n.a.	9.8572
None	9.8572	9.8572	9.8572

cannot be carried forward, can be carried forward but at zero interest rates and can be carried forward at forward rates implied in the current term structure. For each of the optimisations we report the replication costs. Bear in mind, that our benchmark is $l = 9.875$ ie, the market value of liabilities. The results are summarised in Table 1.

We see that allowing replication costs can largely differ, and replication is sometimes not even feasible. If we do not allow excess cash to be carried forward and at the same time do not allow investments into bonds that match the longest maturity, we cannot replicate all cashflows.

To see that matching (hedging) and pricing are highly related concepts, we can set up the dual to the previous problem.

$$\max_{d} 1^T d \quad \text{subject to} \tag{3.22}$$

$$Cd \le B \tag{3.23}$$

$$\mathbf{R}^T\mathbf{d} \leq 0 \qquad (3.24)$$

We start with (3.23). If the equality sign was satisfied ($\mathbf{C}^T\mathbf{d} = \mathbf{B}$) we arrive at the formula for valuing coupon bonds:

$$B^{C_k}(0,t_i) = \sum_{i=1}^{n} C_{k,t_i} d(0,t_i) \qquad \text{for all } k \qquad (3.25)$$

So $\mathbf{d}$ is the vector of existing zero bond prices, containing $\mathbf{d} = (d(0,t_1),\ldots d(0,t_n))^T$, which can also be used for liability valuation.

$$l = \mathbf{1}^T\mathbf{d} = \sum_{i=1}^{n} l_{t_i} d(0,t_i) \qquad (3.26)$$

Finally, we can interpret (3.24) as imposing no-arbitrage restrictions on the set of discount factors. Expanding $\mathbf{R}^T\mathbf{d}$ yields

$$\left(1+r_{t_i}\right)d\left(0,t_{i+1}\right) \leq d(0,t_i) \qquad (3.27)$$

This essentially enforces $d(0,t_{i+1}) \leq d(0,t_i)$ for positive reinvestment rates. Longer-dated zero bonds must always trade at a lower price than shorter-dated zeros. If we use market forward rates implied by the pricing of the available bond universe

$$r_{t_1} = \frac{d(0,t_i)}{d(0,t_{i+1})} - 1 \qquad (3.28)$$

constraint (3.24) will hold, as substituting (3.28) into (3.27) yields

$$-d(0,t_i)+\left(1+r_{t_1}\right)d(0,t_{i+1})$$
$$=-d(0,t_i) + \left(1+\frac{d(0,t_i)}{d(0,t_{i+1})}-1\right)d(0,t_{i+1})=0 \qquad (3.29)$$

What can we conclude from this section? First of all it seems artificial to allow excess cash to be carried forward at current forward rates, as we could use the same forward rates to replicate all cashflows without even investing into physical bonds. The most practical insights are twofold. If we have one bond for each cashflow maturity, we will be able to replicate all future cashflows at minimum costs. Even if we do not have the required number of bonds, we can considerably reduce the replication costs if we allow cash to be carried forward at least at zero rates. Note that the same technique applies to real bonds.

One consideration is still missing. We have not looked at credit risk. If we allow bonds with credit risks, which would carry a larger coupon at par, we will implicitly get a new term structure

$$d^{BBB}\left(0,t_i\right)<d^{AAA}\left(0,t_i\right)$$ (3.30)

and therefore also arrive at lower liability value

$$\sum_{i=1}^{n} l_{t_i} d^{BBB}\left(0,t_i\right)<\sum_{i=1}^{n} l_{t_i} d^{AAA}\left(0,t_i\right)$$ (3.31)

Suppose a company has a *BBB* rating for its outstanding debt. But, since there is not enough liquidity in *BBB* bonds as well as too little scope for diversification, individual credit risk would be too large. Even worse, available credits would be unlikely to span the whole maturity curve. How would we set up a liability benchmark? Luckily, the arrival of credit derivatives allows the separation of interest rate and credit risk. We could therefore use (3.14) to (3.24) and find a replicating portfolio of government bonds. The price of this portfolio would be too large for the companies underlying credit risk. In order to create (almost) the same credit risk and to reduce the costs of the respective portfolio the pension fund can sell an add-up basket credit default swap. The pension fund would therefore provide a payoff for defaults in any of the basket reference entities. The proceeds of this sale would reduce the costs of this portfolio to *BBB* funding level while at the same time generically creating *BBB* exposure.

NAIVE REPLICATION USING DURATION
Duration matching is one of the oldest methodologies for imperfect replication of cashflows (see Fabozzi, 1999). It has been used in early attempts of index replication or fixed-income risk management and is therefore a natural starting point for our discussion of imperfect replication.

Before we start calculating market exposures, we need to establish market values. How could we otherwise ever hope to correctly calculate liability risks if we can't even correctly price liability cashflows? We start with the valuation of pension liabilities using fair-value calculations from Chapter 2. The present value of future liabilities is derived using market-based discount factors and can be calculated from Table 2.

$$l = l_{t_1} d\left(0, t_1\right) + l_{t_2} d\left(0, t_2\right) + \cdots + l_{t_n} d\left(0, t_n\right)$$
$$= \sum_i l_{t_i} d\left(0, t_i\right) = 26.52 \tag{3.32}$$

The calculation in (3.32) also allows us also to calculate the internal rate of return for a set of pension liabilities from the solution of

$$l - l(y) = l - l_{t_1} \frac{1}{(1+y)^{t_1}} - l_{t_2} \frac{1}{(1+y)^{t_2}} - \cdots - l_{t_n} \frac{1}{(1+y)^{t_n}} = 0 \tag{3.33}$$

with respect to y. The solution for (3.33) is $y = 4.29\%$. We can think of y as the yield to maturity of a bond that pays cashflows l_{t_i} for the next $i = 1, \ldots, 50$ years and is priced at 26.52.

The idea of duration replication is to approximate changes in the present value of our liability stream from a (2nd order) Taylor approximation of $l = l(y)$.

$$\frac{\Delta l}{l} \approx -D\Delta y + \frac{1}{2} C\left(\Delta y\right)^2 \tag{3.34}$$

where D and C are called duration and convexity. The corresponding values are given in

$$D = \frac{\delta l}{\delta y} \frac{1}{l} = \sum_i w_{t_i} t_i = 16.39 \tag{3.35}$$

$$C = \frac{d^2 l}{dy^2} \frac{1}{l} = \sum_i w_{t_i} t_i^2 = 384.85 \tag{3.36}$$

$$w_{t_i} = \frac{l_{t_i} \frac{1}{(1+y)^{t_i}}}{l} \tag{3.37}$$

A value of $(\delta l / \delta y)(1/l) = 16.39$ means that pension liabilities are expected to fall by 16.39%, for a 100-basis-points (1%) increase in the discount rate. Note that the convexity term in (3.34) is positive, no matter whether rates fall or rise. It also becomes larger if yield changes increase in absolute value. For two bonds exhibiting the same duration, higher convexity is always preferable. However,

Table 2 Liability cashflows.
The table shows sample liabilities for a DAX 30 corporate.
Multiplying each cashflow (Column 2) with its respective discount
factor (Column 3) yields the present value of a given liability
payment. Relating this present value to the present value of total
liabilities gets the respective weight in present value terms (Column
5). Multiplying each weight its respective the time index (Column 6)
it allows us to calculate duration and convexity. The total value of
liabilities is $\sum_i l_{t_i} d(0, t_i) = 26.52$ with a yield to maturity of 4.29%

i	l_{t_i}	$d(0, t_i)$	$d(0, t_i)l_{t_i}$	$w_{t_i} = \dfrac{l_{t_i}\frac{1}{(1+y)^{t_i}}}{l}\%$	$w_{t_i}t_i$	$w_{t_i}t_i^2$
1	1.00	0.978	0.98	3.61	0.04	0.04
2	1.02	0.952	0.97	3.55	0.07	0.14
3	1.08	0.923	1.00	3.59	0.11	0.32
4	1.12	0.892	1.00	3.56	0.14	0.57
5	1.16	0.859	0.99	3.54	0.18	0.88
6	1.20	0.825	0.99	3.52	0.21	1.27
7	1.25	0.792	0.99	3.52	0.25	1.73
8	1.30	0.758	0.99	3.50	0.28	2.24
9	1.35	0.725	0.98	3.48	0.31	2.82
10	1.40	0.693	0.97	3.46	0.35	3.46
11	1.44	0.662	0.95	3.43	0.38	4.14
12	1.49	0.631	0.94	3.39	0.41	4.89
13	1.53	0.602	0.92	3.34	0.43	5.64
14	1.57	0.574	0.90	3.29	0.46	6.45
15	1.61	0.546	0.88	3.23	0.48	7.27
16	1.65	0.520	0.86	3.17	0.51	8.10
17	1.67	0.495	0.83	3.09	0.52	8.92
18	1.69	0.471	0.79	2.98	0.54	9.67
19	1.70	0.448	0.76	2.88	0.55	10.41
20	1.71	0.426	0.73	2.78	0.56	11.13
21	1.72	0.405	0.70	2.68	0.56	11.80
22	1.72	0.385	0.66	2.57	0.57	12.43
23	1.72	0.366	0.63	2.46	0.57	13.02
24	1.70	0.348	0.59	2.34	0.56	13.46
25	1.68	0.331	0.56	2.21	0.55	13.83
26	1.66	0.314	0.52	2.10	0.54	14.16
27	1.62	0.298	0.48	1.96	0.53	14.31
28	1.58	0.283	0.45	1.83	0.51	14.35
29	1.52	0.269	0.41	1.69	0.49	14.25
30	1.47	0.255	0.37	1.57	0.47	14.09
31	1.40	0.244	0.34	1.43	0.44	13.76
32	1.33	0.233	0.31	1.30	0.42	13.34
33	1.25	0.223	0.28	1.18	0.39	12.83
34	1.17	0.213	0.25	1.06	0.36	12.26
35	1.09	0.203	0.22	0.95	0.33	11.60
36	1.02	0.194	0.20	0.84	0.30	10.94

LIABILITY HEDGING AND PORTFOLIO CHOICE

Table 2 (continued)

i	l_{t_i}	$d(0, t_i)$	$d(0, t_i)l_{t_i}$	$w_{t_i} = \dfrac{l_{t_i}\frac{1}{(1+y)^{t_i}}}{l}$ %	$w_{t_i} t_i$	$w_{t_i} t_i^2$
37	0.94	0.186	0.17	0.75	0.28	10.25
38	0.87	0.177	0.15	0.66	0.25	9.57
39	0.79	0.170	0.13	0.58	0.23	8.83
40	0.72	0.162	0.12	0.51	0.20	8.13
41	0.65	0.155	0.10	0.44	0.18	7.34
42	0.59	0.148	0.09	0.38	0.16	6.68
43	0.53	0.141	0.07	0.33	0.14	6.04
44	0.47	0.135	0.06	0.28	0.12	5.38
45	0.42	0.129	0.05	0.24	0.11	4.82
46	0.37	0.123	0.05	0.20	0.09	4.32
47	0.33	0.118	0.04	0.17	0.08	3.86
48	0.30	0.113	0.03	0.15	0.07	3.44
49	0.26	0.108	0.03	0.13	0.06	3.01
50	0.23	0.103	0.02	0.11	0.05	2.64

this is true only in the simplified world where only parallel yield changes take place. But as parallel yield curve changes are not arbitrage-free (guaranteed profit of a position with equal duration but higher convexity, while all bonds earn the same yield), engineering high convexity is not always a good idea.

To see how well (3.34) approximates to actual liability changes, we can run through an example. Suppose interest rates increase by 100 basis points (1%) from 4.29% to 5.29% across all maturities. The resulting exact change amounts to

$$\frac{l(y+\Delta y)-l(y)}{l(y)} = \frac{l(4.29\%+1\%)-l(4.29\%)}{l(4.29\%)} = -14.04\% \quad (3.38)$$

Pension liabilities will fall by 14.04% if the yield to maturity rises by 100 basis points. Using duration alone will provide us with an approximated change that is considerably different.

$$\frac{\Delta l}{l} \approx -D\Delta y = -16.39\Delta y = -16.39\% \quad (3.39)$$

The reason for this is called convexity. Liability values react less heavily to interest rate rises than to interest rate falls. In other words a 100-basis-point drop in rates will lead to a larger change in

76

Table 3 Tracking universe.
For simplicity we focus on a three-bond universe. Each bond has a different maturity t_n (ranging from 1 to 30 year). All bonds are coupon paying (par) bonds $B^C (0, t_n)$

	B^C (0, t_n)	C_n	t_n	D	C
#1	100	2.202	1	1.000	1.000
#2	100	3.654	10	8.554	80.487
#3	100	4.373	30	17.259	410.016

value than a 100-basis-point rate increase. To some extent we can take account of this by including convexity next to duration:

$$\frac{\Delta l}{l} \approx -D\Delta y + \frac{1}{2}C(\Delta y)^2 = -16.39\Delta y + \frac{1}{2}384.84\Delta y^2 = -14.47\% \quad \textbf{(3.40)}$$

Now we arrive at a much closer approximation. Adding convexity significantly improved our ability to track changes in liabilities.

How can we use the above measures to find a liability-mimicking portfolio? Let's assume investors face an investment opportunity set of three par bonds (bonds that trade at par, ie, 100) at hand as given in Table 3.

All bonds are priced from Table 2, where coupons are given by

$$C_n = \frac{1-d(0, t_n)}{\sum_{i=1}^{n} d(0, t_n)} \times 100 \quad \textbf{(3.41)}$$

in order to arrive at par (under the current yield curve). The resulting bond characteristics are summarised in Table 3.

In order to track valuation changes for pension liabilities we employ three different strategies:

1. Duration equivalence. No short sales allowed. Maximise convexity to enforce unique solution.
2. Duration equivalence. No short sales allowed. Minimise convexity to enforce unique solution.
3. Duration equivalence. Short sales allowed. Create convexity of 500.

Table 4 Matching strategies.
Each strategy has a different (unique) solution. Strategies that try to create high convexity (#1 and #3) tend to be barbell strategies, where more weight is given to very long and very short bonds (even shorting intermediate maturity bonds as in strategy #3)

Strategy	θ_1	θ_2	θ_3	$D_{portfolio}$	$C_{portfolio}$
#1	5.30%	0.00%	94.70%	16.39	388.34
#2	0.00%	9.90%	90.10%	16.39	377.40
#3	59.38%	−101.01%	141.63%	16.39	500.00

The results of these strategies are given in Table 4. Mathematically, Strategy 1 is expressed as maximising portfolio convexity ($C_{portfolio}$), which is the value weighted average of individual convexities.

$$\max_{\theta_1, \theta_2, \theta_3} C_{portfolio}, \text{ subject to}$$

$$\sum_{i=1}^{3} \theta_i D_i = D_l$$
$$\sum_{i=1}^{3} \theta_i = 1$$
$$\theta_i \geq 0$$

Although Strategy 1 matches liability duration and convexity very closely we can see the cashflow mismatch in Figure 1.

Each mismatched cashflow exposes the investor to real-world reinvestment risk. For example, in Year 30, the 30-year bond pays $100 + 4.373$. However, as the strategy owns only 94.7%, this amounts to a payment of 98.841. Proper scaling (total amount of liabilities is 26.52 and not 100, which is the price of a weighted portfolio of par bonds) gives us a cashflow of 26.21 in Figure 1, which is considerably higher than the 1.46 liability cashflows. If rates drop, receiving a cashflow of 26.21 and reinvesting it at lower rates will not suffice to cover future cashflows. Also, any changes in yields between the 30- and 50-year sector of the curve will expose the plan sponsor to considerable yield curve risk (in this case the risk that the yield curve flattens). A barbell portfolio (investing at the "ends"

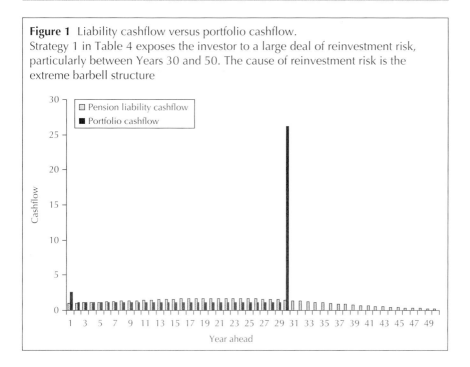

Figure 1 Liability cashflow versus portfolio cashflow.
Strategy 1 in Table 4 exposes the investor to a large deal of reinvestment risk, particularly between Years 30 and 50. The cause of reinvestment risk is the extreme barbell structure

of the yield curve, while leaving the medium-term sector) will not track liabilities very well in reality.

DURATION ANALYSIS WHEN LIABILITY CASHFLOWS ARE UNAVAILABLE

So far we have seen that duration analysis can provide only a first shot at the liability hedging problem. However, why do so many investors focus on a flawed approximation? The reason for this is (mostly) data availability. As actuaries do not think in terms of liability cashflows and discounting takes place on the assumption of a flat yield curve, cashflow data are available only at additional costs. However, while we have used individual cashflows to calculate duration and convexity in the previous section we can also calculate these numbers numerically. Suppose liabilities are dependent on two factors, eg, real interest rates (r) and inflation (π).

$$l = l(r, \pi) \tag{3.42}$$

We can now take a first-order Taylor approximation of l around current actuarial estimates of real interest rates $\bar{r}$ and inflation $\bar{\pi}$.

$$l(r, \pi) = l(\bar{r}, \bar{\pi}) + D_r^l \Delta r + D_\pi^l \Delta \pi + \tfrac{1}{2} D_{rr}^l \Delta r^2$$
$$+ \tfrac{1}{2} D_{\pi\pi}^l \Delta \pi^2 + D_{\pi r}^l \Delta \pi \Delta r \tag{3.43}$$

where D_i^l measure the sensitivity of liabilities with respect to $i \in \{\pi, r\}$. The same notation is used for higher-order derivatives, ie, $D_{\pi r}^l$ measures the real rate sensitivity if inflation rises.

No cashflows are needed as long as we can calculate liability values for any given parameter constellation. The derivatives in (3.43) can be approximated using their discrete counterparts.[1]

$$D_r^l \approx \frac{l(r+h, \pi) - l(r-h, \pi)}{2h} \tag{3.44}$$

$$D_\pi^l \approx \frac{l(r, \pi+h) - l(r, \pi-h)}{2h} \tag{3.45}$$

$$D_{r\pi} \approx \frac{[l(r+h, \pi+h) - l(r+h, \pi-h)] - [l(r-h, \pi+h) - l(r-h, \pi-h)]}{4h^2} \tag{3.46}$$

$$D_{rr}^l \approx \frac{[l(r+h, \pi) - l(r, \pi)] - [l(r, \pi) - l(r-h, \pi)]}{4h^2} \tag{3.47}$$

$$D_{\pi\pi}^l \approx \frac{[l(r, \pi+h) - l(r, \pi)] - [l(r, \pi) - l(r, \pi-h)]}{4h^2} \tag{3.48}$$

This liability approximation allows non-actuaries to develop simple models for asset liability management, even without any knowledge of the liability side. All that is required are the values for $l(r + h, \pi)$, $l(r - h, \pi)$, ..., $l(r - h, \pi - h)$. The derivatives in (3.44) and (3.45) can be thought of as real rate duration and inflation duration. Note that $D_\pi^{ABO} < D_\pi^{PBO}$ by its very definition. Targeting the *PBO* results in hedging wage growth, which has not even been decided upon and therefore overstates inflation risk. Hedging the *PBO* is equivalent to hedging the future wage bill of the firm. The same methodology can also be applied to evaluate the sensitivity of pension liabilities to other driving factors, such as productivity growth and accumulated inflation. Moreover, the methodology can also be applied to the sensitivity of service costs.

In order to find the risk-minimising (liability-hedging) solution we need to find the matching combination of inflation linked and nominal bonds. Let us define the following duration measures. The real duration (sensitivity to real yield changes) of real bonds is given by D_r^r, the real duration of nominal bonds by D_r^n, the inflation duration of nominal bonds by D_π^n, while the inflation duration of inflation bonds is obviously 0 (indexation makes real bonds react only to changes in real yields but not in inflation, which is the whole point of inflation protection). The equivalent duration measures for the liability side are given by D_r^l, D_π^l. We can now solve the following set of two linear equations with respect to the optimal weightings

$$\begin{bmatrix} D_r^r & D_r^n \\ 0 & D_\pi^n \end{bmatrix} \begin{bmatrix} w_r \\ w_n \end{bmatrix} = \begin{bmatrix} D_r^l \\ D_\pi^l \end{bmatrix} \tag{3.49}$$

The solution to (3.49) provides us with weighting of real (w_r) and nominal bonds (w_n), which achieves duration neutrality.

Instead of using physical investments we could also use inflation swaps. We need to first establish real rate and inflation duration of inflation swaps. The initial value of an inflation swap is given by

$$swap = b(0, t_i) - d(0, t_i) \cdot (1 + K_{t_i})^{t_i} = 0 \tag{3.50}$$

where $b(0, t_i) = (1 + r_{t_i})^{-t_i}$ and $d(0, t_i) = (1 + r_{t_i})^{-t_i}(1 + \pi_{t_i})^{-t_i}$ are the prices of real and nominal bonds of maturity t_i, while K is the agreed fixed side in an inflation swap (see Chapter 2). Note that real bond plus inflation swap equals nominal bond. We can now calculate the sensitivity of (3.50) to changes in inflation and real rates.

$$\frac{dswap}{dr}\bigg|_{K_{t_i}=\pi_{t_i}} = \frac{db(0, t_i)}{dr} - \frac{dd(0, t_i)}{dr}(1 + K_{t_i})^{t_i}$$

$$= -t_i(1 + r_{t_i})^{-t_i-1} - -t_i(1 + \pi_{t_i})^{-t_i}(1 + r_{t_i})^{-t_i-1}(1 + K_{t_i})^{t_i}$$

$$= 0 \tag{3.51}$$

$$\left.\frac{dswap}{d\pi}\right|_{K_{t_i}=\pi_{t_i}} = \frac{db(0,t_i)}{d\pi} - \frac{dd(0,t_i)}{d\pi}\left(1+K_{t_i}\right)^{t_i}$$

$$= 0 - -t_i\left(1+\pi_{t_i}\right)^{-t_i-1}\left(1+r_{t_i}\right)^{-t_i}\left(1+K_{t_i}\right)^{t_i}$$

$$= t_i\frac{b(0,t_i)}{\left(1+\pi_{t_i}\right)} \tag{3.52}$$

Note that for (3.50) to hold we need $K_{t_i} = \pi_{t_i}$, which also ensures (3.51) and (3.52). Suppose a plan sponsor already used duration to hedge interest rate risk. It has now to decide on how many zero-inflation swaps have to be purchased in order to hedge inflation risks. The hedge ratio ϕ can be set (almost) independently from the underlying bond portfolio, as inflation swaps do not a carry real rate duration.

$$\phi = \frac{D_\pi^l - D_\pi^n}{D_\pi^{swap}} \tag{3.53}$$

Suppose the inflation duration of liabilities is -5 years. A 1% increase in inflation would, other things being equal (ie, keeping

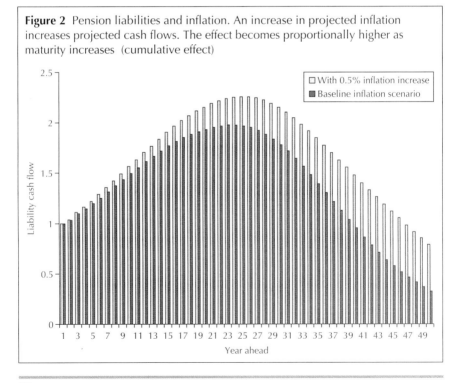

Figure 2 Pension liabilities and inflation. An increase in projected inflation increases projected cash flows. The effect becomes proportionally higher as maturity increases (cumulative effect)

Table 5 Inflation and real rate duration for alternative mortality assumptions.
As life expectancy increases, cashflows reach out far longer and so real rate duration also increases. Note that inflation duration is negative. If inflation rises, liabilities fall. This is due to the partial indexation of liabilities. Rising inflation implies an increase in liability cash flows, but also an increase in the discount rate. The net effect is negative. Under perfect indexation, inflation duration would be zero.
Negative inflation duration means that pension liabilities are actually long inflation risk. Falling inflation would increase liabilities. The optimal hedging policy would be to enter a contract that increases in value if inflation falls. This is opposite to the demand of most investors. They want to be protected against rising inflation

	Inflation duration	Real rate duration
Actuarial mortality	−5.83	−15.29
Life insurance mortality	−5.87	−17.49

real rates constant), lead to a 5% decrease in liabilities. The value of liabilities would remain constant only if liabilities were perfectly indexed. Assume further the inflation duration of nominal bonds is −10 years, while the inflation duration of an inflation swap is assumed to be 10 years. The swap value rises if inflation increases. Substituting these values into (3.53) yields a 50% hedge ratio. The inflation swap hedges whatever inflation exposure is left. Suppose instead pension liabilities are fully indexed ($D_\pi^l = 0$). In this case the optimal hedge ratio is 100%.

$$\phi = -\frac{D_\pi^n}{D_\pi^{swap}} = -\frac{-10}{10} = 1 \qquad (3.54)$$

The asset liability manager has to completely hedge out the inflation risk (nominal bond prices fall when inflation rises), as pension liabilities in this example do not carry any inflation risk. The portfolio of nominal bonds needs to be protected against rising inflation by an offsetting inflation hedge. Also, note that inflation swaps can be used to transform any nominal bond into a real bond plus the respective yield pick-up. That is why it has been sometimes recommended to invest in corporate bonds, and inflation swaps make pension assets work harder. In fact, derivatives allow us to decouple interest, inflation and credit risk. This allows pension funds to choose any warranted exposure.

How can we apply this framework in practice? The scenario calculations in Tables 6–8 allow us to calculate the required numbers for Table 5. We distinguish between actuarial mortality tables used in liability valuation (which are slowly updated to reflect changes in life expectancy) and life insurance mortality tables (which reflect current mortality assumptions and are used in pricing life insurance policies).

While we have seen at the end of Chapter 1 that using one mortality table rather than the other will result in largely differing liability values, we also see that real rate exposure values largely differ. It is worthwhile to further investigate the difference between both mortality tables in Tables 9 and 10.

Comparing both tables, we see that durations under insurance mortalities are significantly higher. This is not surprising. As life expectancy lengthens, cashflows stretch further out. Also, as cashflows become more back-loaded, convexity increases. All exposure measures increase under life insurance mortality tables. A second observation is also worth noting. If inflation rises, interest rate duration increases ($D_{r\pi} > 0$). This should come as no surprise. Inflation will increase distant cashflows and hence we should see an increase in both duration and convexity.

So far we decomposed changes in interest rates into real rate and inflation changes. Why have we done so?

❑ First, because we can easily decompose the reaction of financial instruments into real rate and inflation changes. Real bonds do not react to changes in inflation per se (as we have seen in the previous chapter). They rather move with real rates, while nominal bonds and real bonds both move with real rates (leaving inflation constant).

❑ Second, because empirically there is virtually zero correlation between changes in real yields and inflation, as can be seen in Figure 3. Not only does it make risk calculations extremely convenient, but it is also what we would expect. There is little reason (apart from "money illusion") why real and nominal variables should show any correlation.

Under the assumption of parallel yield curve changes we can calculate the liability risks from the following calculations. The

Table 6 Base-case liabilities for different assumptions on salary growth and mortality.
Each column shows liability cashflows. We arrive at present values using the appropriate discount factors

Year	Inflation					
	2% (= current)					
	Margin on inflation 0.5%		Margin on inflation 1% (current)		Margin on inflation 1.5%	
	Current mortality	Life insurance mortality	Current mortality	Life insurance mortality	Current mortality	Life insurance mortality
2004	1.00	1.00	1.00	1.00	1.00	1.00
2005	1.02	1.04	1.02	1.04	1.02	1.04
2006	1.08	1.11	1.08	1.11	1.08	1.11
2007	1.11	1.16	1.12	1.16	1.12	1.16
2008	1.16	1.22	1.16	1.22	1.16	1.22
2009	1.20	1.28	1.20	1.29	1.20	1.29
2010	1.25	1.35	1.25	1.36	1.26	1.36
2011	1.30	1.42	1.30	1.42	1.31	1.43
2012	1.34	1.49	1.35	1.49	1.35	1.50
2013	1.39	1.56	1.40	1.57	1.41	1.58
2014	1.43	1.63	1.44	1.63	1.45	1.64
2015	1.48	1.70	1.49	1.70	1.50	1.72
2016	1.52	1.76	1.53	1.77	1.54	1.78
2017	1.56	1.82	1.57	1.84	1.58	1.85
2018	1.60	1.89	1.61	1.90	1.62	1.92
2019	1.63	1.95	1.65	1.97	1.66	1.99
2020	1.65	2.00	1.67	2.02	1.69	2.04
2021	1.67	2.05	1.69	2.07	1.71	2.09
2022	1.68	2.09	1.70	2.12	1.72	2.14
2023	1.69	2.13	1.71	2.15	1.74	2.19
2024	1.69	2.16	1.72	2.19	1.75	2.23
2025	1.69	2.19	1.72	2.22	1.75	2.26
2026	1.68	2.20	1.72	2.24	1.75	2.28
2027	1.66	2.22	1.70	2.25	1.74	2.30
2028	1.64	2.22	1.68	2.26	1.72	2.31
2029	1.61	2.21	1.66	2.26	1.71	2.31
2030	1.57	2.20	1.62	2.25	1.67	2.31
2031	1.53	2.18	1.58	2.23	1.63	2.29
2032	1.47	2.14	1.52	2.19	1.58	2.26
2033	1.41	2.09	1.47	2.15	1.53	2.22
2034	1.34	2.04	1.40	2.11	1.46	2.18
2035	1.27	1.99	1.33	2.05	1.39	2.13
2036	1.19	1.92	1.25	1.99	1.32	2.07
2037	1.12	1.85	1.17	1.92	1.24	2.00
2038	1.04	1.78	1.09	1.85	1.16	1.93

Table 6 (continued)

Year	Inflation					
	2% (= current)					
	Margin on inflation 0.5%		Margin on inflation 1% (current)		Margin on inflation 1.5%	
	Current mortality	Life insurance mortality	Current mortality	Life insurance mortality	Current mortality	Life insurance mortality
2039	0.96	1.71	1.02	1.77	1.08	1.86
2040	0.89	1.63	0.94	1.70	1.00	1.78
2041	0.82	1.56	0.87	1.63	0.92	1.71
2042	0.75	1.49	0.79	1.56	0.85	1.63
2043	0.68	1.42	0.72	1.48	0.77	1.56
2044	0.61	1.34	0.65	1.40	0.70	1.48
2045	0.55	1.27	0.59	1.33	0.63	1.41
2046	0.49	1.21	0.53	1.26	0.57	1.34
2047	0.44	1.13	0.47	1.19	0.51	1.26
2048	0.39	1.06	0.42	1.12	0.45	1.19
2049	0.35	1.00	0.37	1.05	0.41	1.12
2050	0.31	0.93	0.33	0.98	0.36	1.04
2051	0.28	0.87	0.30	0.92	0.32	0.98
2052	0.24	0.81	0.26	0.85	0.28	0.91
2053	0.21	0.74	0.23	0.79	0.25	0.84

Table 7 Liabilities for 1% inflation increase under different assumptions on salary growth and mortality.
Each column shows liability cashflows. We arrive at present values using the appropriate discount factors

Year	Inflation					
	3% (= current + 1%)					
	Margin on Inflation 0.5%		Margin on inflation 1% (current)		Margin on inflation 1.5%	
	Current mortality	Life insurance mortality	Current mortality	Life insurance mortality	Current mortality	Life insurance mortality
2004	1.00	1.00	1.00	1.00	1.00	1.00
2005	1.03	1.05	1.03	1.05	1.03	1.05
2006	1.10	1.13	1.10	1.13	1.10	1.13
2007	1.14	1.19	1.14	1.19	1.14	1.19
2008	1.19	1.26	1.19	1.26	1.20	1.26

Table 7 (continued)

Year	Inflation					
	3% (= current + 1%)					
	Margin on inflation 0.5%		Margin on inflation 1% (current)		Margin on inflation 1.5%	
	Current mortality	Life insurance mortality	Current mortality	Life insurance mortality	Current mortality	Life insurance mortality
2009	1.24	1.33	1.25	1.34	1.25	1.34
2010	1.31	1.42	1.31	1.42	1.32	1.43
2011	1.36	1.49	1.37	1.50	1.37	1.51
2012	1.42	1.58	1.43	1.58	1.43	1.59
2013	1.48	1.66	1.49	1.67	1.50	1.68
2014	1.53	1.74	1.54	1.75	1.55	1.76
2015	1.59	1.83	1.60	1.84	1.61	1.85
2016	1.64	1.90	1.65	1.92	1.66	1.93
2017	1.69	1.99	1.70	2.00	1.72	2.02
2018	1.74	2.07	1.75	2.09	1.77	2.10
2019	1.78	2.14	1.80	2.16	1.82	2.18
2020	1.81	2.21	1.83	2.23	1.85	2.26
2021	1.83	2.28	1.86	2.30	1.88	2.33
2022	1.86	2.34	1.88	2.37	1.91	2.39
2023	1.87	2.39	1.90	2.42	1.93	2.46
2024	1.88	2.44	1.92	2.48	1.95	2.52
2025	1.89	2.48	1.93	2.52	1.97	2.57
2026	1.89	2.52	1.93	2.56	1.98	2.61
2027	1.88	2.54	1.93	2.60	1.97	2.65
2028	1.86	2.56	1.91	2.62	1.97	2.68
2029	1.85	2.57	1.90	2.64	1.95	2.70
2030	1.81	2.57	1.86	2.64	1.92	2.71
2031	1.76	2.56	1.82	2.63	1.88	2.70
2032	1.71	2.53	1.77	2.61	1.83	2.68
2033	1.65	2.50	1.72	2.58	1.78	2.65
2034	1.58	2.46	1.65	2.54	1.72	2.62
2035	1.51	2.40	1.57	2.49	1.64	2.57
2036	1.43	2.34	1.50	2.43	1.56	2.51
2037	1.34	2.27	1.41	2.36	1.48	2.45
2038	1.26	2.20	1.33	2.29	1.39	2.38
2039	1.17	2.12	1.24	2.21	1.31	2.30
2040	1.09	2.04	1.15	2.13	1.22	2.21
2041	1.01	1.96	1.07	2.05	1.13	2.13
2042	0.92	1.88	0.98	1.97	1.04	2.05
2043	0.85	1.80	0.90	1.88	0.95	1.96
2044	0.76	1.71	0.81	1.79	0.86	1.87
2045	0.69	1.63	0.74	1.71	0.79	1.79
2046	0.63	1.55	0.67	1.63	0.71	1.70
2047	0.56	1.46	0.60	1.54	0.64	1.62

Table 7 (continued)

Year	3% (= current + 1%)					
	Margin on inflation 0.5%		Margin on inflation 1% (current)		Margin on inflation 1.5%	
	Current mortality	Life insurance mortality	Current mortality	Life insurance mortality	Current mortality	Life insurance mortality
2048	0.50	1.38	0.54	1.45	0.58	1.52
2049	0.45	1.30	0.48	1.37	0.52	1.44
2050	0.40	1.22	0.43	1.29	0.46	1.35
2051	0.36	1.14	0.39	1.21	0.42	1.27
2052	0.32	1.06	0.34	1.13	0.37	1.19
2053	0.28	0.98	0.30	1.04	0.32	1.10

Table 8 Liabilities for 1% inflation decrease under different assumptions on salary growth and mortality.
Each column shows liability cashflows. We arrive at present values using the appropriate discount factors

Year	1% (= current − 1%)					
	Margin on inflation 0.5%		Margin on inflation 1% (current)		Margin on inflation 1.5%	
	Current mortality	Life insurance mortality	Current mortality	Life insurance mortality	Current mortality	Life insurance mortality
2004	1.00	1.00	1.00	1.00	1.00	1.00
2005	1.02	1.04	1.02	1.04	1.02	1.04
2006	1.08	1.11	1.08	1.11	1.08	1.11
2007	1.11	1.16	1.12	1.16	1.12	1.16
2008	1.16	1.22	1.16	1.22	1.16	1.22
2009	1.20	1.28	1.20	1.29	1.20	1.29
2010	1.25	1.35	1.25	1.36	1.26	1.36
2011	1.30	1.42	1.30	1.42	1.31	1.43
2012	1.34	1.49	1.35	1.49	1.35	1.50
2013	1.39	1.56	1.40	1.57	1.41	1.58
2014	1.43	1.63	1.44	1.63	1.45	1.64
2015	1.48	1.70	1.49	1.70	1.50	1.72
2016	1.52	1.76	1.53	1.77	1.54	1.78
2017	1.56	1.82	1.57	1.84	1.58	1.85

Table 8 (continued)

Year	Inflation					
	1% (= current − 1%)					
	Margin on inflation 0.5%		Margin on inflation 1% (current)		Margin on inflation 1.5%	
	Current mortality	Life insurance mortality	Current mortality	Life insurance mortality	Current mortality	Life insurance mortality
2018	1.60	1.89	1.61	1.90	1.62	1.92
2019	1.63	1.95	1.65	1.97	1.66	1.99
2020	1.65	2.00	1.67	2.02	1.69	2.04
2021	1.67	2.05	1.69	2.07	1.71	2.09
2022	1.68	2.09	1.70	2.12	1.72	2.14
2023	1.69	2.13	1.71	2.15	1.74	2.19
2024	1.69	2.16	1.72	2.19	1.75	2.23
2025	1.69	2.19	1.72	2.22	1.75	2.26
2026	1.68	2.20	1.72	2.24	1.75	2.28
2027	1.66	2.22	1.70	2.25	1.74	2.30
2028	1.64	2.22	1.68	2.26	1.72	2.31
2029	1.61	2.21	1.66	2.26	1.71	2.31
2030	1.57	2.20	1.62	2.25	1.67	2.31
2031	1.53	2.18	1.58	2.23	1.63	2.29
2032	1.47	2.14	1.52	2.19	1.58	2.26
2033	1.41	2.09	1.47	2.15	1.53	2.22
2034	1.34	2.04	1.40	2.11	1.46	2.18
2035	1.27	1.99	1.33	2.05	1.39	2.13
2036	1.19	1.92	1.25	1.99	1.32	2.07
2037	1.12	1.85	1.17	1.92	1.24	2.00
2038	1.04	1.78	1.09	1.85	1.16	1.93
2039	0.96	1.71	1.02	1.77	1.08	1.86
2040	0.89	1.63	0.94	1.70	1.00	1.78
2041	0.82	1.56	0.87	1.63	0.92	1.71
2042	0.75	1.49	0.79	1.56	0.85	1.63
2043	0.68	1.42	0.72	1.48	0.77	1.56
2044	0.61	1.34	0.65	1.40	0.70	1.48
2045	0.55	1.27	0.59	1.33	0.63	1.41
2046	0.49	1.21	0.53	1.26	0.57	1.34
2047	0.44	1.13	0.47	1.19	0.51	1.26
2048	0.39	1.06	0.42	1.12	0.45	1.19
2049	0.35	1.00	0.37	1.05	0.41	1.12
2050	0.31	0.93	0.33	0.98	0.36	1.04
2051	0.28	0.87	0.30	0.92	0.32	0.98
2052	0.24	0.81	0.26	0.85	0.28	0.91
2053	0.21	0.74	0.23	0.79	0.25	0.84

Table 9 Duration figures for life insurance mortality under different inflation assumptions.
Forward differences approximate duration with a 1% fall in rates, while backward differences use a 1% rise. Due to convexity, both values differ. Hence practitioners are advised rather to use the central difference. We also calculated central differences, as can be seen in (3.44) and (3.45). The change between forward and backward difference can be used to calculate convexity

	Forward difference (1% fall in rates)	Backward difference (1% rise in rates)	Central difference (+/−1% change)	Convexity
Base case	−15.13	−19.45	−17.49	215.90
1% rise in inflation	−15.75	−20.39	−18.07	231.86
1% fall in inflation	−14.48	−17.63	−16.61	202.15

Table 10 Duration figures for actuarial mortality under different inflation assumptions.
Forward differences approximate duration with a 1% fall in rates, while backward differences use a 1% rise. Due to convexity, both values differ. Hence practitioners are advised rather to use the central difference

	Forward difference (1% fall in rates)	Backward difference (1% rise in rates)	Central difference (+/−1% change)	Convexity
Base case	−13.56	−17.30	−15.29	173.15
1% rise in inflation	−15.44	−19.49	−17.49	183.97
1% fall inflation	−13.41	−16.41	−13.50	163.22

covariance matrix of yield changes is given by Ω. Together with the duration exposures we can calculate the standard deviation of liability returns (σ_l) as given below.

$$\Omega = \begin{bmatrix} 0.45^2 & 0 \\ 0 & 0.52^2 \end{bmatrix} \quad \mathbf{d}^l = \begin{pmatrix} D_\pi^l \\ D_r^l \end{pmatrix} = \begin{pmatrix} -15.29 \\ -5.83 \end{pmatrix}$$

$$\sigma_l = \sqrt{\mathbf{d}_l^T \Omega \mathbf{d}_l}$$

$$= \sqrt{\begin{pmatrix} -15.29 \\ -5.83 \end{pmatrix}^T \begin{pmatrix} 0.45^2 & 0 \\ 0 & 0.52^2 \end{pmatrix} \begin{pmatrix} -15.29 \\ -5.83 \end{pmatrix}}$$

$$= 7.66 \tag{3.55}$$

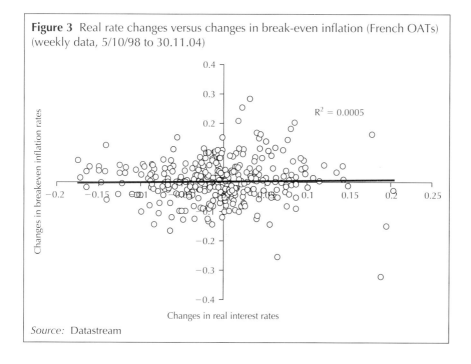

Figure 3 Real rate changes versus changes in break-even inflation (French OATs) (weekly data, 5/10/98 to 30.11.04)

Source: Datastream

Liability volatility is about 7.66. Note that this value critically depends on the volatility of real yield and inflation changes.

Suppose we opt for immunising only changes in nominal rates. How much risks would be left unaccounted? We assume here for simplicity that real and nominal bonds with the equivalent duration numbers are readily available. If we denote $\mathbf{d}_e$ as the vector of excess durations (asset minus liability durations) the following calculations would yield asset/liability risks of still 4.91%.

$$\mathbf{d}_e = \mathbf{d}_a - \mathbf{d}_l = \begin{pmatrix} -15.31 \\ -15.31 \end{pmatrix} - \begin{pmatrix} -15.31 \\ -5.83 \end{pmatrix} = \begin{pmatrix} 0 \\ -9.45 \end{pmatrix}$$

$$\sigma_l = \sqrt{\mathbf{d}_e^{\ T} \Omega \mathbf{d}_e}$$

$$= \sqrt{\begin{pmatrix} 0 \\ -9.45 \end{pmatrix}^T \begin{pmatrix} 0.45^2 & 0 \\ 0 & 0.52^2 \end{pmatrix} \begin{pmatrix} 0 \\ -9.45 \end{pmatrix}}$$

$$= 4.91 \tag{3.56}$$

Please note, that so far we made the simplifying assumption that inflation risks can be perfectly hedged, ie, that there is no difference between the inflation inherent in the hedge instrument (for example, French CPI) and the inflation adjustments in the actual pension plan (for example, German wage growth in the banking sector).

In reality there will be differences (also called basis risk) that will affect the effectiveness of the hedge. We can generalise the problem. What correlation between my proxy (less than perfectly correlated) hedge and the position to be hedged do we need, in order to decrease risk? Clearly if there was no correlation between French inflation and German wage growth in the banking sector (or possibly worse: negative correlation) any hedging attempt would result in an increased overall risk. What is the critical correlation? Define σ_h as the volatility of the attempted hedge.

The inflation attached to the proxying instrument is given by π^* as opposed to the inflation π we target to hedge. For any hedge to be considered, we need the inflation risk after hedging has taken place to be less than before hedging. This is expressed below:

$$\sigma_h^2 = \underbrace{D_\pi^2\left(\sigma_\pi^2 + \sigma_{\pi^*}^2 - 2\rho\sigma_\pi\sigma_{\pi^*}\right)}_{\text{inflation risk after hedging}} < \underbrace{D_\pi^2\sigma_\pi^2}_{\substack{\text{inflation risk}\\\text{before hedging}}} \tag{3.57}$$

Under the assumption that French CPI is as volatile as German wage growth ($\sigma_{\Delta\pi} = \sigma_{\Delta\pi^*}$), we can solve for the required correlation and get the condition that $\rho > 1/2$. How well this requirement is met is an empirical question. Figure 4 graphs the historical (12-month rolling) correlation between European CPI and German CPI. Note that the correlation is not always above 0.5. Note further that German CPI is again quite different from German wage growth in the banking industry. Hence it is not clear that inflation hedging reduces the risk that assets and liabilities might drift apart. If we instead had used French CPI, the number would have looked even worse (because German CPI is already a considerable part of European CPI).

We can also use the above approximation in order to quickly estimate the impact of a 1% decrease in both inflation (π) *and* discount rate ($y = r + \pi$). This is equivalent to a decrease in inflation that leaves real rates unchanged. Hence we can approximate the instantaneous change in liabilities by

Figure 4 Rolling correlation (12-month window) between changes in European inflation and German inflation.
Calculations are based on monthly data and span the time period between June 1995 and October 2004. Raw data have not been seasonally adjusted

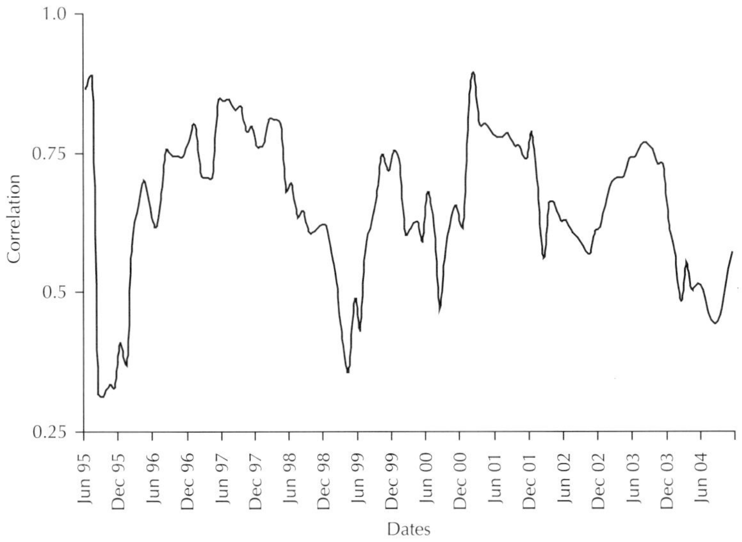

Source: Datastream

$$\frac{\Delta l}{l} \approx D_{\pi}^{l}\Delta\pi + D_{r}^{l}\Delta r$$
$$= D_{\pi}^{l}\Delta\pi + D_{r}^{l}\left(\Delta y - \Delta\pi\right)$$
$$= 5.83 \times (-1\%) + (-15.31) \cdot (1\% - 1\%)$$
$$= -5.83\% \tag{3.58}$$

Changes in discount rates and inflation can have dramatic changes on the fair value of insurance liabilities. An increase in inflation of $\Delta\pi = 1\%$, coupled with a 1% decrease in the discount factor $\Delta y = -1\%$, leads to a percentage change in liabilities of

$$\frac{\Delta l}{l} \approx D_{\pi}^{l}\Delta\pi + D_{r}^{l}\left(\Delta y - \Delta\pi\right)$$
$$= 5.83 \times 1\% - 15.31\left(-1\% - 1\%\right)$$
$$= 36.43\% \tag{3.59}$$

Table 11 Liabilities values.
The table provides a traditional scenario analysis, for changes in inflation ($\Delta\pi$) and discount rate ($\Delta y = \Delta r + \Delta\pi$) using (3.58)

		Inflation		
		1%	**2%**	**3%**
Discount rate	100 bps	21.05	22.93	29.21
	unchanged	24.24	26.52	31.77
	−100 bps	28.23	31.04	36.18

Hence $\Delta l = 26.52 \times (1 + 36.43\%) = 36.18$ as calculated in Table 11. Again, we do not recommend modelling changes in liability fair value as a function of changes in discount rates and inflation, as it is both inconsistent with the pricing of financial instruments and would add an additional term: $Cov(\Delta y, \Delta\pi) = Cov(\Delta r - \Delta\pi, \Delta\pi) = -Var(\Delta\pi)$ for $Cov(\Delta r, \Delta\pi) = 0$, that makes calculations unnecessarily difficult.

HEDGING PENSION LIABILITIES WITH GENERALISED DURATION VECTOR MODELS

The generalised duration vector model tries to calculate interest rate risk *exposure measures* for non-infinitesimal, nonparallel yield curve changes under non-flat-yield curves (see Chambers, Carleton and McEnally, 1988; Chambers and Nawalka, 1997). It is as such an extension of the simple duration model. It is called vector model because it needs to calculate a vector of m durations, ranging from

$$D_m = \sum_i w_{t_i} g\left(t_i\right)^m, m = 1, \ldots, M \tag{3.60}$$

$$w_{t_i} = \frac{l_{t_i} d\left(0, t_i\right)}{\sum_i l_{t_i} d\left(0, t_i\right)} = \frac{l_{t_i} d\left(0, t_i\right)}{l} \tag{3.61}$$

where $g(t) = t^\alpha$, such that $t^\alpha, t^{\alpha 2}, t^{\alpha 3}, \ldots$ for $m = 1, 2, 3, \ldots$. How can we use (3.60) to approximate changes in liability value? After all, we want to describe changes in liability values (Δl) as a function of risk exposures similar to (3.34). Suppose $g(t) = t$. Percentage changes can then be approximated by

$$-\frac{\Delta l}{l} = D_1^l \left[\Delta f(0) \right] + D_2^l \left[\frac{1}{2} \frac{(\delta \Delta f(t))}{\delta t} - (\Delta f(0))^2 \right]_{t=0}$$

$$+ D_3^l \left[\frac{1}{3!} \frac{(\delta^2 \Delta f(t))}{\delta t^2} - 3\Delta f(0) \frac{(\delta \Delta f(t))}{\delta t} + (\Delta f(0))^3 \right]_{t=0} \tag{3.62}$$

where $f(t)$ describes the term structure of (continuously compounded) instantaneous forward rates. Note that in this framework $d(0, t_i) = e^{-\int_0^{t_i} f(s)ds}$. Percentage changes are expressed as the summation product of duration and yield curve change. Yield curve changes range from parallel shifts in the term structure of forward rates $\Delta f(0)$ to changes in slope, curvature, etc. But how can we fill (3.62) with life? How can we check how well (3.62) tracks liability changes? To do so we need to undertake a series of steps.

Step 1. We choose a yield curve model. Suppose we estimate our model of the spot yield curve (from Chapter 2) $s(t_n) = b_0 + b_1 \left(\frac{1-e^{-t_n/\tau}}{t_n/\tau} \right) + b_2 \left(\frac{1-e^{-t_n/\tau}}{t_n/\tau} - e^{-t_n/\tau} \right)$ with the corresponding forward curve function

$$f(t_n) = b_0 + b_1 e^{-t_n/\tau} + b_2 e^{-t_n/\tau} \frac{\tau}{t_n} \tag{3.63}$$

Note that different yield curve models – with each model restraining possible yield curve moves – will lead to varying tracking behaviour.

Step 2. Estimate (3.63) for two discrete points in time and calculate the corresponding forward curves. Suppose we take t and $t + 1$ for the instantaneous forward curve

$$f_{t+1}(t_n) = b_{0,t+1} + b_{1,t+1} e^{-t_n/\tau} + b_{2,t+1} e^{-t_n/\tau} \frac{t_n}{\tau} \tag{3.64}$$

The distance between both points determines the time span for which we want to investigate the liability tracking abilities of the duration vector model.

Step 3. Calculate yield curve changes in (3.62). For example, we can calculate the parallel shift in term structure of forward rates as

$$\Delta f(0) = f_{t+1}(0) - f(0) = \left(b_{0,t+1} + b_{1,t+1} \right) - \left(b_0 + b_1 \right)$$

The same calculations can also be applied to all terms in (3.62), where all higher-order derivatives are taken at $t = 0$. For example we get $\delta f_{t+1}(t)/\delta t \,|_{t=0} = (-1/\tau)b_{1,t+1} - (1/\tau)b_{2,t+1}$.

Step 4. Compare the outcome of (3.62) with the exact change in liability value. The approximation generally works well for large m. What "works well" and "large" exactly mean depends on the assumed yield curve changes and is subject to empirical testing.

How can we use the duration vector model to find the liability-mimicking portfolio? Suppose we are given the liability duration vector with elements $D_1^l, D_2^l, ..., D_k^l, ..., D_m^l$. Further, we can use $k = 1, ... K$ bonds to replicate the duration vector of pension liabilities as closely as possible. Investments into a given bond are expressed as a percentage of total wealth, $\theta_1, \theta_2, \ldots, \theta_k, \ldots, \theta_k$. A portfolio is matched if the following conditions are satisfied

$$D_1^p = \theta_1 D_1^1 +, \ldots, + \theta_K D_1^K = \sum_{k=1}^{K} \theta_k D_1^k = D_1^l$$
$$D_2^p = \theta_1 D_2^1 +, \ldots, + \theta_K D_2^K = \sum_{k=1}^{K} \theta_k D_2^k = D_2^l$$
$$\ldots = \ldots \tag{3.65}$$
$$D_1^p = \theta_1 D_M^1 +, \ldots, + \theta_K D_M^K = \sum_{k=1}^{K} \theta_k D_M^k = D_M^l$$

$$\theta_1 + \theta_2 +, \ldots, + \theta_K = 1 \tag{3.66}$$

Equations (3.65) and (3.66) define $M + 1$ constraints (M duration plus one full investment constraint). We can distinguish the following cases.

❑ $K = M + 1$. A unique solution exists. Note that we allowed $\theta_k < 0$, ie, short sales. If we instead constrain holdings to be positive ($\theta_k > 0$) no exact solution might exist.
❑ $K < M + 1$. No solution exists. Alternatively, we can define an objective function that penalises weighted duration vector deviations. This equivalently tries to minimise

$$Z = \sum_{m=1}^{M} \omega_m Y \left(D(m) - D_l(m) \right)$$

where $Y(\ldots)$ denotes a penalty function like quadratic or absolute loss and ω_m defines the weight given to a particular deviation.

Table 12 Duration vector for tracking universe
Universe of $K = 4$ par bonds. Duration vector for $g(t) = t$

	$B^C(0, t_n)$	C_n	t_n	D_1	D_2	D_3
#1	100	2.20	1	1.00	1.00	1.00
#2	100	3.06	5	4.71	22.99	113.54
#3	100	3.65	10	8.55	80.49	780.47
#4	100	3.98	15	11.58	156.94	2235.68
#5	100	4.17	20	13.95	241.54	4486.48
#6	100	4.29	25	15.81	327.34	7423.86
#7	100	4.37	30	17.26	410.02	10888.50
#8	100	4.39	35	18.49	490.96	14852.20
#9	100	4.40	40	19.48	565.95	19089.51
#10	100	4.42	50	20.91	695.46	27848.51

❏ $K > M + 1$. In this case many solutions exist. In order to enforce a unique solution we apply a little trick and minimise $\sum_{k=1}^{K} \theta_k^2$ subject to (3.65) and (3.66). By this we also enforce diversification among different bonds, which reduces credit risk as well as idiosyncratic yield curve movements.

We can now start to apply the duration vector approach to our liability data in Table 2. The corresponding durations are given below and have been calculated according to (3.60) for $\alpha = 1$.

$$D_1^l = 15.778, \quad D_2^l = 359.205, \quad D_3^l = 9918.427 \tag{3.67}$$

Note that D_1^l and D_2^l differ from duration and convexity in section 0, as numbers in (3.67) have been calculated under the assumption of a non-flat term structure and therefore

$$\frac{\frac{1}{(1+s_n)^{t_n}} l_{t_n}}{l} \neq \frac{\frac{1}{(1+y)^{t_n}} l_{t_n}}{l} \tag{3.68}$$

As weights differ, so will duration measures. We use a universe of $K = 10$ par bonds, all priced according to (3.41) and are described in Table 12.

The strategy we want to review is to match the pension liability duration vector $M = 3$ with $K = 10$ par bonds. Note that this does not allow a unique solution as $K > M + 1$. We therefore need to minimise $\sum_{k=1}^{K} \theta_k^2$ to identify a unique solution. Leaving θ_k unconstrained yields a linear programme with $K + M + 1$ variables, which arises from maximising the following Lagrange function:

$$\underset{\substack{\theta_1,\ldots,\theta_{10} \\ \lambda_1,\ldots,\lambda_4}}{L} = \sum_{k=1}^{K} \theta_k^2 + \lambda_1 \left(\sum_{i=1}^{k} \theta_k D_1^k - D_1^l \right) + \lambda_2 \left(\sum_{i=1}^{k} \theta_k D_2^k - D_2^L \right)$$

$$+ \lambda_3 \left(\sum_{i=1}^{k} \theta_k D_3^k - D_3^l \right) + \lambda_4 \left(\sum_{i=1}^{k} \theta_k - 1 \right) \tag{3.69}$$

$$\frac{\delta L}{\delta \theta_1} = 2\theta_1 + \lambda_1 D_1^1 + \lambda_2 D_2^1 + \lambda_3 D_3^1 + \lambda_4 = 0$$

$$\vdots$$

$$\frac{\delta L}{\delta \theta_{10}} = 2\theta_{10} + \lambda_1 D_1^{10} + \lambda_2 D_2^{10} + \lambda_3 D_3^{10} + \lambda_4 = 0$$

$$\frac{\delta L}{\delta \lambda_1} = \sum_{i=1}^{k} \theta_k D_1^k - D_1^l = 0$$

$$\vdots$$

$$\frac{\delta L}{\delta \lambda_3} = \sum_{i=1}^{k} \theta_k D_3^k - D_3^l = 0$$

$$\frac{\delta L}{\delta \lambda_4} = \sum_{i=1}^{k} \theta_k - 1 = 0 \tag{3.70}$$

The solution to (3.70) is shown in Figure 5, where we have plotted the total cashflow position from the portfolio of 10 par bonds given in Table 12. While all duration measures are exactly matched, cashflow profiles remain very different.

The duration vector model allows us to calculate exposures (the duration vector distance between liability and bond portfolio) but not track risk. In order to put a risk number on duration deviations we need to calculate both exposure to risk factors and risk-factor volatility. We will look further at this in the next section.

COVARIANCE APPROACH TO LIABILITY RISK ANALYSIS: KEY RATE ANALYSIS

This section follows the basic idea that any smooth (zero coupon) yield curve change can be modelled as a linear combination of a much smaller set of yield changes. These zero rates are also called

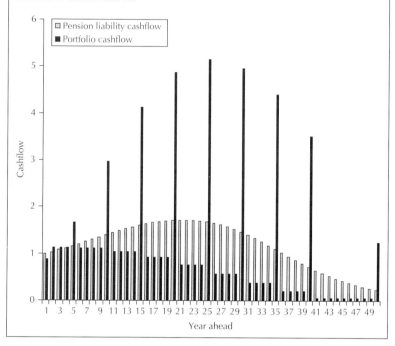

Figure 5 Pension liability cashflows versus portfolio cashflows for duration vector model.
Reinvestment risk is still very large but significantly smaller than in Figure 1. The humped shape of the liability cashflow stream is at least somehow accounted for

key rates (see Ho, 1992; Golub and Tilmann, 2000). The purpose is to allow a parsimonious modelling of complex yield curve changes. We start with the simplest case, where we assume that we model as many key rates as we face liability cashflows. Further, we assume that the maturity of key rates and the timing of liability cashflows perfectly coincide. The exact value of corporate liabilities depends on n cashflows occurring at times $t_1, t_2, \ldots, t_n$ discounted at n key rates, maturing at the very same maturity points:

$$
\begin{aligned}
l = l\left(s_{t_1}, s_{t_2}, \ldots, s_{t_n}\right) \\
= l_{t_1} d\left(0, t_1\right) + l_{t_2} d\left(0, t_2\right) + \cdots + l_{t_n} d\left(0, t_n\right) \\
= \frac{l_{t_1}}{\left(1 + s_{t_1}\right)^{t_1}} + \frac{l_{t_2}}{\left(1 + s_{t_2}\right)^{t_2}} + \cdots + \frac{l_{t_n}}{\left(1 + s_{t_n}\right)^{t_n}}
\end{aligned}
$$

(3.71)

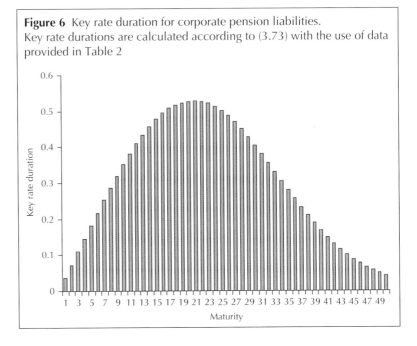

Figure 6 Key rate duration for corporate pension liabilities. Key rate durations are calculated according to (3.73) with the use of data provided in Table 2

In other words: For each cashflow we model a key rate with the corresponding maturity. Linearisation of (3.71) with respect to our key rates yields

$$\tfrac{\Delta l}{l} \approx KRD_1^l \Delta s_1 + KRD_2^l \Delta s_2 \ldots + KRD_n^l \Delta s_n$$

$$= \sum_{i=1}^{n} KRD_i^l \Delta s_i \qquad (3.72)$$

$$KRD_i^l = \frac{\delta l}{\delta s_i} \frac{1}{l} = -t_i \frac{\dfrac{l_{t_i}}{(1+s_{t_i})^{(t_i+1)}}}{l} \qquad (3.73)$$

The corresponding key rate duration measures (for each of the 50 cashflows) are given in Figure 6.

Note that the sum of all key rate durations comes close to the traditional duration measure.

$$\sum_{i=1}^{50} KRD_i^l = -\sum_{i=1}^{50} t_i \frac{\dfrac{l_{t_i}}{(1+s_{t_i})^{(t_i+1)}}}{l}$$

$$= -(0.036 + 0.071 + \cdots + 0.042) = -15.13 \qquad (3.74)$$

In the same way, we can also define key rate convexities, as (3.72) represents only a first-order approximation of liability changes.

$$\frac{\Delta l}{l} \approx \sum_{i=1}^{n} KRD_i^l \Delta s_i + \frac{1}{2} \sum_{i=1}^{n} \sum_{j=1}^{n} KRC_{ij}^l \Delta s_1 \Delta s_2 \qquad (3.75)$$

$$KRC_{ij}^l = \frac{\delta^2 l}{\delta s_i \delta s_j} \frac{1}{l} \qquad (3.76)$$

Note that all key rate convexities can be represented by a symmetric $(n \times n)$ matrix. The usual portfolio properties apply, ie, portfolio key rate durations and convexities can be the calculated as the value-weighted key rate durations and convexities of individual assets. However, approximation (3.75) is hardly ever used.

We also use (3.72) for various risk calculations. Imposing the variance operator on (3.72) allows us to model liability risk within a covariance framework, familiar from risk or portfolio management applications.

$$Var\left(\frac{\Delta l}{l}\right) \approx Var\left(\sum_{i=1}^{n} KRD_i^l \Delta s_i\right)$$
$$= \sum_{i=1}^{n} KRD_i^l Var\left(\Delta s_i\right) + 2\sum_{i=1}^{n} \sum_{j\neq i}^{n} KRD_i^l KRD_j^l Cov\left(\Delta s_i, \Delta s_j\right) \qquad (3.77)$$

This in turn will allow us to calculate extreme liability scenarios. The liabilities at risk at the $1 - \alpha$ confidence level can be calculated from

$$LaR = l \times \sqrt{Var\left(\frac{\Delta l}{l}\right)} \times z_\alpha \qquad (3.78)$$

where z_α is the α-percentile of the standard normal distribution, eg, $z_{5\%} = 1.645$ or $z_{1\%} = 2.326$. Obviously, (3.77) can also applied for a liability relative risk measure:

$$Var\left(\frac{\Delta l}{l} - \frac{\Delta p}{p}\right) \approx Var\left(\sum_{i=1}^{n} EKRD_i^l \Delta s_i\right)$$
$$= \sum_{i=1}^{n} EKRD_i^l Var\left(\Delta s_i\right)$$
$$+ 2\sum_{i=1}^{n} \sum_{j\neq i}^{n} EKRD_i^l EKRD_j^l Cov\left(\Delta s_i, \Delta s_j\right) \qquad (3.79)$$

where excess key rate durations are given by $EKRD_i = KRD_i^l - KRD_i^p$ and $\Delta p/p$ measure changes in portfolio returns. While the above digression on key rate durations is very general, we still need a more realistic representation of key rate changes. In reality, we neither model as many key rates as cashflows, nor can we assume that future cashflows only take place at key rate maturity. Suppose instead we can only model 6 key rates: 1-year, 5-year, 10-year, 15-year, 20-year and 30-year spot rates, but cashflows range from 1 to 50 years. How do we proceed? We will present a generalised methodology and leave it to the reader to check his/her understanding by recalculating the numbers provided in the text.

We start with the notion that pension liabilities can be decomposed into a portfolio of zero coupon bonds as can be readily seen from (3.71). Let us denote the present value of a liability cashflow at t_i as $l_i = l_{t_i} (1 + s_{t_i})^{-t_i}$. We can now model the sensitivity of pension liabilities with respect to the m-th key rate as

$$KRD_m^l = \sum_{i=1}^{50} \frac{l_i}{l} \left(\frac{\delta l_i}{\delta s_i} \frac{1}{l_i} \frac{\delta s_i}{\delta s_m} \right) \tag{3.80}$$

Equation (3.80) presents a value-weighted (l_i/l) sum of partial durations ($\delta l_i / \delta s_i (1/l_i)$) for each liability cashflow, where each partial duration is adjusted for its sensitivity with respect to changes in the m-th key rate ($\delta s_i / \delta s_m$). All that remains to be done is to define these sensitivities. For a liability cashflow that occurs at t_i the sensitivity with respect to a key rate with maturity t_m is defined as

$$\frac{\delta s_i}{\delta s_m} = \frac{|t_i - t_m|}{|t_{m'} - t_m|} \tag{3.81}$$

where t_m and $t_{m'}$ are the neighbouring key rates. In case t_i has only one neighbouring key rate (either left or right), the sensitivity becomes one. This logic becomes immediately clear when we think about modelling interest rate risk with a single key rate. This would lead us directly back to the traditional duration measure. We can now apply (3.80) and (3.81) to calculate key rate durations with respect to alternative key rate structures as shown in Figures 7 and 8. When the neighbouring key rates t_m and t_m' change, so do the sensitivities in (3.81) and ultimately the numbers in (3.80). Note, however, that the sum of key rate durations does not change with a particular partition.

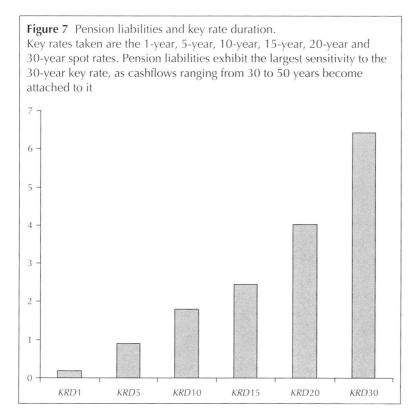

Figure 7 Pension liabilities and key rate duration.
Key rates taken are the 1-year, 5-year, 10-year, 15-year, 20-year and
30-year spot rates. Pension liabilities exhibit the largest sensitivity to the
30-year key rate, as cashflows ranging from 30 to 50 years become
attached to it

We have now all the necessary tools to find the liability tracking
portfolio with the use of key rate durations. Suppose we have an
$M \times 1$ vector of liability key rate durations

$$\mathbf{KRD}^l = \begin{bmatrix} KRD_1^l & KRD_2^l & \ldots & KRD_M^l \end{bmatrix}^T \qquad (3.82)$$

and a $M \times J$ matrix of key rate durations for a given bond universe
available for liability hedging.

$$\mathbf{KRD}^b = \begin{bmatrix} KRD_1^1 & KRD_1^2 & \ldots & KRD_1^J \\ KRD_2^1 & KRD_2^1 & \ldots & KRD_2^J \\ \vdots & \vdots & \ddots & \vdots \\ KRD_M^1 & KRD_M^2 & \ldots & KRD_M^J \end{bmatrix} \qquad (3.83)$$

where J denotes the number of bonds available for liability hedging. In case $J = M$, ie, the number of bonds equals the number of

Figure 8 Pension liabilities and key rate duration under alternative key rates.
Key rates taken are the 1-year, 5-year, 10-year, 15-year, 20-year and 30-year spot rates. Pension liabilities exhibit different key rate exposure from the 10-year spot rate onwards as neighbouring key rates change and this alters the sensitivities in (3.81). Note that this looks much closer to Figure 6

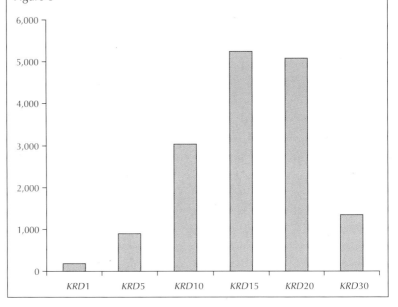

key rate exposures and allows short positions, we can find the vector of bond weights $\boldsymbol{\theta}$ as the solution of

$$\mathbf{KRD}^l = \mathbf{KRD}^b \boldsymbol{\theta}$$

$$
\begin{bmatrix} KRD_1^l \\ KRD_2^l \\ \vdots \\ KRD_M^l \end{bmatrix} = \begin{bmatrix} KRD_1^1 & KRD_1^2 & \cdots & KRD_1^J \\ KRD_2^1 & KRD_2^1 & \cdots & KRD_2^J \\ \vdots & \vdots & \ddots & \vdots \\ KRD_M^1 & KRD_M^2 & \cdots & KRD_M^J \end{bmatrix} \begin{bmatrix} \theta_1 \\ \theta_2 \\ \vdots \\ \theta_J \end{bmatrix} \quad \textbf{(3.84)}
$$

which is readily available as $\boldsymbol{\theta} = (\mathbf{KRD}^b)^{-1}\,\mathbf{KRD}^l$.

In this case we can generate a bond portfolio that has exactly the same key rate exposures as a given liability portfolio. Technically this will amount to zero liability relative risk, as we can see from (3.79). In reality, however, we have only immunised those risks that arise from a limited number of key rates, which by no means establishes a risk-free position. In the unlikely case that we have fewer bonds than key rate exposures, we can no longer arrive at an equal sign in (3.84), and so it becomes

$$\mathbf{KRD}^l = \mathbf{KRD}^b\,\boldsymbol{\theta} + \mathbf{e} \tag{3.85}$$

where $\mathbf{e}$ denotes the $M \times 1$ vector of hedging errors with respect to the M key rates. As (3.85) is written in terms of a linear regression, we can use OLS (ordinary least squares) theory to arrive at the optimal hedge ratio that minimises the sum of squared hedging errors.

$$\boldsymbol{\theta} = ((\mathbf{KRD}^b)^T\,\mathbf{KRD}^b)^{-1}\,(\mathbf{KRD}^b)^T\,\mathbf{KRD}^l \tag{3.86}$$

However standard regression theory assumes the elements of $\mathbf{e}$ to exhibit the same volatilities and show no dependencies. Both assumptions are likely to be violated for the above problem due to the high correlation of yield curve moves as well as interest rate volatilities that depend on maturity. A straightforward change of (3.86) would use GLS (generalised least squares).

$$\boldsymbol{\theta} = ((\mathbf{KRD}^b)^T\,\boldsymbol{\Omega}\,\mathbf{KRD}^b)^{-1}\,(\mathbf{KRD}^b)^T\,\boldsymbol{\Omega}\,\mathbf{KRD}^l$$

All this involves is the inclusion of a weighting matrix $\boldsymbol{\Omega}$ to take out the covariance structure in error terms.

I will close this section with a numerical application of the above theory. As key rates we choose the 1-year, 5-year, 10-year, 15-year, 20-year and 30-year spot rates. The distribution of weekly key rate changes is illustrated in Figure 9. From these data we can calculate the covariance matrix of key rate changes $\boldsymbol{\Sigma}$. The dimension of this matrix is $M \times M$.

$$\boldsymbol{\Sigma} = \begin{bmatrix} Cov\left(\Delta s_1, \Delta s_1\right) & Cov\left(\Delta s_1, \Delta s_5\right) & \cdots & Cov\left(\Delta s_1, \Delta s_{30}\right) \\ Cov\left(\Delta s_5, \Delta s_1\right) & Cov\left(\Delta s_5, \Delta s_5\right) & & \\ \vdots & & \ddots & \\ Cov\left(\Delta s_{30}, \Delta s_1\right) & & & Cov\left(\Delta s_{30}, \Delta s_{30}\right) \end{bmatrix}$$

$$= \begin{bmatrix} 3303.75 & 3314.74 & 2428.45 & 2077.59 & 1859.06 & 1718.46 \\ 3314.74 & 5041.07 & 4223.06 & 3814.52 & 3520.48 & 3321.11 \\ 2428.45 & 4223.06 & 4043.48 & 3788.37 & 3587.81 & 3438.45 \\ 2077.59 & 3814.52 & 3788.37 & 3676.40 & 3528.63 & 3406.73 \\ 1859.06 & 3520.48 & 3587.81 & 3528.63 & 3459.72 & 3368.66 \\ 1718.46 & 3321.11 & 3438.45 & 3406.73 & 3368.66 & 3355.12 \end{bmatrix} \tag{3.87}$$

Figure 9 Key rate changes
Weekly data on European spot rates. Data span from December 1996 to December 2004. The correlation between key rates increases at the long maturity spectrum (scatter plot become less cloudy)

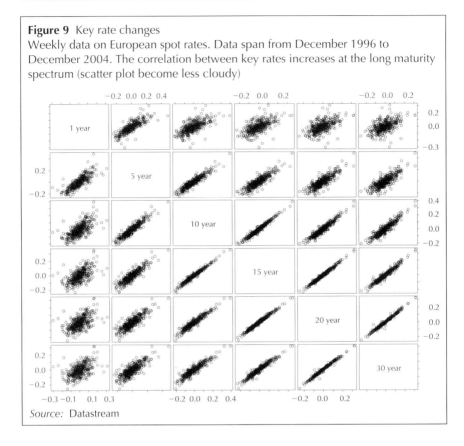

Source: Datastream

The elements in Σ are annual covariances of yield changes (measured in basis points) calculated from the data in Figure 9. For example: the standard deviation of basis point changes in 5-year spot rates is about 70 basis points: $\sqrt{Cov\left(\Delta s_5, \Delta s_5\right)} = \sqrt{5041.47} = 71\,bps$. Next we need the key rate durations of pension liabilities:

$$\mathbf{KRD}^l = [0.186\ 0.897\ 3.035\ 5.243\ 5.078\ 1.340]^T \qquad \textbf{(3.88)}$$

This already allows us to calculate the volatility of pension liabilities using the above key rate decomposition:

$$\sigma\left(\tfrac{\Delta l}{l}\right) = \left(\mathbf{KRD}^l\right)^T \cdot \Sigma \cdot \mathbf{KRD}^l = 9.24\% \qquad \textbf{(3.89)}$$

Suppose now we want instead solve a realistic hedging problem. In particular we want to minimise liability-relative risk with the

Table 13 Key rate duration for tracking universe.
The numbers are calculated according to (3.80) and (3.81). Note that
the table reflects **KRD**^{b} and is properly dimensioned as a 6×10 matrix

Bond	#1	#2	#3	#4	#5	#6	#7	#8	#9	#10
KRD_1	1.00	0.14	0.17	0.18	0.19	0.19	0.20	0.20	0.20	0.20
KRD_5	0.00	4.57	0.71	0.76	0.79	0.80	0.82	0.82	0.82	0.82
KRD_{10}	0.00	0.00	7.68	1.33	1.37	1.39	1.41	1.41	1.41	1.41
KRD_{15}	0.00	0.00	0.00	9.31	1.68	1.70	1.71	1.71	1.72	1.72
KRD_{20}	0.00	0.00	0.00	0.00	9.93	6.78	2.78	2.78	2.78	2.79
KRD_{30}	0.00	0.00	0.00	0.00	0.00	4.94	10.34	11.57	12.55	13.97

portfolio of bonds in Table 12. The vector of excess key rate durations (**EKRD**) can be described as the difference between liability
key rate durations (**KRD**^{l}) and portfolio key rate durations (**KPD**^{p}),
which in turn represent the weighted sum of key rate durations
from a tracking portfolio, ie, **KPD**^{b}**θ**, where the data for **KRD**^{b} can
be found in Table 13.

$$\mathbf{EKRD} = \mathbf{KRD}^l - \mathbf{KRD}^p$$
$$= \mathbf{KRD}^l - \mathbf{KRD}^b \boldsymbol{\theta} \quad (3.90)$$

The liability hedging objective now becomes

$$\min_{\theta} \sigma\left(\tfrac{\Delta l}{l}\right) = \left(\mathbf{EKRD}\right)^T \cdot \Sigma \cdot \mathbf{EKRD} \quad (3.91)$$

In order to be realistic we impose a non-negativity constraint ($\boldsymbol{\theta} \geq 0$)
on individual bond weights. The solution to (3.91) is given below.

$$\boldsymbol{\theta} = [0\% \ \ 3\% \ \ 8\% \ \ 13\% \ \ 27\% \ \ 1\% \ \ 1\% \ \ 1\% \ \ 0\% \ \ 44\%]^T \quad (3.92)$$

The resulting cashflows are graphed in Figure 10.

The main advantage of using the covariance approach in comparison with previous methodologies is the ability to calculate liability-relative risks rather than exposures alone. The approach fits
well into classical mean variance optimisation and hedging and
can therefore be easily integrated into a broader risk management
framework. On the downside, there is little guidance (as with the
other models) on the number of key rates to be selected. Also, from
a theoretical point of view, suggested yield curve moves must
imply rather unrealistic forward-rate changes. Nevertheless the

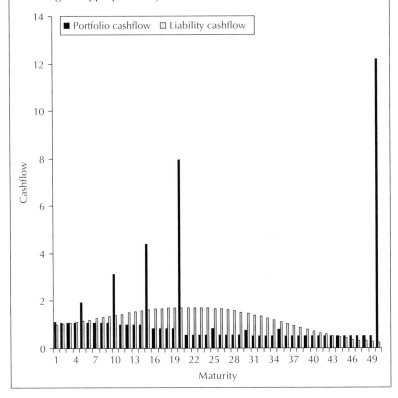

Figure 10 Pension liability cashflows versus portfolio cashflows for key rate duration model.
Due to the shape of liability key rate durations in Figure 7 the shape of liability cashflows is not well captured. This underlines the point of choosing the appropriate key rate durations

key rate duration approach is still the workhorse in fixed-income risk management.

RESTRICTING YIELD CURVE MOVEMENTS: PRINCIPAL COMPONENT DURATION

The main purpose of the previous section was to characterise fixed-income risks as exposures to individual zero yield changes. However, we know that interest rate changes are highly collinear. Can we describe the movement in $m = 1,\dots M$ key rates by a smaller number of $f = 1,\dots F$ factors? Instead of expressing liability risks as in (3.71) and (3.72) we can now write

$$l = l(f_1, f_2, f_3, \ldots) \qquad (3.93)$$

$$\tfrac{\Delta l}{l} = PCD_1 \Delta f_1 + PCD_2 \Delta f_2 + PCD_3 \Delta f_3 + \cdots \qquad (3.94)$$

where $PCD_i = (\delta l / \delta f_1) 1 / l$. One technique to express changes in zero rates by a small number of factor shifts is known as *principal component analysis* (see Bliss, 1977). Suppose $F = 3$, ie, we can explain the overwhelming part (eg, 98%) of yield curve moves by three factors.

$$\Delta s_m = b_{m1} \Delta f_1 + b_{m2} \Delta f_2 + b_{m3} \Delta f_3 \qquad (3.95)$$

Under this model, the movement of the m-th zero rate is a function of three factor movements, where each zero rate has a particular sensitivity (also called *factor loading*, or *factor sensitivity*) to a given factor movements. Suppose for illustration we isolate changes in the first risk factor. This results in a series of zero rate changes across the whole yield curve.

$$\begin{aligned} \Delta s_1 &= b_{11} \Delta f_1 \\ \Delta s_2 &= b_{21} \Delta f_1 \\ &\vdots \\ \Delta s_m &= b_{m1} \Delta f_1 \end{aligned} \qquad (3.96)$$

From (3.96) it becomes easy to see that

$$PCD_1 = \tfrac{\delta l}{\delta f_i} \tfrac{1}{l} = \sum_{i=1}^{m} KRD_i \Delta s_i = \sum_{i=1}^{m} KRD_i b_{i1} \Delta f_1 \qquad (3.97)$$

Each move in f_1 will feed through to $\Delta s_1, \Delta s_2, \ldots, \Delta s_m$. This in turn will change the liability value according to key rate duration exposures. If all loadings were exactly identical, all rates would react identically, ie, the yield curve moves strictly parallel and we are once again back to traditional duration. The principal component duration model is therefore a variation of the key rate duration model in which the covariance matrix is decomposed into a smaller set of factor changes. We will therefore limit our discussion of principal component duration to the absolute minimum.

Under the principal components model, factor changes are uncorrelated (by construction) and exhibit unit variance.

$$Var(\Delta f_i) = 1 \qquad (3.98)$$

$$Cov(\Delta f_i, \Delta f_j) = 0 \qquad (3.99)$$

which largely simplifies risk calculations. For example:

$$Var\left(\Delta s_m\right) = Var\left(b_{m1}\Delta f_1 + b_{m2}\Delta f_2 + b_{m3}\Delta f_3\right)$$
$$= \left(b_{m1}\right)^2 Var\left(\Delta f_1\right) + \left(b_{m2}\right)^2 Var\left(\Delta f_2\right) + \left(b_{m3}\right)^2 Var\left(\Delta f_3\right)$$
$$= \sum_{f=1}^{3}\left(b_{mf}\right)^2$$

(3.100)

$$Cov\left(\Delta s_i, \Delta s_j\right) = Cov\left(b_{i1}\Delta f_1 + b_{i2}\Delta f_2 + b_{i3}\Delta f_3, b_{j1}\Delta f_1 + b_{j2}\Delta f_2 + b_{j3}\Delta f\right)$$
$$= b_{i1}b_{j1} + b_{i2}b_{j2} + b_{i3}b_{j3}$$

(3.101)

Properties (3.100) and (3.101) make principal component analysis extremely useful for risk decompositions and explain its widespread use. Orthogonal factors allow for a unique "budgeting" of risk without having to deal with unattributable covariance terms.

Let us finish this section with a brief digression on principal component analysis, applied to the data used before. Suppose we are given the covariance matrix of spot rate changes Σ. Let us denote the $(M \times 1)$ vector of key rate changes by Δs with the following properties.

$$E(\Delta s) = 0 \qquad (3.102)$$
$$E(\Delta s^T \Delta s) = \Sigma \qquad (3.103)$$

As Σ is symmetric we can decompose it into a product of eigenvalues and eigenvectors.

$$\Sigma = VDV^T \qquad (3.104)$$

where the i-th column of V is an eigenvector with an attached eigenvalue of D_{ii} (i-th element on the main diagonal of D), where D is a diagonal matrix. We can now construct a new vector Δ (with dimension $M \times 1$, containing $\Delta f_1, \dots ,\Delta f_M$) of principal components according to

$$\Delta f = D^{-\frac{1}{2}}V^T \Delta s \qquad (3.105)$$

The expected value and covariance of (3.105) is given below:

$$E(\Delta \mathbf{f}) = \mathbf{D}^{-\frac{1}{2}} \mathbf{V}^T E(\Delta \mathbf{s}) = 0 \qquad (3.106)$$

$$\begin{aligned} E\left(\Delta \mathbf{f} \Delta \mathbf{f}^T\right) &= E\left(\mathbf{D}^{-\frac{1}{2}} \mathbf{V}^T \Delta \mathbf{s} \Delta \mathbf{s}^T \mathbf{V} \mathbf{D}^{-\frac{1}{2}}\right) \\ &= \mathbf{D}^{-\frac{1}{2}} \mathbf{V}^T E\left(\Delta \mathbf{s} \Delta \mathbf{s}^T\right) \mathbf{V} \mathbf{D}^{-\frac{1}{2}} \\ &= \mathbf{D}^{-\frac{1}{2}} \mathbf{V}^T \mathbf{V} \mathbf{D} \mathbf{V}^T \mathbf{V} \mathbf{D}^{-\frac{1}{2}} \\ &= \mathbf{D}^{-\frac{1}{2}} \mathbf{D} \mathbf{D}^{-\frac{1}{2}} \\ &= \mathbf{I} \qquad\qquad\qquad (3.107) \end{aligned}$$

where $\mathbf{I}$ is a diagonal matrix with one along the main diagonal and zero elsewhere. This is exactly the distribution we have used in (3.100) and (3.101). Note that $\mathbf{V}^T = \mathbf{V}^{-1}$, as it contains normalised and orthogonal vectors.

There is one question left. Where does the reduction in dimensionality come from? After all $\Delta \mathbf{f}$ in (3.105) has the same dimension than $\Delta \mathbf{s}$. To put it differently: for M series of spot rate changes, there will also be M uncorrelated series of factors (principal components). In practice we will choose the number of factors that explains "most" (usually well above 95%) of the spot rate variation. To visualise, what principal component analysis does, we can run a regression of principal components against spot rate changes. The regression output, containing factor loadings (regression coefficients) as well as R^2 (measure of how much variation in spot rate changes is explained by factors) is summarised in Table 14.

It appears that the first principal component affects all changes in interest rates by roughly the same amount. That is why the first component is always associated with changes in interest rate levels. The second component will lead to a fall in short rates and a rise in long rates. This again can be interpreted as a change in slope. Finally, the last component affects both short and long end positively, while it leads to a decrease in intermediate rates. We therefore interpret it as a measure of curvature. The key advantage of principal component analysis is that it does rely on particular yield curve points. We also could have defined a slope factor as the change in interest rate difference between 1-year and 15-year rates, but factor volatilities as well as factor loadings would change considerably with a change in factor definition. On the negative side we know that changes in rate levels (proxied by Δf_1) are empirically

Table 14 Regression diagnostics.
The table shows regression coefficients as well as R^2 of a linear regression of the form $\Delta s_m = b_{m1}\Delta f_1 + b_{m2}\Delta f_2 + b_{m3}\Delta f_3 + \varepsilon$, based on weekly data in Figure 9. If the first principal component takes on a one-standard-deviation change, the 5-year spot rate will change by 9.4 basis points. Each regression explains more than 99% of spot rate changes showing the appropriateness of a three-factor model

	Δf_1	Δf_2	Δf_3	R^2
Δs_1	5.8123	−5.2420	1.5000	0.9996
Δs_5	9.3829	−2.2917	−1.8077	0.9960
Δs_{10}	8.7227	0.5884	−0.6896	0.9890
Δs_{15}	8.2362	1.5446	0.0741	0.9933
Δs_{20}	7.8447	2.0706	0.6815	0.9964
Δs_{30}	7.5539	2.3662	1.0990	0.9899

Table 15 Floating-rate pricing.
Floating-rate note cashflows consist of a series of one-year forward rates, derived from the current term structure. However discounting these payments at the current spot rates will yield to a value of 1

Time	t_1	t_2	t_3	t_4	...	t_n
Cash flow	$\dfrac{1}{d(0,t_1)}-1$	$\dfrac{1}{d(t_1,t_2)}-1$	$\dfrac{1}{d(t_2,t_3)}-1$	$\dfrac{1}{d(t_3,t_4)}-1$		$\dfrac{1}{d(t_{n-1},t_n)}$
Discount factor	$d(0,t_1)$	$d(0,t_2)$	$d(0,t_3)$	$d(0,t_4)$	...	$d(0,t_n)$

Table 16 Coupon bond pricing.
The swap rate K is adjusted such that the present value of cashflows equals one. This I why swap rates are interpreted as par rates

Time	t_1	t_2	t_3	t_4	...	t_n
Cashflow	K	K	K	K		$1 + K$
Discount factor	$d(0,t_1)$	$d(0,t_2)$	$d(0,t_3)$	$d(0,t_4)$	...	$d(0,t_n)$

correlated with slope changes (proxied by Δf_2). If interest rates fall, the yield curve becomes steeper and it tends to flatten with rising rates. While this can be explained with mean reversion it is somewhat lost in principal component analysis.

INTEREST RATE SWAPS AND LIABILITY HEDGING

Hedging interest rate sensitive liability streams is often pursued within overlay structures. A pool of actively managed and ideally market-neutral assets (which are subject to an optimised multi-manager structure to achieve the maximum active return per unit of active risk) is overlaid with interest-rate-sensitive derivatives. While the underlying managers try to create risk- (β) adjusted out-performance, ie, so called α (in order to turn a capital market investment into a positive net-present-value project), the overlay structure aims at passively generating desired risk exposures (called β) to either fixed-income or equity markets. This leads to an unbundling of expensive and well-sought-after α and cheap and readily available creation (or hedging) of market exposures. It also allows a separation of roles, responsibilities and accountability. Swap structures in pension funds do not require additional cash (as collateral), as the whole underlying assets serve as collateral. Asset managers focus on beating their respective benchmarks, while overlay management manages the misfit between actual assets and liabilities. Asset liability management can hence be understood as managing the misfit between the sum of manager benchmarks and a pension liability benchmark.

How can interest rate swaps help to hedge liability risks. Interest rate swaps are agreements where two parties exchange cashflows based on a notional at times $t_1, t_2, \ldots, t_n$.[2] One party pays a fixed rate (denoted K and usually an annual quote), while the other party pays a floating rate L_{t_i} (also an annual quote and usually Libor). The fixed-rate receiver is effectively long a coupon bond $B^K(0, t_n)$, which pays a coupon K, while at the same time being short a float-ing-rate note FRN, paying out Libor.

$$swap_{receiver} = B^K(0, t_n) - FRN \qquad \textbf{(3.108)}$$

When entering a swap the value of this (leveraged position) is usually set zero. In order to understand the mechanics of interest rate swaps, we need to understand how they are priced. We will look at both components in isolation.

Suppose a floating-rate note pays one-year Libor at $t_1, \ldots, t_n$, but the Libor rate has already been fixed at period $t_0, \ldots, t_{n-1}$. It is straightforward to see that at t_1 the current one-year Libor rate is paid. However, what rate is paid at time t_2? From today's perspective it will be the one-year spot rate in one year's time, ie, the one-year forward rate. In other words $d(t_1, t_2) = d(0, t_2)/d(0, t_1)$. Note that no convexity adjustment is necessary, as this cashflow can be perfectly hedged with today's forward rates. Extending this argument up to time t_n yields the price of a floating-rate note at the reset date (beginning of the interest rate period). In the absence of credit risk it will be priced at par (and without mark up or discount).

$$
\begin{aligned}
FRN &= \left(\frac{1}{d\left(0, t_1\right)} - 1 \right) d\left(0, t_1\right) + \left(\frac{1}{d\left(t_1, t_2\right)} - 1 \right) d\left(0, t_2\right) \\
&\quad + \left(\frac{1}{d\left(t_2, t_3\right)} - 1 \right) d\left(0, t_3\right) + \cdots + \left(\frac{1}{d\left(t_{n-1}, t_n\right)} \right) d\left(0, t_n\right) \\
&= \left(\frac{1}{d\left(0, t_1\right)} - 1 \right) d\left(0, t_1\right) + \left(\frac{1}{\frac{d(0,t_2)}{d(0,t_1)}} - 1 \right) d\left(0, t_2\right) \\
&\quad + \left(\frac{1}{\frac{d(0,t_3)}{d(0,t_2)}} - 1 \right) d\left(0, t_3\right) + \cdots + \left(\frac{1}{\frac{d(0,t_n)}{d(0,t_{n-1})}} \right) d\left(0, t_n\right) \\
&= 1 - d\left(0, t_1\right) + d\left(0, t_1\right) - d\left(0, t_2\right) + d\left(0, t_2\right) - d\left(0, t_3\right) \\
&\quad + \cdots + d\left(0, t_{n-1}\right) \\
&= 1
\end{aligned}
\tag{3.109}
$$

Given the fact that $FRN = 1$ (at the reset date), we need to find K such that the bond price also equals 1 in order to let the swap trade (initially) at 0.

$$
0 = \underbrace{1}_{FRN} - \underbrace{\left(K \sum_{i=1}^{n} d\left(0, t_i\right) + d\left(0, t_n\right) \right)}_{\text{Coupon bond}}
\tag{3.110}
$$

$$
K = \frac{1 - d\left(0, t_n\right)}{\sum_{i=1}^{n} d\left(0, t_i\right)}
\tag{3.111}
$$

For any time between $t_0 < t < t_1$ (between inception in t_0 and first coupon date t_1) the swap value will change with interest rates. The value of the FRN will change due to changes in s_{t_i}. However these changes will play a minor role, as the time to the next reset date (where the FRN must again trade at 1) is a maximum of 1 year. Changes in credit risk will have a much larger impact on the FRN pricing as it affects the discounting of all future cashflows. That is why we see floating rate notes to substantially trade below par.

$$swap\left(s_{t_1}, s_{t_2}, \ldots, s_{t_n}\right) = B^K\left(s_{t_1}, s_{t_2}, \ldots, s_{t_n}\right) - FRN\left(s_{t_1}\right) \quad \textbf{(3.112)}$$

If interest rates rise the receiver swap will fall in value (become negative) and vice versa. One difficulty remains. How do we calculate interest rate sensitivities? Applying standard calculations for key rate durations (or generalised duration vectors) would not give us sensible results as

$$KRD_{s_m}^{swap} = \frac{\delta swap\left(s_{t_1}, \ldots, s_{t_m}, \ldots, s_{t_M}\right)}{\delta s_{t_m}} \frac{1}{swap\left(s_{t_1}, \ldots, s_{t_m}, \ldots, s_{t_M}\right)} \quad \textbf{(3.113)}$$

becomes either ill defined (if $swap = 0$), or very large for small swap values. A useful way out is to calculate the swap key rate duration as the weighted duration positions of a long bond and short floating-rate note portfolio, where portfolio weights are given by the swap notional. The swap notional N is the amount all payments relate to. A notional of 500 million would trigger fixed payments of $500 \cdot K$, where K reflects a percentage payment.

$$KRD_{s_m}^{swap} = \left(\tfrac{B^K}{N}\right)KRD_{s_m}^{B^K} - \left(\tfrac{FRN}{N}\right)KRD_{s_m}^{FRN} \quad \textbf{(3.114)}$$

Calculations in (3.114) are repeated in Table 17 for swaps ranging from 1 to 10 years.

We can decompose any swap contract into key rate exposures, duration vectors, principal component durations and so on, and use this result to construct a hedging portfolio. Note also, that swap agreements are not limited to receive a fixed cashflow K. Instead we could have set the fixed side equal to our liability cashflows. Doing this would allow us to eliminate any yield curve risk between

Table 17 Key rate durations for swaps of different maturity.
Key rate durations have been approximated as the weighted durations of a portfolio of floating-rate notes and coupon bonds. The key rate durations for swaps can be used in the same way as the key rate durations for the hedging universe in the previous sections

Swap term	KRD_1^I	KRD_2^I	KRD_3^I	KRD_4^I	KRD_5^I	KRD_6^I	KRD_7^I	KRD_8^I	KRD_9^I	KRD_{10}^I
1	−0.98	0.00	0.00	0.00	0.00	0.00	0.00	0.00	0.00	0.00
2	−0.02	−1.90	0.00	0.00	0.00	0.00	0.00	0.00	0.00	0.00
3	−0.03	−0.05	−2.77	0.00	0.00	0.00	0.00	0.00	0.00	0.00
4	−0.03	−0.05	−0.08	−3.57	0.00	0.00	0.00	0.00	0.00	0.00
5	−0.03	−0.06	−0.08	−0.11	−4.29	0.00	0.00	0.00	0.00	0.00
6	−0.03	−0.06	−0.09	−0.11	−0.13	−4.95	0.00	0.00	0.00	0.00
7	−0.03	−0.06	−0.09	−0.12	−0.14	−0.16	−5.54	0.00	0.00	0.00
8	−0.03	−0.06	−0.09	−0.12	−0.14	−0.17	−0.19	−6.06	0.00	0.00
9	−0.03	−0.07	−0.10	−0.12	−0.15	−0.17	−0.19	−0.21	−6.52	0.00
10	−0.03	−0.07	−0.10	−0.13	−0.15	−0.18	−0.20	−0.21	−0.23	−6.93

pension liabilities and swap portfolio, as it is essentially cashflow replication. I will show this in a more general way in the next section.

LIABILITY HEDGING AND FORWARD STARTING SWAPS

The trouble with interest rate swaps is that they need the exchange of cashflows. To avoid this (and therefore leave the management of underlying pension assets unaffected), forward starting swaps are often used by practitioners.

A forward starting swap is essentially a swap like the one analysed in the previous section with the difference that it does not start now, but in the future. I have argued that the vanilla swap previously explained is equivalent to a long short/portfolio in a floating-rate note (FRN) and a coupon bond, where the coupon (K) is set such that the initial value of the swap amounts to zero. In a forward-rate swap the same principle applies. We simply enter a vanilla swap at a future date. Suppose we are at time $t_0 = 0$ and want to enter a swap that starts at t_m. We know that a floating-rate note in m years will still trade at 1 (on the reset date). Hence we can price the floating leg of this swap as $d(0, t_m)$ 1. The fixed leg (coupon bond) pays a constant rate K^f (forward swap rate) and can be priced as a straightforward bond. In order to enforce an initial value of 0, we need to set the forward swap rate such that

$$\underbrace{d\left(0, t_m\right)}_{PV(FRN)} - \underbrace{\left(K^f \sum_{i=1}^{n} d\left(0, t_{m+i}\right) + d\left(0, t_{m+n}\right)\right)}_{PV(Bond)} = 0 \qquad (3.115)$$

Solving for K_f we get the swap rate for a forward starting swap.

$$K_{m,n}^f = \frac{d\left(0, t_m\right) - d\left(0, t_{m+n}\right)}{\sum_{i=1}^{n} d\left(0, t_{m+i}\right)} \qquad (3.116)$$

We immediately see from (3.115) that changes in interest rates must have opposite effects for different key rates. A fall in the spot rate for maturity t_m will increase the value of our forward starting swap, while a fall in the spot rate associated with maturity t_{m+n} will decrease its value. The largest key rate duration exposures will be at the key rates that coincide with the start (t_m) and the maturity (t_{m+n}) of the swap. This is more easily understood if we think of swap that starts in 5 years with a 25-year maturity as a long position in a swap with 30-year maturity and a short position in a 5-year maturity swap.

Although the theme of this book is that hedging corporate pension liabilities is always in the best interest of shareholders, I will briefly comment on how to implement option strategies in liability-relative investing. In August 2005, many investors wanted to hedge against the risk of falling rates in order to protect their liability-relative position. At the same time they felt that rates have been too low to immunise pension liabilities. Investors wanted to keep upside, ie, they wanted their liability-relative position to improve if rates were instead rising. The most widespread instrument to protect portfolios either from a fall or rise in rates swaptions. These are options to enter a swap agreement at some future date, ie, options on a forward starting swap. One way to benefit from falling rates is with a receiver swaption. This option allows entering a receiver swap, ie, a swap where fixed rates are received (to pass them through to employees) at a previously fixed rate. Let us be more precise. At time t_0 a receiver swaption with maturity t_m allows to enter a receiver swap with maturity t_{m+n} at rate $\overline{K}$. The payoff from a receiver swaption is[3]

$$\max\left[\bar{K}-K^f_{m,n},0\right] \tag{3.117}$$

where $\bar{K}$ is the contractually agreed swap rate. Should rates on forward starting swaps fall the option value increases. We have two ways of evaluating (3.117), which essentially is a put option on swap rates.

First, we know that at option maturity the floating-rate side of the swap we enter is 1. Hence (3.117) can be priced as an option to buy an n-year bond with coupon $\bar{K}$, at par. If interest rates fall it should not trade at par, but above it. We can use the valuation technology described in Chapter 2 to value this claim.

Alternatively, practitioners use Black's Model to price European swaptions. The time t_0 value of (3.117) is given by

$$p = N\sum_{i=1}^{n} d\left(0,t_{m+i}\right)$$

$$\left(\bar{K}\cdot N\left(-\frac{\ln\left(\frac{K^f_{m,n}}{\bar{K}}\right)-\frac{1}{2}\sigma^2 t_m}{\sigma\sqrt{t_m}}\right)-K^f_{m,n}\cdot N\left(-\frac{\ln\left(\frac{K^f_{m,n}}{\bar{K}}\right)+\frac{1}{2}\sigma^2 t_m}{\sigma\sqrt{t_m}}\right)\right) \tag{3.118}$$

where $K^f_{m,n}$ is the t_0 rate for a swap, which starts at t_m and matures at t_{m+n}, while σ is the swap rate volatility. We used the symbol p to indicate that we value a put on swap rates. As (3.118) is rather complex we need to evaluate key rate durations numerically

$$KRD^p_{s_t} \approx \frac{p\left(\cdots,s_t+\varepsilon,\cdots\right)-p\left(\cdots,s_t-\varepsilon,\cdots\right)}{2\varepsilon}\frac{1}{p} \tag{3.119}$$

However, note that values in (3.119) might change dramatically with volatility changes. From a liability hedging perspective, this is a further source of risk that shareholders are not willing to take.

It is not clear, why shareholders should spent money on an option premium. As with equity investments they could more efficiently do this in their private account.

THE MANY SOURCES OF LIABILITY RISKS: CASH BALANCE PLANS
In the previous section we (implicitly) dealt with final salary plans, ie, plans where we have been exposed to interest rate, inflation and

Table 18 Cash balance plan.
The cash balance grows with the crediting rate (set at the previous year and hence known at the beginning of 2005). Each year a contribution is added to the cash balance. The size of the contribution is unknown at the beginning of 2005 to both the employee as well as the plan sponsor

Date	Balance	Contribution
2005	1	—
2006	1 times crediting rate (constant maturity, fixed in 2004)	θ% of 2005 compensation
Total	1 times crediting rate + θ% of 2005 compensation	
...		

longevity risk. However cash balance plans increasingly catch attention due as they expose the plan sponsor to an inflation exposure of virtually zero. Let us introduce the mechanics of cash balance as described in Table 18 first.

As 2005 compensation serves as a base for calculating the contribution to an employees cash balance it depends both on inflation and liability growth. However note, that this does not mean that the cash balance is inflation sensitive. Inflation risk will affect contribution risk, but we can not hedge future contributions that arise because of future (yet uncommitted) liabilities with assets based on current liabilities. Each active employees account will be credited with annually compounded interest rate. The exact amount is based on a constant maturity bond yield. For example it could be the 10 year Bund yield at the end of 2005. Future contributions are calculated as percentage (θ) of compensation and are not incorporated in the PBO calculation as they have neither been made nor firmly committed to. When the employee retires he will have accumulated an individual (due to his compensation history) cash balance. At retirement the employee will either receive a series of lump sum payments or a fixed rate annuity depending on the plans characteristics. Assuming that pensions in payment are mostly annuity payments we can distinguish two separate risk characteristics as there are essentially two distinct fixed income streams that make up the PBO (in which case it is useful to break

Table 19 Risk comparison.
Cash balance plans can be hedged at greater precision due to
hedging instrument (CMS) and virtually zero inflation sensitivity

	Final Salary Plan	
Riskfactor	**Risk**	**Hedge**
Interest rate	Falling rates increase market value of pension liabilities	Interest swaps
Inflation	Increase in inflation increases projected cash flows (if indexed) but also discount rate: net effect?	Inflation swaps
Longlevity	Lower mortality lengthens liability duration and increases market vlaue of pension liabilities	?

	Cash Balance Plan	
Riskfactor	**Risk**	**Hedge**
Interest rate	Crediting rate is synthetic. No matching cash investment	Constant maturityswaps
Inflation	No	Not necessary
Longlevity	Lower mortality lengthens liability duration and increases market vlaue of pension liabilities	?

the PBO up into two separate pieces).[4] While the cash balances are
similar to a floating rate money market account with a constant
maturity crediting rate annuity payments show traditional fixed
income characteristics. The economic risks embedded in a cash balance plan can be hedged with a constant maturity swap (CMS),
where the investor receives the market rate of a bond with constant
maturity (10 year swap rate) in exchange for one year Libor. A risk
comparison between cash balance plans can be found below.

In this arrangement the maturity of the crediting rate needs to
coincide with the constant maturity of the CMS. If the notional on
this swap is 100 million, we need to invest this amount into one
year Libor in order to replicate the paying obligations that come
with it. In order to hedge the market risk arising from a particular annuity payment we can use a plain vanilla amortising swap

(a swap whose notional declines over the swap life) that pays a fixed rate (again in exchange for 1 year Libor).

LIABILITY REPLICATION WITH *FRA* STRIPS

We have seen that a swap agreement involves the exchange of multiple cashflows (fixed for floating or vice versa). Let us focus instead on single cashflows. Suppose we are in $t_0 = 0$. A forward-rate agreement (*FRA*) allows us to exchange a yet unknown Libor payment that is set at t_n and paid at t_{n+1} in exchange for a fixed payment of K in t_{n+1}. In other words payments at t_{n+1} amount to

$$FRA(t_n, t_{+1}) = N[K(t_n, t_{n+1}) - L(t_n, t_{n+1})] \qquad \textbf{(3.120)}$$

where $L(t_n, t_{n+1})$ is the yet unknown future spot rate between t_n and t_{n+1}, while is notional amount the *FRA* relates to. An investment in one-period Libor at t_n will lock in $K(t_n, t_{n+1})$ between period t_n and period t_{n+1}. In the same way $FRA(t_{n-1}, t_n)$ locks in a fixed payment of $K(t_{n-1}, t_{n-1})$ between t_{n-1} and t_n. A series of forward-rate agreements would then lock in a guaranteed return between period t_0 and t_{n+1}. All we need to do is to invest in one-period Libor at $t_0 = 0$. The investment return of this is obviously a guaranteed $L(0, t_1) = s_{t_1}$. This amount is then invested in $FRA(t_1, t_2)$. We proceed in the same way until we reach the end of the desired hedging period. This guarantees a risk-free investment that yields

$$\left(1 + s_{t_1}\right) \cdot \left(1 + K\left(t_1, t_2\right)\right) \cdot \left(1 + K\left(t_2, t_3\right)\right) \cdot \ldots \cdot \left(1 + K\left(t_n, t_{n+1}\right)\right) \qquad \textbf{(3.121)}$$

An opportunity like this can exist only if the series of contractually agreed rates are equal to the series of one-period forward rates implied in the current yield curve.

$$1 + K\left(t_n, t_{n+1}\right) = \frac{d\left(0, t_n\right)}{d\left(0, t_{n+1}\right)} \qquad \textbf{(3.122)}$$

Substituting (3.122) in (3.121) yields

$$\left(1 + s_{t_1}\right) \cdot \frac{d\left(0, t_1\right)}{d\left(0, t_2\right)} \frac{d\left(0, t_2\right)}{d\left(0, t_3\right)} \frac{d\left(0, t_3\right)}{d\left(0, t_4\right)} \ldots \frac{d\left(0, t_n\right)}{d\left(0, t_{n+1}\right)}$$
$$= \frac{d\left(0, t_1\right)}{d\left(0, t_{n+1}\right)} = \left(1 + s_{t_n}\right)^{t_n} \qquad \textbf{(3.123)}$$

All we need to do is to invest $l_{t_{n+1}} (1+s_{t_{n+1}})^{-t_{n+1}}$ in one-period Libor and roll-over forward-rate agreements. Note that the notional N will change in a deterministic way, ie, dependent on the locked-in forward rates.

Finally, we need to determine the pricing of (3.120), ie, what is the replicating portfolio? Note that a synthetic position in one-period Libor between t_n and t_{n+1} can be achieved by buying a zero bond maturing at t_n and selling a zero bond that matures at t_{n+1}, while the fixed side of a forward-rate agreement is discounted with current yields, ie, multiplied with the respective zero coupon bond. The value of a forward-rate agreement at time $t_0 = 0$ amounts to

$$FRA = N \cdot K\left(t_n, t_{n+1}\right) \cdot d\left(0, t_{n+1}\right) - N\left[d\left(0, t_n\right) - d\left(0, t_{n+1}\right)\right]$$
$$= N \cdot \left(d\left(0, t_{n+1}\right)\left[1 + K\left(t_n, t_{n+1}\right)\right] - d\left(0, t_n\right)\right)$$

$$\text{(3.124)}$$

If $K(t_n, t_{n+1})$ is set appropriately, ie, to market conditions defined in (3.122) we arrive at

$$FRA = N \cdot \left(d\left(0, t_{n+1}\right) \frac{d\left(0, t_n\right)}{d\left(0, t_{n+1}\right)} - d\left(0, t_n\right) \right) = 0 \qquad \text{(3.125)}$$

for the time we enter a forward-rate agreement. We can hence leave pension assets invested in cash (one-period Libor, where we have arbitrarily chosen a period of one year for ease of exposition) without the need for additional funding. On top of this we can run an overlay portfolio of FRA series designed to create the desired liability cashflows. Alternatively, we could invest assets into market fixed-income, equity or hedge fund products that promise to generate *Libor* + α. While this would allow us to earn a positive NPV on pension assets, it would also endanger the replicating portfolio. Investors will get less than (3.121) if pension assets underperform the Libor rate that has been promised to be delivered into the forward-rate agreement.

RISKS IN USING SWAPS

The main risk in using swaps to hedge pension liabilities comes as credit risk. It takes either the form of *basis risk*, ie, changes in swap rates move opposite to changes in liability discount rates and *coun-*

terparty risk, ie, the swap counterparty defaults on its promised cashflows.

We start with basis risk. So far we implicitly assumed that liabilities react to the same rates as our hedging instruments (bonds or swaps), ie, there was no basis risk. This is, however, a strong simplification. We will, for example, see in Chapters 5 and 6 that the economically relevant discount factor will depend both on the strength of the plan sponsor and on the chosen asset allocation in the dedicated pool of assets. We will also see that the only correct way to arrive at a discount factor is to apply a contingent-claims framework in which the discount factor is determined after the fair value has been determined. Let us here ignore these issues and focus on a simpler more traditional valuation model. In a market-value framework, pension claims are just another form of corporate debt. It is hence obvious that the economic discount rate depends on the sponsor's credit risk. For example, the market value of pension liabilities for *AAA* industrial companies is calculated by discounting liability cashflows at rates that reflect the particular financial and operational leverage.

For a *BBB* airline company the market-value approach would use a considerably higher rate (one that reflects the larger risks of a cyclical industry as well as company-specific risks) to discount pension liabilities. Some practitioners have a problem with this. How could a deteriorating credit actually get a relief (lower market value of pension liabilities) on its debt? In a fair-value framework a downward-spiralling credit would need fewer and fewer assets to remain economically funded as liabilities fall with increased credit risk. While it is true that in a pure market-value framework default would never occur, as it ensures that the market value of assets always equals the market value of liabilities, it much better anticipates the value of stakes after default has taken place and it is the only framework that gives stakeholders a fair picture of their current wealth. A liability-hedging strategy would therefore invest in assets that ideally default at the same time as the underlying sponsor (buying its own corporate bonds). By this the plan sponsor transfers potential extra funding into those states of the world where funding does not take place, because the plan sponsor also defaults simultaneously. To see the advantage of this strategy let us imagine the situations for an AA-plan sponsor that invests into a diversified portfolio of AA bonds.

Suppose an economic downturn hits the whole economy with default rates rising. In this case defaults in the company's pension fund would trigger additional funding. In case the plan sponsor is less affected by the economic downturn than other companies of the same original rating, this is bad news for all shareholders and bondholders, as contributions might bring the plan sponsor down and will dilute the other stakeholders' claims. If the plan sponsor itself defaults, while all other companies do relatively well, it has no benefit from this. What happens if we use swaps as a proxy for AA bonds? In an accounting framework that continues to discount liabilities at AA swap rates, nothing happens. There will be no basis risks. Whatever the swap rates do to the value of the liability hedging portfolio, liabilities will move in tandem.

Economically there will be two sources of basis risk. The first obviously arises from a difference in swap spreads that are a proxy for banking sector risks (we will come back to this point shortly), while the plan sponsor might be an airline company that is subject to different sectoral exposures. The second applies directly to the nature of swap spreads. Due to the nature of how Libor rates are set (quarterly poll from the strongest credits in the banking sector, ie, weak credits get dropped), a 30-year swap rate does not reflect the credit risk for an average financial institution over 30 years. Instead it relates to a rolling quarterly credit from the very best banks. A 30-year bond from any financial distribution will be much riskier. It should be clear that discounting pension liabilities using swap rates will lead to pension liabilities that behave like high-quality banking liabilities that will also adjust for deteriorating credits in the banking sector. For most companies this will overvalue pension liabilities and create a large sector exposure.

The second source of risks from using swaps is counterparty risk. Luckily, this risk can be managed to a large extent. First of all, credit risk arises only when the pension fund has a claim against the swap counterparty. In other words, when the P&L of the swap (entered at 0) becomes positive.

$$swap_{receiver} = B^K(0, t_n) - FRN > 0 \qquad \textbf{(3.126)}$$

How large can this exposure become? Suppose the swap duration is 15 years with a notional of €4 billion. Also, assume swap spreads could drop by 25 basis points over the next 24 hours. If the plan sponsor has bought a single bond it would have exposed him to credit risk on €4 billion. However, in the swap case the immediate exposure is

$$4 \ billion \cdot 15 \cdot 0.0025 = 150 \ million \qquad (3.127)$$

in the worst-case scenario. If this scenario has happened, the swap counterparty has to deposit a collateral of €150 million. If they fail to do so, the contract is closed (the €150 million profit is taken) and a new contract with a more solid counterparty opened. Apart from this, all conventional methods of reducing credit risks can (and should) be applied, such as diversification among counterparties and allocation of credit lines dependent on perceived counterparty risk.

SUMMARY

This chapter has given readers a brief review of fixed-income risk management and hedging in connection with pension liabilities. Applying these principles will allow plan sponsors to find the appropriate liability-matching (replicating) portfolios. Pension liability management is fixed-income risk management. Pension plans do not need a new asset management framework, but rather the application of sound fixed-income hedging strategies.

1 Note that we used central differences to calculate numerical derivatives. The corresponding forward difference to (3.44) would be $D_r^i \approx h^{-1} \left(l(r-h, \pi) - l(r, \pi) \right)$.
2 This section will not attempt to replicate far better books on financial engineering, such as Neftci (2004). Instead it attempts to introduce readers to the basic idea of using swaps in a unified framework.
3 This section follows Hull (2003, p 522).
4 Note that for cash balance plans ABO and PBO are essentially the same as projected salary developments have no impact on the PBO.

REFERENCES

Bliss, R., 1997, "Movements in the Term Structure of Interest Rates", Economic Review, Federal Reserve Bank of Atlanta.

Chambers, D., W. Carleton, and R. McEnally, 1988, "Immunising Default-Free Bond Portfolios with a Duration Vector", Journal of Financial and Quantitative Analysis 19(3), pp 233–52.

Chambers, D. and S. Nawalka, 1997, "The M-Duration Model: Derivation and Testing of the M-Square Model" *Journal of Portfolio Management* **23(2)**.

Fabozzi, F., 1999, "Duration Convexity and Other Bond Risk Measures", Fabozzi Associates.

Golub B. and L. Tilmann, 2000, *Risk Management: Approaches for Fixed Income Markets* (New York: John Wiley & Sons).

Ho, T., 1992, "Key Rate Durations: Measures of Interest Rate Risk", *Journal of Fixed Income*, pp 29–44, September.

Hull, J., 2003, *Options Futures and Other Derivatives*, 5th edn (Prentice Hall).

Neftci, S.N., 2004, *Principles of Financial Engineering* (Elsevier Academic Press).

4

Liabilities and Portfolio Theory

This chapter deals with asset-liability management as it is taught in asset-management classes. More precisely, we define asset-liability management as the derivation of optimal asset-allocation policies relative to a set of exogenously defined liabilities that rely on risk premiums and some kind of risk preferences trading off expected surplus risk and surplus return. (For an exhaustive review, see Ziemba and Mulvey, 1998). Asset risk is replaced by liability-relative risks. However, this idea is not always shared by practitioners: "I think in different terms. The fall in interest rates did not cause our pension fund deficit. We simply had too much weight in Vodafone."[1] Investors of this type simply try to outrun their liabilities by investing in higher-yielding assets. They have chosen to simply ignore the problem. We will see that this form of happy-end investing is encouraged through actuarial analysis that evaluates contingent claims under the real-world probability measure. The (very) brief survey of asset-liability modelling provided in this chapter is restrictive. I feel therefore obliged to comment on this selection.

❏ Liabilities are proxied by liability benchmarks instead of full cashflow modelling. This is done for ease of exposition. Melting macro data on asset classes (equities, bonds, hedge funds, real estate) with micro data on security-specific information such as liability cashflows and varying discount rates is challenging in notation, without adding further insights to the problem. What is important, though, is that liability discount rates are the same discount as are used to price the investment universe. The section on liability benchmarking underscores this point.

❏ Liabilities are not a choice variable – ie, they are given as exog -nous. Principally, liabilities could also be made endogenous – incorporated as decision-variable into the optimisation problem. However, for corporate pension plans this option hardly exists. Therefore, this modelling aspect was left out.

❏ Asset-liability management is done in a single-period framework. There is a strand of literature that stresses the importance of multi-period decision making (see Scherer 2003). However, the author is very sceptical about the contribution of this field. Not only are these models difficult to solve, but most of them actually either ignore the underlying plan sponsor or model its objective in a fashion inconsistent with corporate finance theory. Most importantly, however, the optimal solution is a self-rebalancing hedging strategy that does not require multi-period optimisation technology.

Consequentially, this chapter is meant to provide insight into mainstream asset-management thinking. It is not a blueprint of how to perform asset-liability management. In fact, it is highly recommended to disregard surplus risk–return tradeoffs in practical decision making. The reasons are made clear in Chapter 5.

TOTAL-RETURN MANAGEMENT *VERSUS* LIABILITY-RELATIVE MANAGEMENT

Our chapter on asset-liability management starts with total-return management, which is employed by many liability-driven investors, but funnily is not asset-liability management at all. The traditional wisdom in total-return management runs as follows: "If a corporate pension plan promises its employees a 6% return on their pension contributions, it surely must earn 6% on its investment portfolio to finance its liabilities. This might mean that we need to invest in equities in order to stay funded over time. But as we don't like the tyranny of the benchmark (it is used only as an excuse by asset managers, anyway) we would prefer a total-return product that promises to return 6% on average over the full cycle." In fact, this could have been recorded in almost every single client meeting after 2002. And

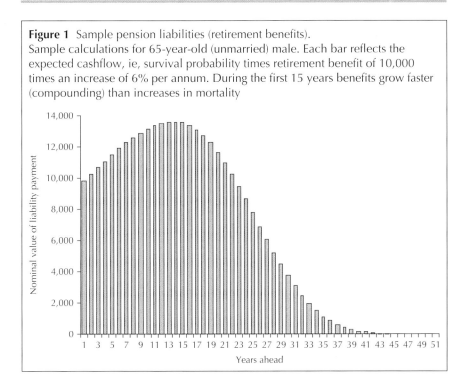

Figure 1 Sample pension liabilities (retirement benefits).
Sample calculations for 65-year-old (unmarried) male. Each bar reflects the expected cashflow, ie, survival probability times retirement benefit of 10,000 times an increase of 6% per annum. During the first 15 years benefits grow faster (compounding) than increases in mortality

of course there have been plenty of asset managers and consultants who jumped on the total-return bandwagon, offering new business (after the collapse of the equity business).

> We see a trend to give asset managers more room to move within a total risk budget. Sometimes even the traditional guidelines are abolished, as long as the manager makes more return and total risk is kept within the boundaries"[2]

However, it will be shown that total-return management has its origin in a simplified (and false) interpretation of the asset-liability problem. Suppose a pension plan offers the following retirement benefit. It promises that pensioners will receive a 6% increase in retirement income every year. For simplicity, we look at 65-year-old unmarried males. The nominal value of future expected payments is calculated in Figure 1.

Interest-rate volatility is assumed to be 0.7% (70 basis points per anum) and constant across maturities. Additional to bonds there is also an equity investment available. It is uncorrelated with bonds and offers a 10% (μ_E) return on average with 20% (σ_E) annual volatility. We will now answer the following questions.

❏ What is the expected liability growth?
❏ What is the most attractive investment?
❏ What is the least attractive investment?
❏ Which one is the most risky with respect to liabilities?

First we calculate the implied liability-growth rate. By how much would the present value of liabilities grow, if interest rates remain unchanged (if only time passes by)? The present value of future pension payments discounted at the current spot curve equals €195,351. This translates into a yield to maturity of 4.077%. In case liabilities are discounted with a constant discount rate, it will grow with this discount rate over term. In no circumstance will the liability growth be 6%. This is a gross misunderstanding of present-value calculations. Even if retirement benefits were to grow by 100% a year, liability growth would be roughly around the internal rate of return of this portfolio.

We will now calculate the most attractive total-return product. A total-return product is initially defined as the combination of available assets that offer the highest return (over one year cash) per unit of risk, defined by the Sharpe Ratio:

$$\text{Sharpe Ratio} = \frac{R_p - S_1}{\sigma_p} \tag{4.1}$$

where $R_p = w_{s_i} s_i + (1 - w_{s_i}) \mu_E$ and $\sigma_p^2 = w_{s_i}^2 D_{s_i}^2 \sigma_{s_i}^2 + (1 - w_{s_i})^2 \sigma_E^2$. Figure 2 plots Sharpe Ratios for combinations of zero bonds (w_{s_i}) and equities ($1 - w_{s_i}$). A maximum Sharpe Ratio is obtained with 18% equity and 82% bonds with a four-year duration. The least attractive investment is a 30-year zero bond (Sharpe Ratio of 0.11), as it offers little yield advantage with equity-like volatility.

So much for total risk and return. How would the optimal total-return portfolio perform against a liability benchmark? The interest-rate duration of the liability stream in Figure 2 is 10.37. Repeating our arguments in Chapter 3, a drop in rates by 100 basis points will increase liabilities by (approximately) 10.37%. Assets will return 4.1% on average. Suppose a pension fund is investing in the total-return product. Its hypothetical balance sheet looks like the one in Figure 3.

Figure 2 Sharpe Ratio and asset allocation.
The portfolio Sharpe Ratio depends on both duration and equity allocation. Increases in duration improve risk-adjusted returns only for short durations, as risk is linear in duration, while expected return does not grow linearly. Equity allocations provide a large increase in a portfolio's Sharpe Ratio; that, however, flattens out as portfolios become too concentrated

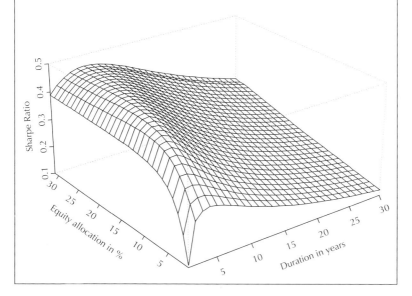

Figure 3 Pension fund balance sheet.
Pension fund liabilities (l) are assumed to behave like a 10.37-year-duration bond. The pension fund is initially 100% funded with an 18% allocation to equities (e) and 82% into short-term bonds (b). Note that the asset allocation has been motivated by a total-return objective

Assets		Liabilities	
e	18	100	$l\,(D = 10.37)$
$b\,(D = 4)$	82	0	s

Now let's assume an exceptional year for our total-return product. Equities rally by 20% and rates fall by 200 basis points. How would the economic situation change? Note that we approximate bond performance by Babcock's formula: $R \approx s_i - D_{s_i} \Delta s_i$.

Figure 4 Pension fund balance sheet: Scenario 1.
Equities rally by 20% and rates fall by 200 basis points.
The total-return product (asset side) outperformed its return
expectations of 6%. However, liabilities increase by much more
than assets and though the absolute return has been positive,
the pension fund shows a deficit of 11

Assets			Liabilities	
e	22	125	l	
b	92	−11	s	

Figure 5 Pension fund balance sheet: Scenario 2.
Interest rates rise by 200 basis points, equities rally by 20%.
The total-return product underperformed its return expectations
of 6%. However, liabilities fall by much more than assets and,
though the absolute return has been around zero, the pension
fund shows a surplus of 17

Assets			Liabilities	
e	22	83	l	
b	79	17	s	

The economic situation (market value of assets minus market value of liabilities) did sharply deteriorate (11 million deficit), even though the total-return product outperformed by far its return expectations, delivering about 13% return instead of the anticipated 4%. An asset-only view would congratulate itself on the excellent risk-adjusted performance. The naïve asset-liability view (incorporating liabilities as a fixed rate of 4.38%) would also be upbeat as reserves (relative to the 4% target) have been created. The reason for this pension fund disaster is that owning equities and short-term bonds opened up a large duration gap of about seven years.

It is certainly true that a rise in rates would have reversed the above situation. Assume a 200-basis-points rise in rates instead. The new balance sheet looks like the one in Figure 5. Economically, this creates a surplus of 17. We will see in the next chapter that shareholders have no interest in surplus volatility, as gains and losses have an asymmetric impact on funding requirements. Even though the economic situation did improve, the so called total-return product would have offered a dismal 0.3% total return.

Again, looking at the total-return manager in isolation would most likely result in replacing the existing mandate with a more "promising" asset-management house and leave the pension officer in great frustration. After all, assets underperformed liabilities in his naïve world.

Let us summarise. Hiring a total-return manager will give false signals about the true status of a company's pension plan (most likely in the opposite direction) and expose the sponsor to a large risk of funding the resulting pension shortfall. A duration position of 10 years is entirely different with 5 or 10 years liability duration. How big is this risk? Assume the plan sponsor invests in the most attractive total-return product. They will then be exposed to a surplus volatility of

$$\left(w_{s_i}D_{s_i} - D_l\right)^2 \sigma_{\Delta s}^2 + \left(1 - w_{s_i}\right)^2 \sigma_E^2 \tag{4.2}$$

In the above case this amounts to 6.13%. We can price this risk using the spread-option approach from Chapter 2. The implied value of this guarantee is 2.44 for one year. Note that the guarantee is repeated every year.

Diehard critics would say that we did not address total-return management at all. All we did was to identify a strategic benchmark portfolio. They would argue that total-return management is either the application of large asset-allocation bets or the creation of (total) returns independent of the performance of broad asset classes. Let us incorporate this view. Suppose you are CIO (chief investment officer) of a large asset-management company and are asked to create a successful total-return product. The objective is to provide a total return of 6% with a minimum value-at-risk (VAR) at the one-year time horizon with 99% confidence. You are given (zero) bonds with maturity ranging from one to five years, equities and tactical asset-allocation skills. We summarise these skills in the information ratio (IR), defined as the active return per unit of active risk (tracking error) on a scalable asset-allocation portfolio with risk (σ_α^2). Active risks can be scaled with θ. How can the CIO satisfy the provided objective? It turns out to be a straightforward optimisation exercise. Minimise VAR

$$\min_{w_1,\ldots,w_6,\theta} \left(z_\alpha \sigma_p\right) \tag{4.3}$$

subject to a series of constraints

Table 1 Risk decomposition for total return mandates.
The optimal total-return mandate will consist of little TAA, unless we
assume unrealistically high information ratios. Risk allocations are calculated from (4.7). Total-return mandates look suspiciously like normal
benchmark mandates

Information ratio	0.25%	0.5%	1%	1.5%
1 Y Bond	0.00	0.00	0.00	0.00
2 Y Bond	0.00	0.00	0.00	0.00
3 Y Bond	0.00	0.00	0.00	0.00
4 Y Bond	0.00	0.00	0.00	0.00
5 Y Bond	11.41	26.74	43.22	27.3
Equity	58.36	26.84	10.09	6.4
TAA	30.23	46.42	46.68	66.3

$$\sigma_p^2 = \sum_{i=1}^n \sum_{j=1}^n w_i w_j \sigma_{ij} + \theta^2 \sigma_\alpha^2 \tag{4.4}$$

$$\bar{\mu} = \sum_{i=1}^n w_i \mu_i + \theta IR \sigma_\alpha \tag{4.5}$$

$$w_i \geq 0 \tag{4.6}$$

where individual asset weights are given by w_i, covariances between
assets are denoted by σ_{ij} and expected individual asset returns by μ_i.
The objective (4.3) is to minimise VAR of a portfolio $(z_\alpha \sigma_p^2)$, where z_α
is the z-value of a standard normal and $\alpha = 0.01$.[3] Portfolio risk
(σ_p^2) in (4.4) consists of underlying asset positions $(\sum_{i=1}^n \sum_{j=1}^n w_i w_j \sigma_{ij})$
plus active management risk $(\theta^2 \sigma_\alpha^2)$. Additionally, we employ a total-
return constraint $(\bar{\mu})$ in (4.5) together with non-negativity constraints
(4.6). Suppose our return requirement is 6%. How would the optimal
risk decomposition look if we allow for alternative degrees of investment skill? Table 1 shows the results of the exercise above.

We calculate percentage contributions to risk in order to
find out the true character of a given product. Define
$\boldsymbol{\omega}^T = [w_1, \ldots, w_6 \quad \theta]$, $\sigma_p^2 = \boldsymbol{\omega}^T \boldsymbol{\Omega} \boldsymbol{\omega}$ and $(d\sigma_p/d\boldsymbol{\omega}) = \boldsymbol{\Omega}\boldsymbol{\omega}$. Percentage
contributions to risk are then given by

$$\frac{d\sigma_p}{d\omega_i} \frac{\omega_i}{\sigma_p} \tag{4.7}$$

where $(d\sigma_p/d\omega_i)$ is the i-th element of $(d\sigma_p/d\boldsymbol{\omega})$. Note that
$\sum_i \omega_i (d\sigma_p/d\omega_i) = \sigma_p$. Heuristically, we might define a total-return

product as a product that contains more than 50% non-benchmark risk. It is interesting to see that, for realistic information ratios (below 1), the percentage contribution to risk is below 50%. Asset-class risk dominates, even though it has been labelled as a total-return product. So most of the risk (more than 50%) is repackaged asset-class risk. Only for unrealistically highly skilled investors will there be more than 50% of non-benchmark risk. Although the example was somewhat synthetic, it showed us a general point: most total-return products will carry a considerable proportion of asset-class risk. They are just normal benchmark products in disguise. In summary, I made the point that so called total-return mandates might create uncontrollable liability-relative risks and are often not even different from normal benchmarked mandates.

IN SEARCH FOR THE LIABILITY ASSET

The calculation of corporate pension liabilities is costly, both in computational and monetary terms. Unfortunately, market-value-based modelling of pension fund surplus requires frequent recalculation of liabilities in order to perform surplus calculations both across time and in different countries. In order to provide the required transparency on corporate pension liabilities I introduce the concept of a *liability asset*.[4] I define it as a portfolio of real or synthetic securities priced according to available market information, which tracks the liabilities as closely as possible. As such, it is by definition a best hedge (see Chapter 3).

The use of a liability asset rests on the assumption that the market value of pension obligations is independent of the underlying assets. This is in general the case. The value of pension liabilities does depend only on the projected cashflows discounted at the correct (risk-adjusted) discount rate. Both inputs do not depend on the asset allocation chosen for a pension fund – with one exemption: credit risk. Decreasing the likelihood that plan members will actually receive the promised payments will decrease the value of theses cashflows due to increased credit risk. However, if assets closely track the liability benchmark, credit risks might well be negligent, which in turn leads to the independence of asset allocation and liability pricing. Admittedly, this makes the concept of a liability asset somewhat circular. However, as pensioners and equity holders generally have the same incentive to call for matched liabilities (see

Chapter 5), this is of little practical relevance. Liability tracking also relies on the assumptions that all systematic risks can be replicated with tradable securities. How about actuarial risks? We have already argued in Chapter 1 that, as long as actuarial risks are uncorrelated with priced risk factors, their presence does not impact valuations. Only if actuarial risks cannot be diversified (because they become too large due to inhomogeneous workforce or longevity risks that affect all plan members at the same time) need they be insured.

So far, I have defined a liability asset as a liability-tracking portfolio, but what exactly do we mean by liabilities? Let us recall three key concepts in valuing liabilities from US GAAP accounting. The projected benefit obligation (PBO, called DBO under IFRS) is the present value of (currently earned) benefit payments based on projected future salaries. In contrast, the accumulated benefit obligation (ABO, no counterpart under IFRS) does not include further salary increases as they might take place (to the discretion of management) but are not guaranteed yet. Lastly, the vested benefit obligation (VBO, no counterpart under IFRS) equals the ABO for employees who have earned their claim on the ABO, even if they leave the company or the plan is terminated. ABO, VBO and PBO coincide at the last day of service. They are all different before this day. Why do these differences matter? The legal obligation of the plan sponsor (in case of bankruptcy) is limited to the VBO. To the extent that external pension funding reflects the PBO rather than the VBO, the pension plan is overfunded. Both equity as well as debtholders experience a wealth transfer. For debtholders this is particularly troubling, as originally junior claims (difference between PBO and VBO) became senior (collateralised).

The second problem concerns inflation sensitivity. PBO calculations include anticipated but neither granted nor guaranteed future wage increases (arising from inflation, career trend or productivity gains) as current liabilities. This is troublesome for several reasons. For a start, most inputs a plan sponsor requires (wages, raw materials, energy and so forth) are inflation-sensitive, but no company would account for these as current liability. The inflation-sensitivity could well be largely overestimated. To put it bluntly, the direct impact from a future wage increase at Deutsche Bank has a first-order importance on its P&L, but is left unaccounted for, while the second-order impact on the pension fund (derivative of the wage bill) is accounted for. Clearly, this makes little sense and is not even consistent with a going-concern approach. That approach would not only need to reflect future wage increases as current liabilities, but also to account for future profits (generated by the same employees) as current assets. Finally it is not clear why companies should hedge inflation if their revenues are positively correlated with inflation. In this case the ongoing business is already a hedge against inflation. Given the fact that wage increases are awarded only if the economic situation of the company allows, every pension plan for a profitable company must by definition be overfunded.

Let us summarise. Tracking PBO rather than VBO overestimates both the economic value of liabilities as well as inflation VBO we recognise that many practitioners will focus mainly on accounting figures – the PBO/DBO. This is rather regrettable from an academic point of view, but still a great improvement on ignoring pension liabilities in the first place.

What do we need the liability asset for? The liability asset reflects the asset allocation that maintains the current funding situation (as much as possible) across all economic scenarios. It is therefore a benchmark against which all active pension fund management needs to be judged. Asset-liability management effectively becomes benchmark-relative portfolio optimisation. A duration position of 10 years in the asset portfolio creates a completely different risk exposure for a liability benchmark of five or fifteen years' years duration. In the first case the plan sponsor benefits from rising rates, while it benefits from falling rates in the second case. A liability benchmark also yields up-to-date information on the current funding status, which directly impacts asset-allocation policies (reduces liability-related risks if funding status falls or net periodic pension costs threaten to become negative) and plan contributions (cash transfer to avoid a kick against shareholders' equity in case of minimum additional liabilities). The introduction of liability benchmarks is also likely to revolutionise asset management. Risk management needs to be operated against liability benchmarks, rather than standard bond portfolios as calculated by bond index providers. The same applies to performance management systems that often cannot deal with cashflow-based benchmarks. Finally, it will shift the attention of plan sponsors towards an unbundling of alpha- and beta-related risks. While asset-management firms are very likely to be marginalised to providing alpha generation, investment banks will sell exposure to interest, inflation and sometimes equity risk via cheap derivative structures.

The precision to which we can model the liability asset (sometimes also called the liability benchmark portfolio) depends on the information available to construct the best hedge. If we are provided with only a duration number we can at best approximate the liabilities with a corporate bond issued by the plan sponsor. Note that, if future cashflows cannot be provided by the plan actuary, convexity risks or more general yield-curve risks will remain unmanaged. If no information on the borrowing costs of the sponsor company is available we could still use bonds of similar maturity and credit risk (eg, from the swap market). However, beware of the dangers of the latter approach. If the creditworthiness of the sponsor company deteriorates this must by definition lower the value of the pension promise (liabilities) as pension payments become less likely. This is not necessarily reflected in a broad market measure of credit risk.

In order to get an understanding how liability exposures to changes in bond yields, credit spreads and inflation vary between already retired pension beneficiaries and active employees, let us examine a fairly typical liability structure from a German industrial company. If we ignore the volatility in pension liabilities, by projecting liabilities with the use of a deterministic base scenario, we will effectively decouple assets from liabilities. We then arrive at an asset-only problem that can be solved without recurrence to the liability profile. However, it is the existence of liabilities that necessitates the availability of assets in the first place. In order to realistically model the asset-liability problem we therefore have to find a computationally less costly way of approximating pension liabilities.

Suppose the value of liabilities depends on a single discount rate l (applied to all future cashflows, as it is the case under IAS accounting) as well as on the projected future inflation π: $l = l(y, \pi)$. We can think of l in quite general terms. It could reflect the accrued benefit obligation, the projected benefit obligation, plan contributions and payments or any other plan characteristic that depends on the assigned values (see Scherer 2004; Scherer and Jasper 2003). In order to calculate the sensitivity of l with respect to the assumed-value drivers above, we take a first order Taylor approximation around the central actuarial scenario.[5] The Taylor approximation leads to

$$\hat{l}_s = \underbrace{l\left(y, \pi\right)}_{\substack{central \\ scenario}} + \underbrace{\frac{dl}{dy}\Delta y_s + \frac{dl}{d\pi}\Delta\pi_s}_{\substack{deviations\ from \\ central\ scenario}} \tag{4.8}$$

where $y + \Delta y_s$ indicates the new (flat) discount rate in scenario s. Application of (4.8) requires the calculation of the identified key sensitivities. A scenario in this context is a deterministic liability path for modified variable values. For each variable we calculate two additional scenarios, where we exclusively change values for this variable, but leave the other variables constant. Effectively, we numerically create partial derivatives.

$$\frac{dl}{dy} = \frac{l\left(y+\Delta y\right) - l\left(y-\Delta y, \pi\right)}{2\Delta y} \tag{4.9}$$

$$\frac{dl}{d\pi} = \frac{l\left(y, \pi+\Delta\pi\right) - l\left(y, \pi-\Delta\pi, \pi\right)}{2\Delta\pi} \tag{4.10}$$

Suppose we are interested in estimating the volatility of annual liability reform (σ) in order to assess the relative riskiness of a given asset allocation. We use historical yield, spread and inflation changes to generate a series of liability returns in order to approximate corporate liabilities for $s = 1 \ldots S$ economic scenarios (ie, realisations of yield and inflation changes) and calculate

$$\sigma_l = \sqrt{\frac{1}{S}\Sigma_{s=1}^{S}\left(\frac{\hat{l}_s - l}{l} - y\right)^2} = \sqrt{\frac{1}{S}\Sigma_{s=1}^{S}(r_l - y)^2} \tag{4.11}$$

where liability returns (r_l) grow on average with the discount rate (y) used for the central scenario (assuming no convexity effects). The result of this calculation – where $\hat{l}_s$ is calculated from (4.8) – is shown in Figures 6 and 7.

We can also examine total liability volatility in its sources. In the current (one-period) example we identify changes in government bond yields (Δg), credit spreads (Δs) and inflation ($\Delta\pi$). Note that liabilities legally need to be discounted by AA corporate bond yields ($\Delta y = \Delta g + \Delta s$).

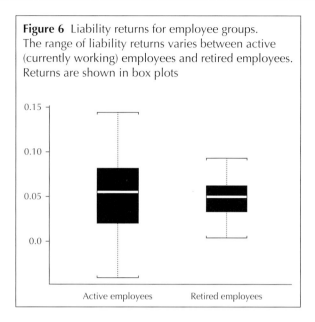

Figure 6 Liability returns for employee groups. The range of liability returns varies between active (currently working) employees and retired employees. Returns are shown in box plots

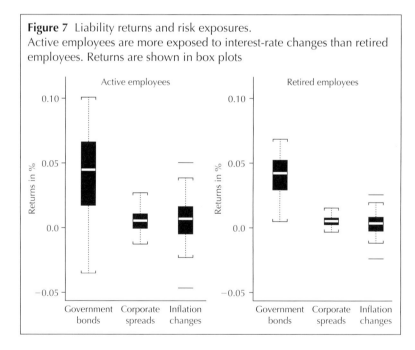

Figure 7 Liability returns and risk exposures. Active employees are more exposed to interest-rate changes than retired employees. Returns are shown in box plots

Table 2 Pension liabilities and economic sensitivities.
In a given actuarial base scenario (5% nominal rates and 2% inflation), pension liabilities (DBO) are valued at €957 million. Should only nominal rates increase with inflation unchanged (increase in real yields), liabilities fall to €880 million. If inflation rises by 1% while bond yields have remained constant, liabilities increase to €1,000 million

	Base Scenario	Scenario 1	Scenario 2
Interest Rate	5%	6%	5%
Inflation	2%	2%	3%
Subsidiary 1	67787137	62249068	70491555
Subsidiary 2	27933394	25809975	30177882
Total	95720531	88059043	100669437

In matrix notation we write

$$\Sigma = \begin{pmatrix} \sigma^2_{\Delta g} & \sigma_{\Delta g, \Delta s} & \sigma_{\Delta g, \Delta \pi} \\ & \sigma^2_{\Delta s} & \sigma_{\Delta s, \Delta \pi} \\ & & \sigma^2_{\Delta \pi} \end{pmatrix}, L = \begin{pmatrix} \dfrac{dl}{dg} \\ \dfrac{dl}{ds} \\ \dfrac{dl}{d\pi} \end{pmatrix} \quad (4.12)$$

where $\sigma^2_{\Delta g}$, $\sigma^2_{\Delta s}$, $\sigma^2_{\Delta \pi}$ denotes the variance of government yield changes, spread changes and inflation changes, while $\sigma_{\Delta g, \Delta s}$ $\sigma_{\Delta g, \Delta \pi}$, $\sigma_{\Delta s, \Delta \pi}$ reflect the covariance between government yield changes and spread changes, government yield changes and inflation changes, and spread changes and inflation changes. We can hence create the covariance matrix that drives liability risk from $\Omega_{ll} = L\Sigma L$. Total volatility can now be calculated from $\sigma^2_l = I^T \Omega_{ll} I$, where I denotes a 3x1 vector of ones. Marginal and percentage risks are calculated from $(d\sigma^2_l / dI) = \Omega_{ll} I$ and $(d\sigma^2_l / dI)(1/\sigma^2_l) = (\Omega_{ll} I / I^T \Omega_{ll} I)$.

So far we have investigated the nature of liability returns. Next we want to provide a simple but robust methodology to liability hedging in the absence of exact cashflow data. We assume the actuary is able to calculate pension liabilities across a range of economic scenarios as stylised in Table 2.

Given changes in valuation due to isolated changes in macroeconomic risks (interest rates and inflation) we can now calculate the

Figure 8 Liability hedging properties.
Liability returns are plotted against asset returns. Government bonds
(grey squares) show both close liability tracking and a positive correlation,
while equities (dark squares) exhibit a negative and very loose
relationship between equities and government bonds. Numbers are based
on monthly observations from January 1999 to March 2005

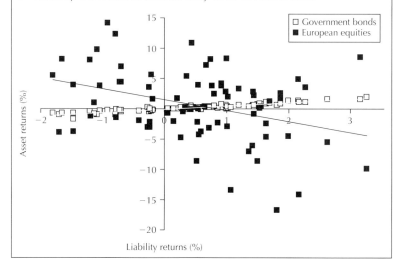

relevant numbers for interest-rate duration and inflation duration.
All we need to do is to use the entries in Table 2 to calculate the
numerical approximations to the respective durations.

$$D_{\Delta y} \approx \frac{\frac{88059043}{95720531}-1}{0.01} = -8.00, \; D_{\Delta\pi} \approx \frac{\frac{100669437}{95720531}-1}{0.01} = 5.17 \quad \textbf{(4.13)}$$

Suppose we centre the expected liability return on the actuarial rate
of 5% and assume further that we have calculated figures for both
changes in bond yields and inflation. With this we can build a
series of historical liability returns.

$$r_l = y_{actuarial} + D_{\Delta y}\Delta y + D_{\Delta\pi}\Delta\pi \quad \textbf{(4.14)}$$

If we regress r_l against duration equivalent bonds (r_b) or
equity returns (r_e) we will obtain the straight lines in Figure 8.
The liability-hedging asset tracks liabilities as closely as it possibly gets – ie, it < minimises the variance of the error term in
$r_l = \beta_0 + \beta_1 r_b + \varepsilon$.

Suppose now we want to more generally express the liability-tracking problem. First we need estimates on the covariance structure between all k assets provided by the $k \cdot k$ covariance matrix $\boldsymbol{\Omega}_{aa}$, the covariance structure between assets and liabilities expressed in the $k \cdot 1$ covariance vector $\boldsymbol{\Omega}_{al}$ and the volatility of liability returns σ_l. Note that the k-th element of $\boldsymbol{\Omega}_{al}$, denotes the covariance between the k-th asset and pension liabilities.

There is some discussion on the individual entries in $\boldsymbol{\Omega}_{al}$, particularly with respect to the covariance between equities and liabilities. Assets that exhibit large covariances with liabilities are natural hedges. One theory brought forward to rescue equity investments in an asset-liability world uses the concept of equity duration.[6] Stocks are assumed to have an infinite (or at least very long) lifetime. It follows directly from the logic of the simple dividend discount model that equities (particularly growth stocks that pay low dividends) have long interest-rate durations. The same conclusion arises from viewing equities as real call options. Lower risk-free rates would also increase option values. If equities had a high enough interest-rate sensitivity they could also be used as a hedging instrument, but with much larger return-generating abilities. Financial economists become very sceptical. Large correlation paired with high return differentials promises unusually high risk-adjusted returns – too high to be consistent with equilibrium returns on other assets. And indeed empirically the correlation between equities and bonds drifts around zero with changing signs and recently has even become negative.

Liability tracking aims at minimising the tracking risk between a portfolio of investable securities and synthetic liability returns.

$$\sigma_{TE}^2 = \begin{bmatrix} \mathbf{w} \\ -1 \end{bmatrix}^{\mathrm{T}} \begin{bmatrix} \boldsymbol{\Omega}_{aa} & \boldsymbol{\Omega}_{al} \\ \boldsymbol{\Omega}_{al}^{\mathrm{T}} & \sigma_l^2 \end{bmatrix} \begin{bmatrix} \mathbf{w} \\ -1 \end{bmatrix} \tag{4.15}$$

We will illustrate the formal derivations with an underlying example. Assume the following numerical values. The asset universe consists of real bonds, nominal bonds and equities.

$$\boldsymbol{\Omega}_{aa} = \begin{bmatrix} 5.66 & 10.04 & -15.33 \\ & 32.47 & -42.42 \\ & & 416.83 \end{bmatrix}, \boldsymbol{\Omega}_{al} = \begin{bmatrix} 9.21 \\ 21.53 \\ -30.35 \end{bmatrix}, \sigma_l^2 = 16.84 \tag{4.16}$$

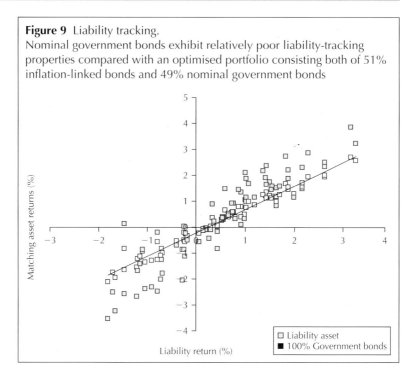

Figure 9 Liability tracking.
Nominal government bonds exhibit relatively poor liability-tracking properties compared with an optimised portfolio consisting both of 51% inflation-linked bonds and 49% nominal government bonds

Minimising (4.15) with respect to w_a yields the liability-hedging solution.

$$\mathbf{w}^* = \begin{bmatrix} 51\% \\ 49\% \\ 0\% \end{bmatrix}$$

It consists of 51% real bonds and 49% nominal bonds. The remaining risk is less than 1 per cent. The quality of benchmark tracking is largely improved, as we can see in Figure 9.

The key advantage to the hedging model is that it is not based on risk premium estimates that are well known to carry large estimation errors. This not only reduces the amount of subjectivity but also leads to a solution well rooted within corporate finance theory.

Suppose we found a liability hedging benchmark. As hedging and pricing are strongly related concepts, the yield on the liability-hedging portfolio also provides a realistic guess about expected asset growth. Often, however, actuarial guesses are influenced by sponsors' interests, which are more concerned with higher interest rates in order to reduce the present value of future liabilities and hence improve the accounting treatment of a given funding situation. Suppose actuaries used a 5% discount rate, while the fair market rate is at 4.5%. Given a duration of 15 years, liabilities are 7.5% undervalued. Investing in a matching portfolio would yield a 0.5% return gap (per annum). The hedging portfolio would contribute to a deterioration of accounting numbers. However, investing in riskier assets that provide the prospect of a (on average) stable funding ratio exposes the company to excess risks. Manipulation of liability valuations might hence lead to economically dangerous asset-allocation policies.

ASSET-LIABILITY MANAGEMENT: SURPLUS RISK

Even though I have already used the terms *surplus*, and *surplus volatility*, I want to introduce surplus risk and surplus return more formally. In fact, I want to express the asset-liability optimisation problem in terms of well-known mean-variance optimisation. First, I define (economic) surplus as the difference between assets and liabilities: $s = a - l$. Assets (a) and liabilities (l) are assumed to be valued at market prices. The change in surplus (Δs) is given by $\Delta s = \Delta a - \Delta l$, while the current funding ratio (sometimes called solvency ratio) can be expressed as $f = (a/l)$. In percentage terms we arrive at $(\Delta s / s) = (\Delta a - \Delta l) / s$. However, if we start with a fully funded position (surplus equals zero), liability returns would be undefined (dividing by zero), and, for small surpluses, surplus returns would reach 1,000 per cent or more. What is needed is an alternative definition of surplus returns. Let us instead normalise changes in pension fund surplus with current assets $(\Delta s / a) = (\Delta a - \Delta l / a)$. We can rewrite this as

$$R_{s(a)} = R_a - \frac{l}{a}\frac{\Delta l}{l} = R_a - \left(\frac{1}{f}\right)R_l \qquad (4.17)$$

where $R_{s(a)}$ denotes surplus returns, if a given surplus (or deficit) is normalised with current assets. Also, note that $R_a = \Sigma_{i=1}^{k} w_{a_i} R_{a_i}$ denotes the return of an asset portfolio weight, with individual returns and weights given by R_{a_i} and w_{a_i}. How can we arrive at an expression for surplus risk (σ_s^2) and return (μ_s)? After applying the variance and expectations operator on (4.17) we get

$$\sigma_s^2 = \sigma_a^2 + \left(\tfrac{1}{f}\right)^2 \sigma_l^2 - 2\left(\tfrac{1}{f}\right)\sigma_a\sigma_l\rho \qquad (4.18)$$

$$\mu_s = \mu_a - \left(\tfrac{1}{f}\right)\mu_l , \qquad (4.19)$$

where ρ denotes the correlation between assets and liabilities. For optimisation purposes – ie, when we choose the optimal asset allocation $(w^*_1, ..., w^*_k)$ – we can ignore all terms where asset weights are not involved. Note that for increasing solvency ratios $(1/f \to 0)$, liabilities become less and less important for surplus optimisation.

We can sharpen our intuition with a continuation of the above example. The assumed values for assets and liabilities have been ($a = 94, l = 90$). Suppose asset returns are 6%, while liabilities have grown by 12%. Also, assume surplus risk in the order of 10%. By how much did our initial surplus of $s = a - l = 4$ change? Substituting the relevant values into (4.19) yields $\mu_s = 6\% - (1/(94/90))12\% = -5.49\%$. What does this number mean in terms of a change in surplus? We know that by definition $\Delta s = a\mu_s$. Surplus dropped by -5.49% of assets – by 5.16 million. As the initial surplus has been 4 million, the new surplus must have moved into a 1.16 million deficit. Alternatively, we could have calculated this directly by s = 94 · 1.06 − 90 · 1.12 = −1.16. Surplus volatility (in millions) is measured by $a\sigma_s$, which amounts to 90 · 10% = 9 millions. Incorporating the expected surplus return into our surplus at risk calculation

$$SaR = a\left(\mu_s - \sigma_s z_\alpha\right) \qquad (4.20)$$

we arrive at a value of 19.7 million. We see that SaR in (4.20) can (normally) be directly derived from mean-variance inputs. There is no difference in minimising surplus volatility or surplus at risk. Both frontiers will share the same set of efficient solutions. A portfolio that minimises surplus volatility for unit of surplus return, will also minimise surplus risk for the same return target.

The literature on surplus optimisation typically assumes that pension funds operate in a mean-variance framework, where surplus return increases utility while surplus risk decreases utility and is therefore penalised by λ (risk-aversion) (see Sharpe and Tint 1990).

$$u = \mu_s - \lambda\sigma_s^2 \qquad (4.21)$$

Any asset-liability model uses an objective function similar to (4.21), although the functional form as well as the chosen risk measures might differ. Often, we find measures such as contribution risk, contribution at risk and average contribution. It is, however, completely unclear how these specifications are rooted in corporate finance theory. This applies to the used risk measures as well as to the idea of a corporate risk aversion. Corporate plan sponsors are not living individuals. They are only investment vehicles through which equity holders and bondholders aim to take risks. Unless we speak of a large shareholder who has tied up most of their wealth in a particular company (family business), specifications like (4.21) have no economic foundation whatsoever.

We can now expand (4.21) to a simple allocation between equities and bonds. Suppose we found the returns for a liability asset (r_l) to follow a linear relationship with the returns of a given bond benchmark index (r_b):

$$r_l = \beta r_b + \varepsilon \tag{4.22}$$

where β reflects the regression coefficient and ε the usual error term. In this context any error term arises from imperfect hedging. Asset returns are generated by a portfolio of equities (r_e) and bonds (r_b):

$$r_a = w r_e + (1-w) r_b \tag{4.23}$$

The optimal condition relates marginal surplus returns to marginal surplus risks:

$$\frac{d\mu_s}{dw} = \lambda \frac{d\sigma_s^2}{dw} \tag{4.24}$$

Equity weights are given by w. Marginal surplus returns (with respect to changes in equity holdings) and marginal surplus risks are given below.

$$\frac{d\sigma_s^2}{dw} = w\sigma_b^2 + (1-w)\sigma_e^2 - 2w\rho\sigma_e\sigma_b - (1-\beta)\frac{1}{f}\left(\sigma_b^2 - \sigma_e\sigma_b\rho\right) \tag{4.25}$$

$$\frac{d\mu_s}{dw} = r_e - r_b \tag{4.26}$$

Substituting (4.25) and (4.26) into (4.24) yields a closed-form solution for the optimal equity allocation (w^*):

$$w^* = \frac{\frac{1}{\lambda}(r_e - r_b) - (1-\beta)\frac{1}{f}\left(\sigma_b^2 - \sigma_e\sigma_b\rho\right)}{w\sigma_b^2 + (1-w)\sigma_e^2 - 2w\rho\sigma_e\sigma_b} \tag{4.27}$$

It is useful to look at (4.27) in more detail. First we note that w^* does not depend on the amount of hedging error ε. The unhedgeable cannot be hedged with equities.

The equity allocation increases with the risk premium of equities *versus* bonds and decreases with risk aversion. However, as we will argue in Chapter 5, shareholder-value-maximising companies should not take surplus risks in their pension funds. In this case $\lambda \to \infty$ and (4.27) becomes

$$w^* = \frac{(1-\beta)\frac{1}{f}\left(\sigma_b^2 - \sigma_e\sigma_b\rho\right)}{w\sigma_b^2 + (1-w)\sigma_e^2 - 2w\rho\sigma_e\sigma_b} \tag{4.28}$$

At a first look this seems to imply a non-zero equity allocation even in the case of surplus risk minimisation. However, we have restricted ourselves to a portfolio of equities and duration mismatched bonds. In other words we ignored duration as a choice variable. A portfolio of liability-mimicking bonds would exhibit $\beta = 1$, in which case

$$w^* = 0 \tag{4.29}$$

independent from funding assumptions. Additionally we can ignore estimation risks in al, other parameters, which would make (4.30) w^* a rather arbitrary number.

LIABILITIES AND THREE-FUND SEPARATION

This section identifies the properties of asset-liability-based portfolio optimisations (stochastic liabilities and non-zero correlations relative to liabilities) relative to asset-only solutions (static liabilities). I define utility in the usual mean-variance form

$$u = \mu_s - \tfrac{\lambda}{2}\sigma_s^2 \tag{4.31}$$

$$\mu_s = \mu - \left(\tfrac{1}{f}\right)\mu_l = \mathbf{w}^T\boldsymbol{\mu} - \left(\tfrac{1}{f}\right)\mu_l \tag{4.32}$$

$$\sigma_s^2 = \mathbf{w}^T\boldsymbol{\Omega}_{aa}\mathbf{w} - \tfrac{1}{f}2\mathbf{w}^T\boldsymbol{\Omega}_{al} + \tfrac{1}{f^2}\sigma_l^2 \tag{4.33}$$

where $\boldsymbol{\mu}$ represents the $k \cdot 1$ vector of expected asset returns.[7] The $k \cdot k$ covariance matrix $\boldsymbol{\Omega}_{aa}$, the covariance structure between assets and liabilities expressed in the $k \cdot 1$ covariance vector $\boldsymbol{\Omega}_{al}$ and the volatility of liability returns σ_l are defined as before. For optimisation purposes we can ignore all fixed terms $(1/f)\mu_l$ and $(1/f^2)\sigma_l^2$. The optimisation problem becomes

$$\min \ \sigma_s^2 = \mathbf{w}^{\mathsf{T}}\mathbf{\Omega}_{aa}\mathbf{w} - \left(\tfrac{1}{f}\right)2\mathbf{w}^{\mathsf{T}}\mathbf{\Omega}_{al} \qquad (4.34)$$

subject to a targeted return requirement $\bar{\mu}$ in (4.35) and a portfolio constraint (4.36).

$$\mathbf{w}^{\mathsf{T}}\boldsymbol{\mu} = \bar{\mu} \qquad (4.35)$$

$$\mathbf{w}^{\mathsf{T}}\mathbf{I} = 1 \qquad (4.36)$$

The Lagrange function in to this problem is expressed in (4.37), where θ_1 and θ_2 denote the multipliers attached to each constraint.

$$L = \mathbf{w}^{\mathsf{T}}\mathbf{\Omega}_{aa}\mathbf{w} - \left(\tfrac{1}{f}\right)2\mathbf{w}^{\mathsf{T}}\mathbf{\Omega}_{al} + \theta_1\left(\bar{\mu} - \mathbf{w}^{\mathsf{T}}\boldsymbol{\mu}\right) + \theta_2\left(1 - \mathbf{w}^{\mathsf{T}}\mathbf{I}\right) \qquad (4.37)$$

Taking first-order derivatives with respect to $\mathbf{w}$ and the multipliers yields

$$\frac{dL}{d\mathbf{w}} = 2\mathbf{\Omega}_{aa}\mathbf{w} - \left(\tfrac{1}{f}\right)2\mathbf{\Omega}_{al} - \theta_1\boldsymbol{\mu} - \theta_2\mathbf{I} = 0 \qquad (4.38)$$

$$\frac{dL}{d\theta_1} = \bar{\mu} - \mathbf{w}^{\mathsf{T}}\boldsymbol{\mu} = 0 \qquad (4.39)$$

$$\frac{dL}{d\theta_2} = 1 - \mathbf{w}^{\mathsf{T}}\mathbf{I} = 0, \qquad (4.40)$$

we can now solve (4.38) for $\mathbf{w}$:

$$2\mathbf{\Omega}_{aa}\mathbf{w} = \left(\tfrac{1}{f}\right)2\mathbf{\Omega}_{al} + \theta_1\boldsymbol{\mu} + \theta_2\mathbf{I}$$
$$\mathbf{w} = \left(\tfrac{1}{f}\right)\mathbf{\Omega}_{aa}^{-1}\mathbf{\Omega}_{al} + \tfrac{1}{2}\left(\theta_1\mathbf{\Omega}_{aa}^{-1}\boldsymbol{\mu} + \theta_2\mathbf{\Omega}_{aa}^{-1}\mathbf{I}\right) \qquad (4.41)$$

Substituting (4.41) in (4.39) and (4.40) we arrive at the equivalents of (4.39) and (4.40):

$$\mathbf{w}^{\mathsf{T}}\boldsymbol{\mu} = \left(\left(\tfrac{1}{f}\right)\mathbf{\Omega}_{aa}^{-1}\mathbf{\Omega}_{al} + \tfrac{1}{2}\left(\theta_1\mathbf{\Omega}_{aa}^{-1}\boldsymbol{\mu} + \theta_2\mathbf{\Omega}_{aa}^{-1}\mathbf{I}\right)\right)^{\mathsf{T}}\boldsymbol{\mu} = \bar{\mu} \qquad (4.42)$$

$$\mathbf{w}^{\mathsf{T}}\mathbf{I} = \left(\left(\tfrac{1}{f}\right)\mathbf{\Omega}_{aa}^{-1}\mathbf{\Omega}_{al} + \tfrac{1}{2}\left(\theta_1\mathbf{\Omega}_{aa}^{-1}\boldsymbol{\mu} + \theta_2\mathbf{\Omega}_{aa}^{-1}\mathbf{I}\right)\right)^{\mathsf{T}}\mathbf{I} = 1 \qquad (4.43)$$

We can now solve for the Lagrange multipliers (two equations in two unknowns) and reinsert back into (4.41) to find $w_{\bar{\mu}}^*$ – ie, the optimal asset allocation for a given return target. In order to impose some structure on the optimisation problem, we start with setting $\theta_1 = 0$ and arrive at the minimum surplus risk portfolio (*msp*).

$$\mathbf{w}_{msp} = \frac{\mathbf{\Omega}_{aa}^{-1}\mathbf{I}}{\mathbf{I}^{\mathsf{T}}\mathbf{\Omega}_{aa}^{-1}\mathbf{I}} + \left(\tfrac{1}{f}\right)\left[\mathbf{\Omega}_{aa}^{-1}\mathbf{\Omega}_{al} - \frac{\mathbf{I}^{\mathsf{T}}\mathbf{\Omega}_{aa}^{-1}\mathbf{\Omega}_{al}}{\mathbf{I}^{\mathsf{T}}\mathbf{\Omega}_{aa}^{-1}\mathbf{I}}\mathbf{\Omega}_{aa}^{-1}\mathbf{I}\right] \tag{4.44}$$

$$\mathbf{w}_{msp} = \mathbf{w}_{mvp} + \mathbf{w}_{lha} \tag{4.45}$$

Note that $\mathbf{w}_{lha}^{\mathsf{T}}\mathbf{I} = 0$ (the liability-hedging adjustment) is a zero-investment long/short portfolio. Alternatively, we could have solved a different optimisation problem from the start.

$$\min_{\mathbf{w}} \quad L = \mathbf{w}^{\mathsf{T}}\mathbf{\Omega}_{aa}\mathbf{w} - \tfrac{1}{f}2\mathbf{w}^{\mathsf{T}}\mathbf{\Omega}_{al} + \tfrac{1}{f^2}\sigma_l^2 + \theta_2\left(1 - \mathbf{w}^{\mathsf{T}}\mathbf{I}\right) \tag{4.46}$$

$$\frac{dL}{d\mathbf{w}} = 2\mathbf{\Omega}_{aa}\mathbf{w} - \tfrac{1}{f}2\mathbf{\Omega}_{al} - \theta_2\mathbf{I} = 0 \tag{4.47}$$

$$\frac{dL}{d\theta_2} = 1 - \mathbf{w}^{\mathsf{T}}\mathbf{I} = 0 \tag{4.48}$$

Solving for $\mathbf{w}$ we arrive at

$$\mathbf{w}^* = \left(1 - \phi\right)\frac{\mathbf{\Omega}_{aa}^{-1}\mathbf{I}}{\mathbf{I}^{\mathsf{T}}\mathbf{\Omega}_{aa}^{-1}\mathbf{I}} + \tfrac{1}{f}\mathbf{\Omega}_{aa}^{-1}\mathbf{\Omega}_{al} \tag{4.49}$$

where $\phi = (1/f)\,\mathbf{I}^{\mathsf{T}}\mathbf{\Omega}_{aa}^{-1}\mathbf{\Omega}_{al}$. The risk-minimising solution is a weighted average of minimum-variance portfolio and liability-hedging credit. Expanding (4.49) gets us

$$\begin{aligned}
\mathbf{w}^* &= \left(1 - \tfrac{1}{f}\mathbf{I}^{\mathsf{T}}\mathbf{\Omega}_{aa}^{-1}\mathbf{\Omega}_{al}\right)\frac{\mathbf{\Omega}_{aa}^{-1}\mathbf{I}}{\mathbf{I}^{\mathsf{T}}\mathbf{\Omega}_{aa}^{-1}\mathbf{I}} + \tfrac{1}{f}\mathbf{\Omega}_{aa}^{-1}\mathbf{\Omega}_{al} \\[2mm]
&= \frac{\mathbf{\Omega}_{aa}^{-1}\mathbf{I}}{\mathbf{I}^{\mathsf{T}}\mathbf{\Omega}_{aa}^{-1}\mathbf{I}} - \tfrac{1}{f}\mathbf{I}^{\mathsf{T}}\mathbf{\Omega}_{aa}^{-1}\mathbf{\Omega}_{al}\frac{\mathbf{\Omega}_{aa}^{-1}\mathbf{I}}{\mathbf{I}^{\mathsf{T}}\mathbf{\Omega}_{aa}^{-1}\mathbf{I}} + \tfrac{1}{f}\mathbf{\Omega}_{aa}^{-1}\mathbf{\Omega}_{al} \\[2mm]
&= \frac{\mathbf{\Omega}_{aa}^{-1}\mathbf{I}}{\mathbf{I}^{\mathsf{T}}\mathbf{\Omega}_{aa}^{-1}\mathbf{I}} + \left(\tfrac{1}{f}\right)\left(\mathbf{\Omega}_{aa}^{-1}\mathbf{\Omega}_{al} - \mathbf{I}^{\mathsf{T}}\mathbf{\Omega}_{aa}^{-1}\mathbf{\Omega}_{al}\frac{\mathbf{\Omega}_{aa}^{-1}\mathbf{I}}{\mathbf{I}^{\mathsf{T}}\mathbf{\Omega}_{aa}^{-1}\mathbf{I}}\right)
\end{aligned} \tag{4.50}$$

which is exactly the same as in (4.44). I will argue in the next chapter that (4.50) is the main focus of shareholder-value-oriented management. Using the numbers in (4.16) and adding a funding ratio of $f = (a/l) = (90/94)$ we can decompose the optimal solution into

$$\mathbf{w}_{msp}^* = \mathbf{w}_{mvp} + \mathbf{w}_{lha} = \begin{bmatrix} 115\% \\ -18\% \\ -3\% \end{bmatrix} + \begin{bmatrix} -59\% \\ 63\% \\ 2\% \end{bmatrix} = \begin{bmatrix} 56\% \\ 45\% \\ -1\% \end{bmatrix} \tag{4.51}$$

Next we want to relax the constraint on target returns: $\theta_1 > 0$. In this case the optimal solution unravels to

$$\mathbf{w}_{\bar{\mu}}^* = \mathbf{w}_{mvp} + \mathbf{w}_{lha} + \theta_1 \mathbf{w}_{spec} \qquad (4.52)$$

$$\mathbf{w}_{spec} = \mathbf{\Omega}_{aa}^{-1}\mathbf{\mu} - \frac{\mathbf{I}^{\mathrm{T}}\mathbf{\Omega}_{aa}^{-1}\mathbf{\mu}}{\mathbf{I}^{\mathrm{T}}\mathbf{\Omega}_{aa}^{-1}\mathbf{I}}\mathbf{\Omega}_{aa}^{-1}\mathbf{I} \qquad (4.53)$$

The speculative portfolio $\mathbf{w}_{spec}$ is independent from liability risk characteristics and depends solely on expected returns and covariances. In more modern language we might imagine $\mathbf{w}_{mvp} + \mathbf{w}_{lha}$ as the matching portfolio and $\mathbf{w}_{spec}$ as the optimal-growth portfolio consuming a given risk budget. Any efficient frontier portfolio consists of a combination of the minimum-variance portfolio, the liability-hedging adjustment and a speculative part. That is why the title of this section refers to three-fund separation. The speculative part is also the most arbitrary portfolio of the three funds. It is based on estimated returns for the asset classes involved and proves to be particularly prone to estimation error, which will result in as many different asset-liability solutions as suppliers of those solutions.

Suppose we set $\mathbf{\mu} = (0.05, 0.034, 0.04, 0.08)^{\mathrm{T}}$. We can now trace out a complete surplus risk frontier as in Figure 10. Note that technically we can express the asset-liability problem as a special case of dual benchmark optimisation.[8] Suppose we introduce $w_l = (1/1+a)$, $w_s = 1 - w_l$ as well as $\mathbf{w}_a^{\mathrm{T}}\mathbf{I} = w_l + w_s = 1$. A pension fund with liabilities of 90, assets of 95 and hence a surplus of 5 implicitly possesses a benchmark of 94.7% liabilities (represented by an interest- and inflation-duration-matched bond portfolio) and 5.3% cash. We can then use a more traditional representation of the asset-liability problem as shown in (4.54).

$$\min \sigma_s^2 = \begin{bmatrix} \mathbf{w}_a \\ -w_l \\ -w_s \end{bmatrix}^{\mathrm{T}} \begin{bmatrix} \mathbf{\Omega}_{aa} & \mathbf{\Omega}_{al} & 0 \\ \mathbf{\Omega}_{al}^{\mathrm{T}} & \sigma_l^2 & 0 \\ 0 & 0 & 0 \end{bmatrix} \begin{bmatrix} \mathbf{w}_a \\ -w_l \\ -w_s \end{bmatrix} \qquad (4.54)$$

subject to $\mathbf{w}_a^{\mathrm{T}}\mathbf{I} = w_l + w_s = 1$ and $\mathbf{w} \geq 0$. This also gives additional insight into the problem, as we can separate the asset-liability problem into the combination of a hedging portfolio (relative to liabilities) and an optimal growth portfolio (relative to cash).

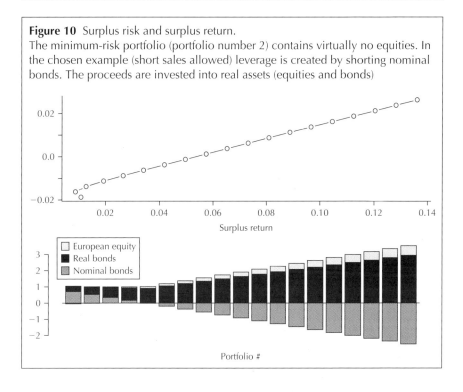

Figure 10 Surplus risk and surplus return.
The minimum-risk portfolio (portfolio number 2) contains virtually no equities. In the chosen example (short sales allowed) leverage is created by shorting nominal bonds. The proceeds are invested into real assets (equities and bonds)

Finally, we extend the above problem allowing a richer covariance structure between assets and liabilities. Suppose liability returns depend on a linear combination of several factor. We can think of these factors as, eg, changes in real yields (productivity growth) or inflation. The assumed dependences take the following form

$$\frac{\Delta l}{l} = \frac{\text{cov}\left(\frac{\Delta l}{l}, \frac{\Delta f_1}{f_1}\right)}{\text{var}\left(\frac{\Delta f_1}{f_1}\right)} \frac{\Delta f_1}{f_1} + \frac{\text{cov}\left(\frac{\Delta l}{l}, \frac{\Delta f_2}{f_2}\right)}{\text{var}\left(\frac{\Delta f_2}{f_2}\right)} \frac{\Delta f_2}{f_2}$$

$$+ \cdots + \frac{\text{cov}\left(\frac{\Delta l}{l}, \frac{\Delta f_n}{f_n}\right)}{\text{var}\left(\frac{\Delta f_n}{f_n}\right)} \frac{\Delta f_n}{f_n} \tag{4.55}$$

$$\frac{\Delta l}{l} = b_1 R_{f_1} + b_2 R_{f_2} + \cdots + b_n R_{f_n} = \sum_{j=1}^{n} b_j R_{f_j} \tag{4.56}$$

Table 3 Asset allocation *versus* asset-liability management
Asset allocation and asset-liability management differ in many ways.
The basic intuition of Markowitz-based portfolio theory does not
carry over to asset-liability management

	Asset allocation	**Asset liability management**
Foundation	Portfolio theory	Theory of the firm
Maximise	Utility	Shareholder value
Liability	Zero covariance	Non-zero covariance
Riskless asset	Cash	Long bonds
Risk-reducing assets	Low-asset correlation	High-liability correlation

where factor returns and factor betas are given by R_{f_j} and b_j. It is
now straightforward express the covariance between the i-th asset
and liabilities as

$$\text{cov}\left(R_i, \tfrac{\Delta l}{l}\right) = \text{cov}\left(R_i, \sum_{j=1}^{n} b_j R_{f_j}\right) = \sum_{j=1}^{n} b_j \, \text{cov}\left(R_i, R_{f_j}\right) \qquad (4.57)$$

From this it follows directly that

$$\mathbf{\Omega}_{al} = \sum_{i=1}^{n} b_j \mathbf{\Omega}_{al,j} \qquad (4.58)$$

where $\text{cov}\left(R_i, R_{f_j}\right)$ denotes the i-th element of $\mathbf{\Omega}_{al,j}$. Leveraging on
the linearity assumption, we can write the liability-hedging adjust-
ment as the sum of beta-weighted factor-hedging portfolios.

$$\mathbf{w}_{lha} = \left(\frac{1}{f}\right) \sum_{j=1}^{n} b_j \left[\mathbf{\Omega}_{aa}^{-1} \mathbf{\Omega}_{al,j} - \frac{\mathbf{I}^{\mathsf{T}} \mathbf{\Omega}_{aa}^{-1} \mathbf{\Omega}_{al,j}}{\mathbf{I}^{\mathsf{T}} \mathbf{\Omega}_{aa}^{-1} \mathbf{I}} \mathbf{\Omega}_{aa}^{-1} \mathbf{I} \right] \qquad (4.59)$$

In other words the liability-hedging adjustment consists of investment portfolios that each hedge out one particular factor risk. The difference between asset-liability solutions (surplus return *versus* surplus
risk) and strategic asset allocation can be summarised in Table 3.

Asset-allocation solutions come in many forms. They deal with
an individual investor's problem of how to allocate wealth among
competing assets in order to trade off risk against expected return,
while asset-liability management is rooted in corporate finance
theory. For a publicly traded firm it is virtually impossible to
summarise corporate finance issues (eg, present value of tax shield,

bankruptcy costs, convexity of tax schedule) in a single risk-aversion parameter. Unless the firm is not owned by a single share-holder who has tied up most of his wealth in the company, portfolio theory is not applicable. Asset-liability management needs to maximise shareholder value instead of utility. Asset-allocation problems therefore implicitly assume zero covariance with liabilities, while the co-movements between assets and liabilities are explicitly modelled in asset-liability problems. In most practical situations long bonds are the riskless (liability-matching) asset. It is also interesting to note that low correlation – ie to say diversification (which is traditionally thought of as risk-reducing) – is not necessarily good news. The more we diversify into alternative asset classes (such as private equity, international equity and hedge funds) the riskier it becomes. Indian private equity might well be diversifying, but it will largely increase liability-relative risks. Low correlation with the local discount factor (used to value liabilities) will increase the probability of assets and liabilities moving apart.

IMPLIED LIABILITY-RELATIVE RETURNS

Suppose we express the optimisation problem as unconstrained utility optimisation. For the sake of comparison we start with mean-variance optimisation with cashlike liabilities, ie, the standard Markowitz framework.

$$\max_{\mathbf{w}} u = \mathbf{w}^T \boldsymbol{\mu} - \frac{\lambda}{2} \mathbf{w}^T \boldsymbol{\Omega} \mathbf{w} \qquad (4.60)$$

Taking first-order derivatives of (4.60) with respect to portfolio weights yields

$$\frac{du}{d\mathbf{w}} = \boldsymbol{\mu} - \lambda \boldsymbol{\Omega} \mathbf{w} = 0 \qquad (4.61)$$

We can either solve (4.61) for optimal portfolio weights (optimal weights given a set of forecasts) or implied returns (returns that make a given set of portfolio weights optimal).

$$\mathbf{w}^* = \lambda^{-1} \boldsymbol{\Omega}^{-1} \boldsymbol{\mu} \qquad (4.62)$$

$$\boldsymbol{\mu}_{impl} = \lambda \boldsymbol{\Omega} \mathbf{w} \qquad (4.63)$$

Investors might it find more useful to think of implied returns in terms of marginal contributions to portfolio risk (β) and expected risk premium:

$$\mu_{impl} = \left(\frac{\mu}{\sigma} \right) \frac{\Omega w}{\sigma} = \beta \mu \qquad (4.64)$$

Note that $\lambda = \mu/\sigma^2$ and $\Omega w/\sigma^2 = \beta$. Marginal contributions to portfolio risk are given by

$$\frac{d\sigma}{dw} = \frac{d(w\Omega w)^{1/2}}{dw} = \frac{1}{2} 2\Omega w (w\Omega w)^{-1/2} = \frac{\Omega w}{\sigma} = MCTR \qquad (4.65)$$

where $(d\sigma/dw_i) = ((w_i\sigma_{ii} + \Sigma_{j \neq i} w_j \sigma_{ij})/\sigma)$. Assets that contribute heavily to portfolio risk command a large risk premium. By definition they must be the highest conviction positions. Other things being equal, these are assets that carry large volatilities and correlations or large positions. We can ask ourselves now: how does the above analysis change with the inclusion of liabilities? Again, we start with a mean-variance-based utility function, but this time we use a specification that includes liability risks

$$\max_{w} \; u = w^T \mu - \frac{\lambda}{2} \left(w^T \Omega_{aa} w - \frac{1}{f} 2w^T \Omega_{al} \right) \qquad (4.66)$$

Again, taking first-order derivatives yields

$$\frac{du}{dw} = \mu - \frac{\lambda}{2} \left(2\Omega_{aa} w - \frac{1}{f} 2\Omega_{al} \right) = 0 \qquad (4.67)$$

We can now solve for implied returns

$$\mu_{impl} = \lambda \left(\Omega_{aa} w - \frac{1}{f} \Omega_{al} \right) \qquad (4.68)$$

Equation (4.68) can also be expressed in terms of (4.63).

$$\binom{implied}{returns} = \binom{mean\ variance}{implied\ returns} - \frac{\lambda}{f} \binom{liability\ hedging}{credit} \qquad (4.69)$$

The usual solution for implied returns is extended by a liability hedging credit. This term $(\lambda/f)\Omega_{al}$ has three influence factors.

❑ assets that have high covariance ($\mathbf{\Omega}_{al}$) with liabilities need to return less than assets with less fortunate hedging properties.

❑ if risk λ aversions is high, liability hedging will become even more important, in that assets that have high covariances with liabilities require even less return.

❑ for pension plans with large surpluses (large f), liability hedging becomes less important and so the importance of the liability hedging credit is reduced.

Conventional thinking is reversed. Assets with large correlations (with liabilities, ie, bonds) require a small risk premium. This is different from (4.63), where large correlations demanded high-risk premiums. Remember that low correlations with liabilities increase the likelihood that assets and liabilities drift apart, ie, they increase surplus risk rather than reduce it.

We could of course extend the above analysis even further to include the factor decomposition (4.58) into (4.68)

$$\mathbf{\mu}_{impl} = \lambda \left(\mathbf{\Omega}_{aa}\mathbf{w} - \frac{1}{f}\sum_{j=1}^{n} b_j \mathbf{\Omega}_{al,j} \right) \tag{4.70}$$

Implied returns can now be traced to the common risk factors that drive the correlations between assets and liabilities. Note that implied return analysis (also cynically called *view optimisation*) serves more as an *ex post* consistency check of implied returns and explicit forecasts.

SURPLUS AT RISK

Surplus at risk (SaR_α) is routinely used in asset-allocation studies. It measures the worst-case, liability-relative loss the sponsoring firm expects to experience from its pension fund in most cases (eg, 95%) at a given time horizon (usually a year). Assuming surplus returns to be normally distributed, the surplus at risk is routinely calculated from $SaR_\alpha = \mu_s - z_\alpha \sigma_s$, where z_α measures the α-quantile from a standard normal distribution. For example $z_{0.05} = -1.6448$ tells us that 5% of all realisations of a standard normal distribution (mean zero and variance 1) fall below –1.6448. If α becomes smaller, losses becomes larger. Any increase in required confidence results in a smaller SaR (higher loss). A second determinant is the mean (μ_s) used for calculation. High expected returns will reduce surplus at risk. In order to make SaR more consistent with economic measures of risk, we prefer to set expected returns to zero, in which case we can transform statistical surplus-at-risk figures into economically relevant option prices.

Surplus at risk attracts a lot of attention, as it seems to allow the sponsoring company to calculate the required risk capital for a given pension fund mismatch. Risk capital is the amount of capital a firm needs to put aside (invest in the risk-free asset) in order to self-insure against bankruptcy in $1 - \alpha\%$ of all cases. If the $SaR = -15\%$ at the 5% quantile, a plan sponsor of a fully funded pension plan with 4,000 million (4 billion) needs to put aside 600 million in cash to make sure that it is fully insured against losses that occur on average not more often than in one out of twenty years. This is consistent with surplus at risk as a statistical risk measure. However, is this also consistent with economic theory? What do we need to tell a corporate treasury department that uses surplus at risk for their capital allocation purposes? First, surplus at risk is an arbitrary statistical risk measure (promoted by an American investment bank) with no guidance on the appropriate confidence level and little rooting in either utility or derivatives pricing theory. Utility rooting is important, since we would like to know what kinds of investors find this statistical risk measure a valid description of their preferences. Foundations in asset pricing (in general contingent claims) is important, since we would like to know whether a statistical risk measure also helps us to define risk capital in economic terms. What is the smallest amount a firm needs to put aside to insure a project against a loss relative to the risk-free alternative (see Merton and Perold 1993). We can translate this into pension fund investments. What is the smallest amount a firm needs to put aside in assets in order to guarantee that the pension plan remains fully funded? We already answered this question in Chapter 2. It equals the value of surplus insurance. All we need to do is to buy a derivative that makes up for any liability-relative losses, ie, that pays

$$c = E^Q \max\left[l - a - SaR_\alpha, 0\right] \tag{4.71}$$

In the above example I calculated that this kind of protection would cost 5.3%. This is quite a difference to our calculations of risk capital above. Also, note that we do not need the arbitrariness of estimated risk premiums or quantile definitions. Second, there are many who would argue that it is not even a proper risk measure (see Artzner *et al*, 1999). It encourages strategies that bet against rare events such as doubling up or write deep out the money puts, but most importantly it does not guarantee that the surplus at risk from a combination of two pension funds (one for a German, the other for an American subsidiary of a UK sponsor) is smaller than the combined surplus at risk from each pension fund in isolation.

At the root of the problem is that *SaR* is not sensitive at all to the likelihood of large losses exceeding surplus at risk. Hence, conditional surplus at risk (expected tail loss) is a better description of risk.

$$CSaR_\alpha = E\left(a - l \mid a - l <= SaR_\alpha\right) \qquad (4.72)$$

Surplus at risk, conditional surplus at risk and option pricing are closely related for short-time horizons, or more precisely for zero means.

$$c = E^Q \max\left(l - a - SaR_\alpha, 0\right) \approx prob\left(a - l \le SaR_\alpha\right) \cdot \left(SaR - CSaR\right) \quad (4.73)$$

I will run a little simulation example to support the arguments above. Suppose a plan invests into assets with 15% volatility, while liabilities vary with 10% volatility. Assets and liabilities are assumed to have 0.5 correlation. Suppose we assume zero expected growth on assets and liabilities. Alternatively, we assume that assets grow by 8%, while liabilities grow by 5%. Risk-free rates are either 0% or 2.5%. What is the required risk capital to cover potential deficits in the pension fund after one year, ie, how much money does the company need to set aside (and invest in cash) to cope with adverse equity market conditions? In order to allow you to easily compute (4.71) to (4.73) we will use Monte Carlo simulation to evaluate the surplus at risk in one year. Assuming that all risk-and-return assumptions have already been made on the assumption of lognormality, the methodology proceeds as follows.

1. simulate e_1 and e_2 from two independent standard normal distributions.
2. set $\varepsilon_1 = e_1$ and calculate $\varepsilon_2 = \rho e_1 + e_2 \sqrt{1 - \rho^2}$.
3. insert ε_1 and ε_2 into the solutions of the stochastic differential equation for asset and liabilities to arrive at year-end asset and liability values

Table 4 Risk measures for alternative asset and liability growth assumptions.

We assume $\alpha = 0.05$. Note that risk-neutral pricing results in a higher option valuation, after interest rates increased to 2.5%. This is counterintuitive, as the option value should fall when rates are rising. However, the strike fell at the same time due to the change in

Risk measure	$\mu_{slf} = r$	0	$\mu_{alf} = r$ 8%, 5%, 2.%
SaR_α		-20.72	-19.12
***		0.243	0.251
***		-25.62	-24.28
***		0.243	0.2579

$$l_1 = l_0 \exp\left(\left(\mu_l - \tfrac{1}{2}\sigma_l\right)1 + \sigma_l \varepsilon_1 \sqrt{1}\right) \qquad \textbf{(4.74)}$$

$$a_1 = a_0 \exp\left(\left(\mu_a - \tfrac{1}{2}\sigma_a\right)1 + \sigma_a \varepsilon_1 \sqrt{1}\right) \qquad \textbf{(4.75)}$$

4. Calculate SaR_α, $CSaR_\alpha$ and c.

We can now present the value of these risk figures for different mean assumptions in Table 4. For a start, we see that surplus at risk falls if return expectations increase.

While this is statistically correct, it makes little economic sense, as the price for insurance is independent from return assumptions (other than the risk-free rate). Only if all returns (including the risk-free rate) are close to zero (eg, for short-term VAR) will there be a direct relationship between statistical measures of risk and option pricing technology. In this case (4.73) yields the same results as risk-neutral pricing in (4.71). We can also see this in Table 4.

Surplus at risk is not consistent with risk-adjusted net-present-value calculations (as it focuses on total rather than systematic risks). It is not useful to rank different projects, nor is it consistent with option pricing technology. It is just one of many risk measures and maybe not even that.

ACTUARIAL MODELS
We will label any model that attempts to cheapen a given stream of liability cashflows as actuarial. Actuarial models (or alternatively money machines) allow this, because they ignore modern valuation

principles: risk premiums do not make assets superior and all guarantees need to be priced under the risk-neutral distribution.

The most naïve approach – which has long has been common in the UK – is called *deterministic funding*. A set of assets is said to fund a given liability cashflow if a deterministic projection of asset return is sufficient to pay off all future pension obligations. Suppose we expect global equities to return 10% per annum. Pension liabilities amount to a single lump-sum payment of €710.67 in 50 years' time. It would be sufficient to invest a mere €6.05 ($710.67/1.1^{50}$) in equities today to fully fund this pension liability. In fact this is equivalent to discounting a debt like payoff with an equity discount rate. If rates for 50-year zero bonds were 4% the pension fund would have needed €100 ($710.67/1.04^{50}$) instead. No wonder that UK pension plans following this type of advice have been seriously underfunded. In order to see how bizarre this approach really is we introduce leverage. Borrowing an additional 100% at a rate of 4% and investing it into equities adds an additional return of 6%, totalling 16%. Now we need only 0.42 to receive the projected 710.67. We could continue this until we virtually need nothing to fund a given liability cashflow.

Actuaries who realised this problem moved to *stochastic funding* or *coverage* models. A liability cashflow is called *funded* if a given asset-allocation policy can pay off all future cashflows with a very high degree of certainty (eg in 95% of all times). Apart from the arbitrariness of a percentile-based certainty measure (what percentile do we choose? why are we not concerned about larger losses?) we can recall from Chapter 2 that the only asset allocation that can always pay off all cashflows is the replicating portfolio. All cost savings relative to this portfolio must come from extra risks that are not priced correctly under a real-world probability measure. The stochastic funding approach to asset liability modelling is best described with a simple example. Suppose again we expect global equities to return 10% per annum, but now we introduce return variability in the order of 15% annual volatility. The yield on a 50-year government (zero) bond is 4%. Liabilities still amount to a single lump-sum payment of 710.67. Would an equity investment of 77.50 stochastically fund liabilities, ie, would the shortfall risk be small enough (5%)? As multi-period security returns are lognormally distributed, we have to transform our return assumptions into the appropriate normal counterparts (we assume for simplicity that 15% is the volatility of log returns).

$$\frac{0.775 \ln\left(1+10\%\right) 50 - \ln\left(1+4\%\right) 50}{15\%\sqrt{50}} = 1.63 \qquad \textbf{(4.76)}$$

The expected end-of-period wealth from a 50-year investment in €77.5 equities is within 1.64 standard deviations' distance from the liability obligation. Using tables for a standard normal, we conclude that this amounts to a probability of 5% of not covering pension cashflows. Again, leverage would reduce the probability of underfunding. While 100% borrowing doubles per-annum volatility to 30%, it increases return to 16%.

$$\frac{0.775 \ln\left(1+16\%\right) 50 - \ln\left(1+4\%\right) 50}{30\%\sqrt{50}} = 1.79 \qquad \textbf{(4.77)}$$

The probability of becoming underfunded in 50 years' time reduces to 3.6%. If instead we attempted to fund liabilities with zero coupon bonds this would cost shareholders 100 (710.67 discounted by 4% over 50 years). Actuarial analysis would conclude that it costs only 77.5 to fund liability cashflows. Leveraged equity funding is cheaper than bond funding. Again this works in the actuarial model as leverage increases the risk premium, while risk is not properly accounted for. Percentile-based risk measures have no relation to modern valuation theory. They are statistical measures of risk and provide no indication of how much risk capital is tied up in a given investment strategy. The economic risk capital can be found by using option pricing theory. We will briefly review how financial economics would deal with the above setting.

Investments in risky equities expose the investor to the risk of falling below the liability value of $l^* = 710.67$. This obligation is equivalent to a short put option on the deficit with strike l^*. The value of this option is 40.41. The sensitivity to changes in volatility (vega) is 245.08. At the same time the investor is long a call option on the surplus (with equal strike). It happens to be that the price of this call is also 40.41 with a volatility sensitivity of 245.08. Risks and rewards are equally distributed. In fact, we can show that this is part of a quite general result. We know that the value of synthetic long position in equities in 50 years' time equals a portfolio of long call and short put with identical strikes of l^*. From put call parity we know that the difference between owning a stock today and owning it tomorrow must equal the time value of money, ie, the present value of liabilities. Expressing this more formally yields

$$a - \left[c\left(a, \sigma, T, r_f, l^*\right) - p\left(a, \sigma, T, r_f, l^*\right) \right] = l = \frac{l^*}{\left(1 + r_f\right)^{50}} \qquad (4.78)$$

where a denotes the current value of assets, and c, p reflect call and puts on assets with strike l^*, which in turn stands for the nominal liability value in 50 years. It now becomes obvious that for a fully funded plan ($a = l$) we also find that:

$$c\left(a, \sigma, T, r_f, l^*\right) - p\left(a, \sigma, T, r_f, l^*\right) \qquad (4.79)$$

The reason for this is that an at-the-money forward put always equals an at-the-money forward call, as the strike is at the centre of the risk-neutral distribution. Volatility increases will increase equity and put value in equal amount. The funding approach does not value liabilities *per se*. It focuses purely on the asset side. This is in sharp contrast to asset-liability models above – in the sections "In search of the liability asset" through "Implied liability-relative returns" – which explicitly used market-based estimates for both liability valuation and liability-related risks.

The third approach to actuarial modelling explicitly incorporates the plan sponsor via future pension fund contributions that become necessary either in the form of future service costs or via additional funding due to pension fund deficits.[9] Peskin (1997) argues, "From the corporations perspective the future stream of contributions looks just like a stream of payments it must make on borrowed money." He concludes, "The sponsor's economic liability is the present value of distributions discounted at the sponsor's term structure of borrowing costs." This means that, "The economic liability is dependent on the assets, the liabilities, the sponsor's borrowing costs as well as the funding method and the investment policy." This contradicts all our thoughts so far. We said that the economic value of pension liabilities is independent from asset-allocation policy.

But where does this discrepancy to financial economics come from? Models that discount future contributions at either the risk-free rate or the sponsors' borrowing costs essentially create a

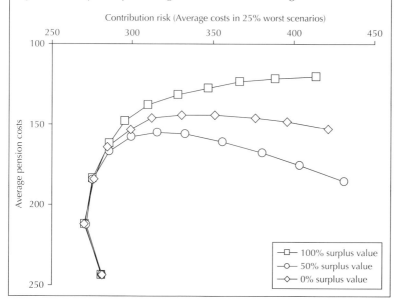

Figure 11 Pension costs and equity allocation in actuarial models. Pension costs are measured as the present value of future contributions discounted with the corporate sponsor's borrowing rate. Efficient allocations are combined with a solid line. Inefficient parts (where pension costs and pension risks are simultaneously rising) are plotted with a dotted line. Equity allocations change from the left to the right within equal steps starting from 10% and reaching 100%

money machine. Equity investment, or more precisely all investments that command a risk premium relative to the chosen discount rate, will reduce the present value of future contributions, since the discount rate does not properly reflect the riskiness of that investment. Riskier investments will lead to, on average, reduced contributions, but, while the uncertainty of pension contributions increases, this is not reflected in the discount factor. An investment of long €100 in equities and short €100 corporate bonds will lead to a positive net present value (NPV), even though we know the NPV must be zero.

We use a highly stylised framework in order to focus on the main assumptions. Suppose current liabilities are worth 100 and grow on average by $\mu_l = 5\%$ with volatility $\sigma_l = 5\%$. Every year there are additional service costs of 3. Corporate borrowing costs are flat across maturities and equal 5%. Equities grow by $\mu_e = 8\%$ (with volatility of $\sigma_e = 15\%$). Additional funding is required if assets underperform liabilities. Any surplus that exists after 30 years can be recovered by the sponsoring company to varying degrees ranging between 0% and 100%.

If the plan sponsor can recover 100% of the pension surplus in 30 years from now, pension costs as defined in the actuarial model (present value of future contributions) must fall. Contributions made in Year 1 are equivalent to additional investments that earn the spread between average growth and discount rate. The advantage of the risky investments fades away as the plan sponsor has limited access to a given pension surplus. Essentially this means that plan sponsors are still short a put option on the pension fund deficit, but the value of their usually offsetting call option is reduced as access to pension fund surplus is restricted.

The trouble in general with actuarial models of any kind is that the value of a given guarantee can only be calculated under the risk-neutral distribution. Actuarial analysis using real-world distribution is arbitrary (dependent on risk premium and risk calculation) and simply wrong. This approach conceals short-term losses using accounting (see next chapter) as well as actuarial tricks to prevent the shareholder from being nervous and hope that a risk premium will materialise to bail you out. However, patience is not a good form of risk management. It is just another form of happy-end investing.

THE CASE OF COMMODITIES: WHAT DEFINES AN ASSET CLASS?

Recent oil price volatility had an unsettling effect on global security markets. Hence investors are becoming more interested in the statistical and economic foundations of commodity investing. We want to investigate whether commodities extend the investment universe for US-based investors. Formally, we need to test whether adding commodities to the investment opportunity set (US equities and US bonds) significantly improves the utility of mean-variance investors. In practical investment management, an asset class is a group of assets that investors regard as homogeneous enough (having high internal correlation) as well as rare enough (having low external correlation) to consider separate strategic allocations worthwhile. For example, investors viewing non-domestic equities as an asset class will allocate parts of their strategic risk budgets towards non-domestic equities in the hope of catching a risk premium ie unique to this asset class and cannot be generated by other investments. The risk premium must arise from economic exposures that can neither be diversified nor generated from other asset classes. Let us introduce an informal statement that can be often heard about commodities to sharpen our intuition: "If an asset earns a risk premium (above cash), shows little correlation to other asset classes and cannot be replicated, it must be an asset class."

Unfortunately, this is wrong. To see why, we will engineer an asset that looks like an asset class from the perspective of the statement above, but actually isn't. Suppose we invest in equities and bonds to generate a risk premium above cash. Suppose, further, we add considerable noise to this asset by buying lottery tickets (uncorrelated to real asset classes with high volatility). The more noise we add on top of our equity/bond exposure, the more likely we will see a decrease in correlation with other asset classes. This noise cannot be replicated. We created an asset from existing assets and added some noise. This obviously does not create an asset class.

So what is the correct (statistical) interpretation of an asset class? Any suspected asset class (R_i) that actually earns a risk premium above cash (c), that cannot be explained by other already existing asset classes ($R_j - c$) is actually an asset class in its own right. Formally we run a regression between the excess returns of a candidate asset class and other established asset classes.[10]

$$(R_i - c) = \alpha + \sum_j \beta_j (R_j - c) + \varepsilon \qquad \textbf{(4.80)}$$

If the constant term in this regression (α) is significantly different from zero, we can consider it as an asset class. This is the basic idea between all tests for mean-variance spanning. We see that correlation plays only an indirect roll. What matters is whether part of the risk premium is not explained by other asset classes. Obviously, the higher the correlation, the more systematic exposures exist. But high correlation is not necessarily enough to justify a negative judgement. Neither is low correlation enough to prove uniqueness. After all, coin flipping is very diversifying. In fact we test whether

Table 5 Unconditional historic correlation and annualised volatility (main diagonal) for investment opportunity set.
All numbers are based on monthly excess returns from January 1989 to January 2005

	GSCI	DBLCI	DBICI-MR	US Bonds	US Equity
GSCI	0.19	0.93	0.85	0.03	−0.10
DBLCI	0.93	0.20	0.92	−0.04	−0.11
DBLCI-MR	0.85	0.92	0.18	−0.04	−0.08
US bonds	0.03	−0.04	0.04	0.05	0.01
US equity	−0.10	−0.11	−0.08	0.01	0.15

Table 6 Monthly risk premium, standard deviation and respective t-value (192 observations) for investment opportunity set.
All numbers are based on monthly excess returns from January 1989 to January 2005

	GSCI	DBLCI	DBICI-MR	US Bonds	US Equity
Risk premium	0.48%	0.75%	0.76%	0.23%	0.60%
Standard deviation	5.47%	5.79%	5.16%	1.32%	4.19%
t-value	1.20	1.79	2.04	2.43	1.97

a given asset class extends the mean-variance frontier (shifts it to the left) in a statistically significant way.

Let us apply the above to a US-based investor. Its current investment universe consists of US equity (proxied by MSCI USA) and US bonds (proxied by JPM US government bonds). We test three commodity indexes for mean-variance spanning: the Goldman Sachs Commodity Index (GSCI), the Deutsche Bank Liquid Commodity Index and the Deutsche Bank Liquid Commodity Index – Mean Reversion (DBLCI – MR). The data range from January 1989 to January 2005. We calculate monthly excess returns (over one month Libor) in dollars. Summary characteristics are given in Tables 5 and 6.

While the three commodity indexes are fairly similar in terms of volatility and correlation, the DBLCI-MR shows the lowest volatility as well as correlation with equities and bonds. At the same time it exhibits the highest monthly risk premium (0.0076%) with the highest t-value ($2.04 = (0.0076/0.0516)\sqrt{192}$). However, this does not necessarily qualify commodity investments as an asset class.

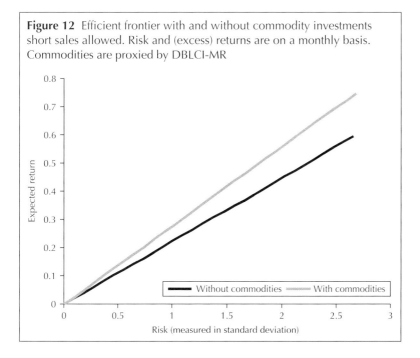

Figure 12 Efficient frontier with and without commodity investments short sales allowed. Risk and (excess) returns are on a monthly basis. Commodities are proxied by DBLCI-MR

Next we plot two efficient frontiers (assets are required to add up to one, but net shorts are allowed) with and without commodity investments in Figure 12.

Both frontiers are straight lines through the origin, as an investment in 100% cash carries neither risk nor risk premium. Portfolios differ only in leverage (positive or negative cash position), but the composition of risky assets remains the same. This explains the straight line. Note that, even though including commodities shifts the efficient frontier to the left, this does not allow us to make a judgement about significance. In fact, sampling error in estimates will assure that every *ex post* observed efficient frontier will always lie to the left of the actual *ex ante* efficient frontier. Even if a new asset class is spanned in large samples, it will always extend the opportunity set in small samples.

To formally test whether commodities extend the investment opportunity set, we need to remove that part of the risk premium ie, already explained by existing asset classes (here equities and bonds) and test whatever is left (α) for significance. Using the

167

Table 7 Mean variance spanning
Estimated parameters from linear regression of commodity excess
returns *versus* equity and bond market excess returns

	GSCI	DBLCI	DBLCI-MR
α	0.0052	0.0088	0.0084
	(0.19)	(0.039)	(0.027)
$\beta_{US\ Bonds}$	0.11	−0.14	−0.16
	(0.70)	(0.64)	(0.55)
$\beta_{US\ Equity}$	−1.13	−0.15	−0.10
	(0.16)	(0.13)	(0.25)

regression approach described above, we arrive at Table 7. It shows the regression coefficients together with their respective p-values. These values calculate the likelihood that a given statistic has been produced by chance, ie, is purely accidental. A p-value of 5% indicates significance at the 5% level, ie, only in 5% of all random samples would we see a value of the test statistic ie, that high.

While we cannot reject the null hypothesis (at the 5% level) that commodities are not a unique asset class for the GSCI, we can do so for DBLCI as well as DBLCI-MR. Investing in DBLCI or DBLCI-MR would have significantly extended the investment universe over this time period. The main reason for this is that the risk premium for the GSCI index has not been significant for the respective time period in the first place. Exposures to significantly rewarded risk premiums are statistically insignificant, confirming the intuition, that commodities live a life of their own.[11] The regression-based approach above is the most widely used procedure in testing for mean-variance spanning. However, it has several shortcomings. First, the implicit assumption in the regression-based approach was that regression betas have been allowed to be positive as well as negative. Note that regression betas effectively are the weights of a tracking error minimising, (replicating) portfolio. In the case of investors facing long-only constraints (or other real-world constraints) we need to check whether diversification benefits rely upon the ability to short asset classes or form leveraged portfolios. Second, we did not include transaction costs. Even if adding a new asset class extends the mean variance frontier to the left (after realistic constraints have been taken into account), that does not necessarily mean it still does so after transaction costs are taken into account. Third, we tested only for statistical significance. This is well known to be different from economic significance. Statistical tests ask the question: how likely is it to see the mean-variance frontier shifting to the left (positive regression intercept) given that excess returns and covariances are measured with sampling error? Economic significance asks the question: by how much did the inclusion of a new asset class increase investors' welfare? We hence need a test procedure that also provides figures for economic significance.

We start with the observation that the inclusion of commodities will increase investors' utility in small samples, no matter whether commodities are spanned (risk premium is explained by existing asset classes) or not. This is true, because an asset allocation with $n + 1$ assets must always lead to a higher utility level than an optimisation with just n assets, as long as one asset is not spanned. In small samples there will always be some differences (sampling error) that ensures the above. We measure the difference in utility as

$$\Delta u = \max(\mathbf{w}^T\boldsymbol{\mu} - \lambda\mathbf{w}^T) - \max(\mathbf{w}_{-c}^T\boldsymbol{\mu}_{-c} - \lambda\mathbf{w}_{-c}^T\boldsymbol{\Omega}_{-c}\mathbf{w}_{-c}^T) > 0 \qquad (4.81)$$

where w and w_{-c} denote the investment weight vectors with and without commodities, $\boldsymbol{\mu}$ and $\boldsymbol{\mu}_{-c}$ describe the risk premiums with and without commodities while $\boldsymbol{\Omega}$ and $\boldsymbol{\Omega}_{-c}$ contain the respective covariances. Assuming $\lambda = 0.15$, the utility difference amounts to

$$\Delta u = 0.1972 - 0.144 = 0.079 \qquad (4.82)$$

Note that this is equivalent to a return difference of eight basis points per month (about 1% per annum). The above difference in utility allows consistent comparisons across investment universes. Measuring the vertical distance between efficient frontiers would not. Different frontier slopes imply different risk aversions. Note that Δu can be calculated for arbitrary constraints, unlike regression-based tests. Next we need to take care of in-sample variation. The process is as follows.

Simulate the return-generating process under the null hypothesis of spanning, ie, the return for commodities is given by $\Sigma_j\hat{\beta}_j(\bar{R}_j - c)$. Therefore, estimated exposure betas are multiplied by the average risk premium. In other words, only the explained part of the risk premium is taken into account.

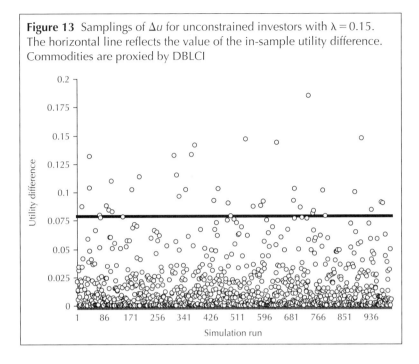

Figure 13 Samplings of Δu for unconstrained investors with $\lambda = 0.15$. The horizontal line reflects the value of the in-sample utility difference. Commodities are proxied by DBLCI

For each simulation we calculate a new value for Δu_i. Repeating this procedure for $i = 1, \ldots, n$ we arrive at the (otherwise) unknown distribution for Δu und the null hypothesis. All we need to do is to compare the in-sample difference (using the historical data) with this distribution and calculate the number of times where the sampling of Δu yielded larger values than our in-sample value. This provides us with the level of significance.

An example of this procedure can be found in Figure 13. Each point reflects one simulated realisation of Δu_i. Note that all samplings are positive, ie, the utility difference between an optimisation with six instead of five assets will always be positive (infinite sample). The horizontal line reflects Δu.

If we count the number of realisations above the horizontal lines (39 cases) and divide this by the total number of runs (1,000) we arrive at a value of 3.9%. Effectively, the value of our test statistic becomes

$$\frac{\#(\Delta u_i \geq \Delta u)}{\#(\Delta u_i)} = \frac{39}{1000} = 0.039 \tag{4.83}$$

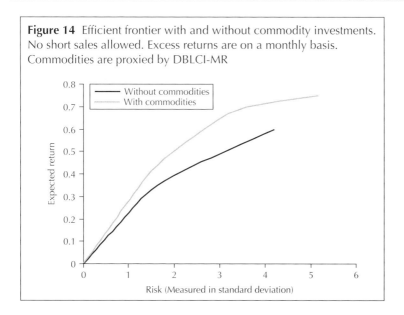

Figure 14 Efficient frontier with and without commodity investments. No short sales allowed. Excess returns are on a monthly basis. Commodities are proxied by DBLCI-MR

This is virtually the same as the p-value for α in Table 7. Our Monte Carlo methodology recovers the regression-based results (as it should). Note that this is irrespective of the assumed risk-aversion coefficient. After all, portfolios along the frontier differ only in leverage. Commodities are an asset class under the above setting as long as DBLCI or DBLCI-MR is used. The GSCI index is too volatile relative to the average historic risk premium to reach statistical significance. This might well be a sample specific phenomenon.

We can now turn to the more interesting question of how real-world constraints affect the above calculations. Do commodities lose their relative attractiveness after short sales constraints have been introduced? Let us start again by plotting both efficient frontiers (with and without short sale constraints).

While both frontiers still start at the origin (100% cash investment remains the least risky portfolio), both frontiers are kinked. Each kink reflects a particular corner solution, ie, one asset hits the non-negativity constraint and leaves the optimal solutions. With three assets (equities, bonds and commodities), there are only two kinks, while there is only one kink in the case of two assets (universe reduced to equities and bonds).

Table 8 Measures of statistical significance (p-values) for three alternative commodity indexes.
Each risk aversion pinpoints a different segment along the efficient frontier

	$\lambda = 0.01$	$\lambda = 0.15$	$\lambda = 0.3$
GSCI	0.005	0.027	0.01
	(0.898)	(0.214)	(0.197)
DBLCI	0.120	0.068	0.039
	(0.507)	(0.052)	(0.047)
DBLCI-MR	0.125	0.076	0.045
	(0.51)	(0.044)	(0.030)

Why is this important? Two-fund separation (each portfolio can be derived from two frontier portfolios) no longer works with long-only constraints. Do we therefore need to check for mean-variance spanning for each single risk-aversion, ie, for every point across the mean-variance frontier? No, because a slight variation of two-fund separation still works. Any portfolio between two neighbouring corner solutions (segment between two kinks) is a linear combination of two portfolios along that segment. It is hence enough to test for mean-variance spanning at a single point within each frontier segment. Note that we can measure risk aversion by $\lambda = (\mu / \sigma^2)$. We can use this to pinpoint individual portfolios within each frontier segment.[12] The results are provided in Table 4. The distribution of our test statistic is sampled via Monte Carlo simulation as described in the previous section.

Two main observations become apparent. First, there is no evidence that commodities improve investment opportunities for very aggressive ($\lambda = 0.01$) investors in the case of long-only constraints. This is entirely intuitive, as the maximum return portfolios are concentrated in one single asset. Given the low correlation between assets (and their low volatilities), it is not surprising that testing for differences in means remains insignificant. Second, commodities still significantly improve US investors' welfare for high and intermediate risk-aversions (depending on the index chosen). The economic-significance range lies between four and eight basis points per month (48 to 96 basis points per annum).[13]

Table 9 Spanning regression for DBLCI-MR.
Time period: August 2000 to January 2005

	Regression including TIPS	Regression without TIPS
α	0.0036	0.0087
	(0.49)	(0.12)
$\beta_{US\ Bonds}$	-1.59	0.31
	(0.02)	(0.87)
$\beta_{US\ Equities}$	-0.51	0.04
	(0.06)	(0.37)
$\beta_{US\ TIPS}$	1.83	–
	(0.001)	

The use of commodities is sometimes motivated by its supposed inflation-hedging properties. Commodities, particularly energy, are an important input factor. An increase in commodity prices is therefore likely to feed through to broader CPI (consumer price index) measures. However, if the correlation between inflation-linked bonds (Treasury inflation-protected securities, also called TIPS) and commodity indexes is substantial – or, more precisely, if part of the risk premium earned by commodities is already explained by inflation-linked bonds – the case for commodities is severely weakened.[14] We can investigate this by running a linear regression of commodity returns against index returns from the chosen universe. For inflation-linked bonds we use monthly returns for US TIPS by Merrill Lynch (Merrill Lynch US Treasury Inflation Linked, available since August 2000). Results are given in Table 9, where numbers in brackets are the respective p-values for the coefficients above.

While none of the regressions produced a statistically significant alpha (not even on the 10% level), we see that a considerable part of the risk premium has been explained by the performance of TIPS. The p-value for the regression intercept (α) drops from 0.12 to 0.49. Including TIPS makes commodities redundant. While there is always a chicken-an-egg problem in mean-variance spanning tests (which asset class came first?), it is more natural to think of TIPS as an asset class, as they allow one to isolate inflation risk and therefore have a unique economic exposure. Interestingly, we see a dramatic shift in sign and size of bond beta (and its significance) when TIPS are included. This indicates that commodity returns are correlated with inflation (difference between nominal and real bonds).

I introduced a general Monte Carlo-based methodology to test for mean variance spanning under arbitrary constraints. It is easy to use for everybody who has a mean-variance optimiser at hand. Apart from calculating statistical significance it also allows to measure economic significance (utility difference). For US-based investors commodities significantly expand the investment universe. This result also holds after we have introduced long-only constraints. Only for very aggressive investors is there no significant improvement in investors' welfare. However, as soon as we incorporate inflation-linked bonds into our analysis, there is no longer any evidence that commodities establish a unique asset class. This is not surprising, since inflation-linked bonds and commodities are both used as inflation hedges.

1 Unknown participant at a UK pension conference in London, February 2005.
2 Brendan Naton, 2005, in IPE, p 7, February.
3 The value-at-risk (VAR) calculation is centred on a return of 0%. This is consistent with most risk management practices and avoids "return-dependent" risk management.
4 Bookstaber and Gold (1988) introduce the term *liability asset*.
5 We could take higher derivations but this would require us also to calculate more scenarios, which would increase the actuarial effort (cost).
6 The concept has been introduced by Leibowitz (1986) and discussed further by Leibowitz *et al* (1989).
7 This section follows Keel and Mueller (1995).
8 On dual benchmark optimisation, see Scherer (2004).
9 Supporters of this view are Peskin (1997); Deert (1995).
10 Most formal tests on mean variance spanning use total returns (not risk premiums). These tests also need the sum of exposures (betas) to existing assets to add up to one. However, as we use excess returns over cash, betas (effectively weights of a replicating portfolio) do not need to add to one. The missing allocation can always be filled up with cash (negative cash in the case of leverage) to create portfolios that add up (to one). For a review on mean-variance spanning tests, see Nijman (2001).
11 More sophisticated statistical procedures that account for missing data and would therefore allow us to account for the covariance structure between commodities and time series that have a longer history implicitly assume mean-variance spanning, which makes them of little appeal.
12 More formally, we identify corner solutions first. Then we calculate the implied risk-aversion for an arbitrary portfolio between two neighbouring corner solutions. This gives us the risk-aversions to work with.
13 Note that the utility difference can be directly translated into a return difference using the security equivalent.
14 Given the high volatility of commodity investments the inflation-hedging argument is already weak, as this kind of "hedge" would expose investors at the same time to considerable (non-inflation-related) noise. It is further weakened by the existence of an asset that can pinpoint inflation risks.

REFERENCES

Artzner, P., *et al*, 1999, "Coherent Measures of Risk", *Math Fin.* **9(3)**, pp 203–28.

Bookstaber, R. and J. Gold, 1988, "In Search of the Liability Asset", *Financial Analysts Journal*, **44(1)**, pp 70–80.

Deert, C., 1995, "Asset-Liability Management for Pension Funds", PhD dissertation, University of Rotterdam.

Keel, A. and H. Müller, 1995, "Efficient Portfolios in the Asset Liability Context", *ASTIN Bulletin*, **25**, pp 33–48.

Leibowitz, M., 1986, "Total Portfolio Duration: A New Perspective on Asset Allocation", *Financial Analysts Journal*, September–October.

Leibowitz, M. L., *et al*, 1989, "A Total Differential Approach to Equity Duration", *Financial Analysts Journal*, September/October, p 30–7.

Merton R. and A. Perold, 1993, "Theory of Risk Capital in Financial Firms", *Journal of Applied Corporate Finance*, **6**, pp 16–32.

Nijman, R., 2001, "Testing for Mean Variance Spanning, a Survey", CEPR, Tilburg University.

Peskin, M., 1997, "Asset Allocation and Funding Policy for Corporate-Sponsored Defined Benefit Pension Plans", *Journal of Portfolio Management*, **23(2)**, pp 66–73.

Scherer B., 2003, *ALM Tools* (London: Riskwaters).

Scherer, B. and T. Jasper, 2003, "Approximating Corporate Liabilities", in Scherer (2003), pp 91–103.

Sharpe, W. F. and L. G. Tint, 1990, "Liabilities – A New Approach", *Journal of Portfolio Management*, **17**, Winter, pp 5–10.

Ziemba, W. T. and J. M. Mulvey, eds, 1998, "World Wide Asset and Liability Modeling" (Cambridge University Press).

5

Theory of the Firm versus *Portfolio Theory*

This chapter will argue that the optimal asset allocation for externally financed pension obligations cannot be answered by looking at the pension fund in isolation.[1] Note that the previous chapter included liabilities within the optimisation problem, but the plan sponsor was at best indirectly addressed. Very much within the tradition of portfolio theory, plan sponsors interests have been captured by a single risk-aversion parameter.

This rests on the simplifying analogy that firms trade off some kind of surplus measure against surplus risk. Depending on corporate risk-aversion, all pension fund asset allocation decisions could be rationalised within these models. An example of this asset-management-centric thinking is Wharing (2004, p 48):

> . . . but the beauty of the surplus optimisation approach is not that it provides a particular answer, but that it enables the plan sponsor consciously to set the surplus beta position for the plan, controlling pension plan financial risk in the process. Risk tolerance is ultimately an individual decision.

While clients might like this statement it is anything but not an individual decision. The impact of asset-allocation decisions on debt capacity, taxation and liquidity costs are simply neglected. Strangely enough, corporate leaders routinely underline the importance to invest in a company's core competencies, while at the same time their pension funds seem to hold diversified global investment portfolios. However, capital market investments (with net present value – or NPV – of zero) are the logical opposite to investing in the core business. Defining the optimal asset allocation for a corporate pension plan, corporate sponsors should not consult the asset management literature or study portfolio theory. The relevant solutions are instead provided by corporate finance theory. Portfolio theory, as we reviewed it in the previous chapter, is applicable to final (end) investors, but not to corporations. The main reason is that firms are investment vehicles through which end investors get exposure to firm specific risks. Asset allocation (decisions on systematic risks) by pension funds can be undone on the investor's level. Any attempt to model pension fund decisions with the help of a corporate risk-aversion parameter is hopelessly flawed.

We will argue that firms should in almost all cases opt for a liability immunisation solution. Efficient frontier analysis reduce to a single point the liability hedging portfolio. It is in the interest of shareholders to avoid liability-relative risks within a pension fund. What about alpha generation? This surely must be a good idea, particularly for underfunded plans. The author agrees that it would be nice to have a money machine. If in deficit, just ask someone with a money-printing machine if they would help you out and print an amount equalling the deficit. Everybody wants this machine, but only children's authors know where to find them.

Pension obligations are nothing more than a form of corporate debt. We therefore need to view all pension-related questions as a corporate finance problem in the first place. There is conceptually little difference between issuing a 100-year corporate bond to the capital market or to employees. In the first case the company receives the proceeds from a bond issue, while in the second case the proceeds come from the present value of lower future wage demands (future pension payments are traded off against current wages). The subtle difference between straight debt and pension obligations is not whether pension claims are inflation-sensitive or carry actuarial risks. It is credit risk. While credit risk is diversifiable to the market as a whole, it is not to employees. In the case of a plan sponsor's default, employees lose their jobs as well as their pensions. The correlation of both events makes pension debt less valuable to employees than to the capital market.

If only pension obligations could be treated like corporate debt, no extra theory of pension finance would be needed. In fact, companies would most probably decide not to issue this form of corporate debt, for the reason explained above. Instead, employees would take the extra cash to buy retirement products from insurance firms (where default risk is uncorrelated with the risk of losing their jobs). However, for some reason, governments continue to think that the pension promise to employees deserves stronger protection than promises made to other creditors of the firm. They require outside funding and/or pension insurance systems. We will include these features in traditional corporate finance arguments as they can found in Grinblatt and Titman (2002) and Brealey and Meyers (2003).

CORPORATE OBJECTIVE: SHARE HOLDER OR STAKEHOLDER VALUE?

The following sections will argue from a corporate finance perspective. In order to understand why shareholder value maximisation is the only feasible objective within corporate finance, we start with a brief statement that describes the mission statement for wealth-creating managers.

> The objective of our company is to increase the intrinsic value of our common stock. We are not in business to grow bigger for the sake of size, nor to become more diversified, nor to make the best of anything, nor to provide jobs, have the most modern plants, the happiest customers, lead in new product development or to achieve any other status which has no relation to the economic use of capital. Any or all of these may be, from time to time, a means to our objective, but means and ends must never be confused. We are in business solely to improve the inherent value of the common shareholders' equity in the company.[2]

Why is this statement true? Shareholders provide a buffer (equity cushion) that protects bondholders, employees and customers from business failures. They take the first loss and receive only residual cashflows. However, in their attempt to maximise their own wealth, they will make sure employees are paid competitively, customers are satisfied with products, interest rates and taxes are paid on time and vendors are treated fairly, so nothing disrupts the production process. Shareholders take risks with their equity investments, but they can diversify company-specific risks. What is left is systematic, economy-wide risk ie, inherent in any economy. The equity market is an efficient platform to trade these risks and spread them across many individuals. The existence of equity markets (with limited liability) allows the separation of ownership and control. Individuals can participate in the airline business without knowing its economics, while airline managers can de-correlate their career (human capital) and investment (financial capital) risk.

This form of risk sharing is an important prerequisite for economic growth (see Bernstein 1998). We could also try to achieve risk sharing with complicated contracts that try to lay down rules on how risk is shared among stakeholders in different states of the world (see Hart 1995). Since it is not feasible to write these ideal contracts, equity ownership developed as a substitute. The question that arises now is: how good is shareholder value maximisation in solving the conflicts of interest with other stakeholders? Firms are a complicated net of contracts between labour, suppliers and customers. All these contracting parties have made investments specific to the firm. Business failure destroys the value of these investments. This unites the interests of stakeholders. We will review the arguments for employees and customers.

Let us start with customers. As long as the return on investments to increase customer satisfaction (increase in quality, service, reliability and so forth) more than outweighs their economic costs, there is no conflict between maximising shareholder value and customer satisfaction. However, if shareholders subsidise customers benefits, this will generally lead to a long-term loss in competitiveness. This is in the interests of neither employees nor creditors.

And so to employees. While in a business upturn there is little talk about conflicts, downsizing seems to be a clear-cut example of equity stakeholders muscling employees. However, the truth is that bondholders would not like a company to cling onto staff who are paid more than their marginal product, and nor would productive employees. When Deutsche Bank announced their job cuts, it was not bondholders or productive employees who marched on the streets.

This does not mean there are no conflicts of interest between stakeholders. In fact, principal agency theory tells us there are many potential conflicts between current shareholders, current bondholders, prospective shareholders, etc. A prominent example that will gain relevance in later sections is asset substitution, arguably the most prominent conflict between *shareholder* and *bondholder* (see Jensen and Meckling 1976). By this we mean the substitution of low-risk by high-risk investments. In the extreme case these are projects with negative NPV in order to leverage on the limited liability of equity. If projects go well the equity holder wins; if they go badly the bondholders lose. Taking excess risks after bonds have been issued maximises the option value inherent in an equity stake. Bondholders will react to the shareholders' opportunity by charging a default premium. Because the shareholder cannot credibly commit not to engage in asset substitution, companies bear higher debt costs and consequentially will be unable to undertake projects that otherwise would have had a positive NPV (underinvestment).

Another conflict arises between *current* and *prospective* shareholders. Suppose it is unknown to investors (prospective shareholders), but not to firms (asymmetric information), whether a good firm (firms that needs to finance positive-NPV projects) or a bad firm (firm whose equity is overvalued and hence raising capital-transfers wealth from new investors to existing shareholders) wants to issue new stocks. Because of the informational asymmetry, the investor will suspect that raising new equity will be attractive to overvalued firms. Consequentially they require compensation for this risk and increase their return requirements. As the costs of equities rises, projects that have been profitable before are now deteriorating in value. This in turn leads to underinvestment as positive-NPV projects are not undertaken, which in turn hurts all stakeholders. Also *shareholders* and *management* have different objectives that are difficult to control in the absence of complete information. Managers prefer to work little and build their own empire (see Jensen 1986). This in turn leads to overinvestment.

However, while the above conflicts exist, it is the shareholders who bear the negative consequence arising from above investment inefficiencies. Among all stakeholders it is usually the shareholder who tries to resolve these conflicts for their own good. Maximising shareholder value is therefore the only way to align the interests of all stakeholders.[3]

MODIGLIANI-MILLER AND PENSIONS

This section introduces an additional stakeholder in corporate assets. Instead of focusing on straight debt, we now consider pension liabilities as an alternative form of debt that has been issued to employees, rather than to the capital market. We assume that these

Table 1 Pension fund

A hypothetical company consists of operating assets (*oa*) and financial assets (a) on the active side of its balance sheet as well as pension liabilities (*l*), bonds (b) and equity (e) on the passive side. External funding means that pension assets in the form of financial assets, ie, capital market investments and bondlike pension liabilities (*l*), are moved into a pension fund

Company I				Company E			
asset		**liabilities**		**asset**		**liabilities**	
oa	60	e	20	*oa*	60	e	20
a	40	b	40			b	40
		l	40				
				Pension	Asset	Pension	Liabilities
				a	40	*l*	40

pension liabilities are held off balance sheet in a so-called pension fund. Assets and liabilities are segregated from the sponsoring company. However, should assets not be sufficient to cover liability payments, the sponsoring company is still obliged to pay the difference. We compare two companies. Company I (internal funding) holds operating assets of 60 and financial assets (equities or bonds) of 40 on balance sheet (see Table 1). Debt claims are 40 for bonds and 40 for pension liabilities. Company E (external funding) resembles exactly the same asset structure. The difference is the that pension liabilities and financial assets are held off balance sheet in a so-called pension fund.

Suppose we start with an idealised Modigliani–Miller (MM) world without transaction costs, liquidity costs, taxes or costs of financial distress.[4] Also, assume that labour markets are perfectly competitive – ie, employees are employed at their marginal productivity. Any change in the value of their pension claim is immediately offset by opposite changes in wage claims. For example, leveraging up the pension fund with geared equity investments will lead to an instantaneous rise in wage claims to equalise the value of compensation (wages plus pension claims) with marginal productivity. Employees will need higher wages to compensate for the increase in credit risk arising from a leveraged pension fund.

Under the above assumptions, shareholders cannot gain from risk shifting in the pension fund. In this setting shareholders have equivalent ways to create exposure to equities. They can hold them directly in their private account. Alternatively they can get indirect exposure if the company they hold shares in invests in equities either on balance sheet (asset funding) or off balance sheet (external funding). The exposure created will be the same for all three options. To see this we can think through one example. A company that removes its equity exposure (source of undiversifiable market risk) will become less risky to investors. Investors can make up for this loss of systematic risk within their private accounts. Asset allocation becomes largely irrelevant. Investors can reallocate their personal portfolios in a way consistent with their risk–return preferences. Whatever is done on the company level will be undone on the investor level in order to restore the utility optimising individual asset mix.

For a corporate plan sponsor to find an optimal portfolio based on risk–return preferences is a hopeless exercise that creates no additional wealth on the shareholder level. In fact, aggressively holding equities in a corporate pension fund comes close to saying that shareholders hold too little in equities for their own good. Or, as John Exley (1997) phrased it, "In this context it seems rather presumptuous to assume that for some reason shareholders of saucepan manufacturers chronically fail to hold enough equities in their portfolio." Arguing that pension plans play a vital role in providing equity capital to an economy extends this rather paternalistic argument to the whole economy.

The irrelevance principle applies to the asset-allocation choice for existing pension funds. But what about funding? Is the decision for internal or external funding irrelevant in an MM world? Before we answer this question we will ask a simpler textbook question. Is debt finance in an MM world irrelevant? The answer is well known to depend on the seniority of additional fixed-income liabilities. If the new bond issue is of equal seniority, there is no net gain to shareholders. However, if the newly issued bonds are more senior than existing bonds, wealth is transferred from old bondholders to shareholders. While the new bondholders get a fair deal, the old bondholders cannot react to the deterioration of their seniority position. Their rating decreases as their claims are pushed down the capital structure.

A similar argument can now also be applied to a move from asset funding (pension assets and liabilities are both held on balance sheet) to external funding (pension assets and liabilities are both held off balance sheet). Employees (who are effectively creditors of the company) get a better deal as credit risk is largely reduced. They not only now have a pension promise but also a collateral from the sponsoring company that they would have shared with other creditors before. However, assuming a perfectly competitive labour market, employees are willing (or forced by competition) to downsize their wage claims. While the total effect on employees is zero, shareholders gain from reduced wage claims, while existing bondholders suffer from their effective drop in seniority. To the degree that outside funding implicitly shifts the seniority structure of existing debt, it will have an impact on shareholders' wealth.

So far we have implicitly come to the conclusion that changing a pension fund's asset allocations does not add shareholder value. Asset liability management (ALM) studies that explicitly try to find an optimal asset allocation are therefore largely irrelevant. While the costs associated with ALM studies directly reduce shareholders' wealth, shareholders do not benefit. In summary, in a Modigliani–Miller world is of no (shareholder) value in asset liability studies. This is bad new for asset managers. After all, convincing pension funds that they should reallocate their assets into the asset managers' own (high-margin) products is a profitable business. We will see in later sections that the irrelevance of pension fund asset allocation (all solutions are possible) changes into corner solutions, with liability matching as the most likely outcome.

Note that this applies to partial models (looking at the pension fund in isolation) as well as to models of the total firm (entity models). In partial models, ALM folk suggest moving into riskier asset classes to outperform the actuarial fixed-return promise. But a riskier allocation that outperforms liabilities by 1% per annum (on average) will not create a single penny in corporate value as the higher return comes from higher risk. After all it is a capital market investment, which by its very definition has a NPV of zero. To put it differently, 100 euro bonds have the same value as 100 euro equities. We will elaborate on this point later.

A related logic applies to *entity models*. We can surely find an allocation that reduces total company risk (volatility of free cashflow,

cashflow at risk or any other corporate risk metrics) by diversifying away from its core business. But what does this mean to the shareholder? Let us take an airline companyie, looking for an optimal asset allocation for its pension fund. The director working for the CFO argues that, in deriving an optimal allocation for the pension fund, the asset manager presenting his ALM proposal should have focused on asset classes that are uncorrelated to the cyclical return of its core business. Cashflow volatility could have been reduced by diversification. Not only is it next to trivial that an airline company is undiversified and carries too much airline risk. After all, it is meant to do so. It is not a global equity fund. However, from the shareholders' point of view, airline risk is diversifiable risk (at least from the point of view of a well-diversified shareholder). Replacing this risk with undiversifiable market risk ie, largely uncorrelated with the airline business but quite correlated with the remaining wealth of diversified shareholders does not seem like a good idea.

Despite the MM irrelevancy principle, the typical actuarial argument has been in the past that equities will almost surely outperform bonds in the long term, so that high-equity allocations make pension promises (priced from bonds) cheaper to finance. More generally, investors still perform some kind of surplus optimisation trading off average pension fund contributions against contribution risk (risk of unexpectedly large contributions). While it is certainly true that average contribution falls with an increase in equity allocation, contribution risk increases. But this does not make it a trade-off in the eyes of shareholders. However, companies are not quasi-individuals. Corporate firms do not buy Big Macs. The Modigliani–Miller arguments made it clear that managing a company in the interests of its shareholders does not include utility optimisation on their behalf.

PENSION FUND ALLOCATION AND NET PRESENT VALUE

In this section three points should be made that are strongly related to the optimal allocation of pension fund investments.

(1) The existence of a risk premium for equities does not generate positive NPVs for shareholders.
(2) All capital market investments carry a zero NPV.

Table 2 Payoff table
We observe three assets in three countries. For each of the assets there is a particular payoff in different countries. Stocks are priced at 50, but they can trade as low as 10 in case the economy is in recession and as high as 90 if the economy booms

	Stock	Corporate bond	Government bond
Recession	10	60	106
Unchanged	60	110	103
Boom	90	112	100
Price	50	98	100

(3) Positive NPV projects are much more likely to be found in a company's core business.

Asset-liability studies usually conclude that, by some clever rearrangement of existing asset classes or introduction of new asset classes, plan sponsors would gain another 50 basis points per annum in risk premium. This is then interpreted as an increase in shareholder wealth. Even though I am confident that asset managers and consultants will continue to tell this tale for years to come, it is nevertheless plain wrong. To show this we start with a simple economy given in Table 2. It differentiates between three asset classes: equities, corporate bonds and government bonds. Stocks trade at 50, corporate bonds at 98 and government bonds at 100. The payoffs are highly stylised but they catch the fundamental properties of these asset classes. Corporate bonds do badly in recession, while government bonds are recession hedges. Consequentially, corporate bonds have their lowest cashflows in the recession state, where government bonds perform best. Equities show considerable volatility, ranging from 10 to 90. We assume the real-world probability of a recession to be 5%, while the probabilities for an unchanged economy or boom are 70% and 25%. The expected return on equities is 22%. This is a considerable risk premium relative to corporate bonds (7.55%) and government bonds (2.7%).

Given the payoff table (Table 2), we start by calculating the value of state price securities. These are primitive securities that pay off one monetary unit in a given state but zero in all other states (see Chapter 2). If the market is in equilibrium (all assets are correctly priced without arbitrage opportunities), we can recover market prices by multiplying each cashflow with the corresponding state price. This is equivalent to paying for the respective cashflows. What we need to is to solve the following set of three equations (one for each asset) in three unknowns. The solution to this system will be a set of state prices that price all assets in our economy.

$$\mathbf{P} = \mathbf{C} \cdot \mathbf{AD}$$

$$\begin{bmatrix} 50 \\ 98 \\ 100 \end{bmatrix} = \begin{bmatrix} 10 & 60 & 90 \\ 60 & 110 & 112 \\ 106 & 103 & 100 \end{bmatrix} \begin{bmatrix} AD(1) \\ AD(2) \\ AD(3) \end{bmatrix} \qquad (5.1)$$

We denote the payoff table by $\mathbf{C}$, the vector of state price securities by $\mathbf{AD}$ and the security prices by $\mathbf{P}$. The solution to (1) is given by

$$\mathbf{AD} = \mathbf{C}^{-1}\mathbf{P} = \begin{bmatrix} 0.1664 \\ 0.7886 \\ 0.0114 \end{bmatrix} \qquad (5.2)$$

We can check this result by pricing government bonds. Each cash-flow is multiplied by its price. Receiving a cashflow of 106 in the recession state is equivalent to owning 106 recession securities with a price of 0.1664. Evaluating the holdings of all state price securities recovers the government bond price.

$$100 = 106 \cdot 0.1664 + 103 \cdot 0.7886 + 100 \cdot 0.0114$$

The careful reader will have noticed that a payoff of 1 in State 1 costs about 0.17. This is much higher than for state 3. The reason is that payments in state 1 (recession) are more valuable than in state 3 (boom). Marginal utility from an extra euro is higher when wealth is low. Note that a portfolio of all state price securities replicates a risk-free investment (payment of one in every state of the world) and hence

$$\frac{1}{\sum_{i=1}^{3} AD(i)} = (1+r) = 1.0348$$

We do not necessarily need a risk-free security to recover the risk-free rate. If we in turn multiply each state price security with the

Table 3 Return matrix
The numbers above are (1 + return) for security payoffs. For example 0.2 means a 80% loss (1 − 0.8) = 0.2. For each state, $S \in \{$Recession, Unchanged, Boom,$\}$real world probabilities (π_s), risk-neutral probabilities ($\bar{\pi}_s$), state price securities (AD_s) and state price deflators (Λ_s) are also given

	Stock	Corporate bond	Government bond	π_s	$\bar{\pi}_s$	AD_s	Λ_s
Recession	0.20	0.61	1.06	0.05	0.17	0.17	3.33
Unchanged	1.20	1.12	1.03	0.7	0.82	0.79	1.13
Boom	1.80	1.14	1.00	0.25	0.01	0.01	0.05

risk-free rate we arrive at what is called the *vector of risk-neutral probabilities*: $\bar{\pi} = \begin{pmatrix} 0.17 & 0.82 & 0.01 \end{pmatrix}^T$ with elements $\bar{\pi}_s, = s = 1, ..., 3$ Note that the sum of all risk-neutral probabilities equals one. Multiplying each cashflow with the risk-neutral probabilities and discounting by the risk-free rate prices all securities in our economy.

$$P_i = \sum_{s=1}^3 C_{is} AD(s) = \frac{\sum_{s=1}^3 C_{is} AD(s)(1+r)}{1+r} = \frac{\sum_{s=1}^3 C_{is} \bar{\pi}_s}{1+r} \quad (5.3)$$

Alternatively, we can extend the first part of (5.3) by the real-world probabilities for each state to arrive at the state price deflator Λ_s. State price deflators are stochastic discount factors (one discount factor for each state of the world) that have the advantage that they work under the real, rather than some abstract, risk-neutral distribution. The state price deflator is defined as the state price divided by its objective probability.

$$P_i = \sum_{s=1}^3 C_{is} \frac{AD_s}{\pi_s} \pi_s = \sum_{s=1}^3 C_{is} \pi_s \Lambda_s \quad (5.4)$$

We can apply the above principle to value risky stocks.

$$P_{Stock} = 10 \cdot 0.05 \cdot 3.33 + 60 \cdot 0.7 \cdot 1.13 + 90 \cdot 0.25 \cdot 0.05 = 50$$

The state price deflators (one for each state) have passed the litmus test. Not only can we use them to recover market prices for risky securities. We can now use (5.4) to virtually price every asset or long/short position in our economy. However, before we do that, we will transform the cashflow matrix in a return matrix and summarise what we have calculated so far in Table 3.

Table 4 Equities *versus* bonds
Probability weighting of return differences leads to a 28% advantage of equities *versus* government bonds. However, discounting each return difference with its arbitrage-free discount factor leads to a net advantage of zero

	$R_{Stock,s} - R_{Bond,s}$	π_s	$(R_{Stock,s} - R_{Bond,s}) \cdot \pi_s$	Λ_s	$(R_{Stock,s} - R_{Bond,s}) \cdot \pi_s \Lambda_s$
Recession	−0.86	0.05	−0.04	3.33	−0.14
Unchanged	0.17	0.70	0.12	1.13	0.03
Boom	0.80	0.25	0.20	0.05	0.01
			0.28		0

A brief look at Table 3 confirms traditional wisdom. Equities outperform government bonds in 95% of all periods.

What would be the net gain of investing in equities rather than bonds? We can think of this as a pension fund that replaces its bonds with equities in the hope of earning a positive NPV on this transaction. To check this claim all we need to do is to first calculate the return difference between both investments and multiply each cashflow with both the real-world probability and the corresponding state price deflator. The necessary calculations are shown in Table 4.

Discounting the return difference with the appropriate discount factors reveals the truth about the equity bond myth. It is as the financial economist suspected: 100 euro bonds have the same value as 100 euro equities.[5]

For value-generating firms, the allocation of risk capital is driven by profitability, which in turn is measured by NPV. So far we have concluded that capital market investments have an NPV of zero. In the absence of taxes, bankruptcy costs and other forms of market imperfections, this makes all capital market investments equal in the eye of the shareholder. But where does a positive NPV come from? We define NPV as the present value of future cashflows minus initial investments discounted at the a risk-adjusted rate. In other words, if projects earn larger returns than their risk-adjusted capital costs, shareholder value is generated via positive NPVs. If all assets in an economy were always efficiently priced, all projects would generate zero NPVs. Positive NPVs require some form of market inefficiency. Where do we find inefficiency? Buying a broadly diversified portfolio of global equities and bonds where residual risk is diversified away is by definition an NPV-equals-zero decision. Financial assets are most likely efficiently priced. Investments in operating assets reflecting a firm's core business are more likely to generate positive NPVs. They are more likely to be generated by firms that have competitive advantages that are difficult to replicate by competitors (patent, technological advantage, unregulated natural monopoly and so on). These firms are likely to earn economic rents. Overweighting equities in a pension fund does not generate an economic rent.[6]

TAX ARBITRAGE

We start with the assumption that pension fund earnings are tax-exempt while employer contributions are tax-deductible. Also, we assume that there are neither transaction nor liquidity costs and there is a zero probability of corporate default (setting expected bankruptcy costs or costs of financial distress equally to zero). In the previous section we established that all capital market investments have an NPV of zero. Now we want to ask the question, Which NPV-equals-zero investment is optimal to the shareholder? The difference is that we now introduce taxes.

Suppose that shareholders have perfect transparency about pension fund asset allocation. The pension fund is currently invested in 100% equities. We will now make a Modigliani–Miller-type argument that selling equities in exchange for buying bonds will increase shareholder value as long as investors adjust their private portfolios accordingly. This is called Tepper arbitrage and works as follows.[7] As the pension fund switches from equities to debt, current shareholders need to readjust their private portfolios. In order to maintain their desired equity allocation, shareholders need to buy equities and sell bonds, which they now hold implicitly in the pension fund. This strategy will provide value as long as personal taxes paid for equity investments (τ_e) are lower than personal taxes on bonds (τ_b). Corporate taxes are assumed to be τ_c. Note that, while we assumed that $\tau_e < \tau_b$, we have not specified the exact difference, as these are the tax rates faced by the marginal investor. Let's be more precise on how arbitrage works in this setting. Changing the present value of pension liabilities (l) into bonds yields a change in investment returns from the pension fund of $l(r_b - \tilde{r}_e)$, where $\tilde{r}_e$ denotes the stochastic outcome of equity investments while zero bond investments yield a certain r_b for the respective maturity. This amount is reduced to $l(r_b - \tilde{r}_e)(1-\tau_c)(1-\tau_e)$ by both corporate and personal taxes. We have not looked at adjustments made by the shareholder yet. Shareholders will shift $l(1-\tau_c)$ from bonds to equities, ie, they give up $l(1-\tau_c)r_b$ from bonds in return for $l(1-\tau_c)\tilde{r}_e$ from equities. After taxation this amounts to $l(1-\tau_c)\tilde{r}_e(1-\tau_e) - l(1-\tau_c)r_b(1-\tau_b)$. The total net gain is the difference between changed cashflows to shareholder

$$
\begin{aligned}
net\ gain &= \left(l(1-\tau_c)\tilde{r}_e(1-\tau_e) - l(1-\tau_c)r_b(1-\tau_b) \right) \\
&\quad - l(r_b - \tilde{r}_e)(1-\tau_c)(1-\tau_e) \\
&= l(1-\tau_c)r_b(\tau_b - \tau_e)
\end{aligned}
$$

Shareholders will always gain as long as $\tau_b > \tau_c$. The present value of this tax arbitrage is to earn $l(1-\tau_c)r_b(\tau_b - \tau_c)$ in perpetuity. Even though this is a cashflow to the equity holder we need to discount it with the risk-free rate (after taxes) as the profit to shareholders actually stems from riskless arbitrage. Hence we get

$$
PV_{Tepper} = \frac{l(1-\tau_c)(\tau_b - \tau_e)}{(1-\tau_b)} \tag{5.5}
$$

The effect of this can be substantial, as has been shown by Gold (2003) Under the assumption that $\tau_c = 0.35$, $\tau_b = 0.4$, $\tau_e = 0.15$, he arrives at a riskless after-tax gain of 16.25% of the riskless bond return in perpetuity. Discounting this at the riskless rate yields a whopping 27.01% of plan assets (assuming assets are fully funded). Even though the tax advantage from Tepper arbitrage will always be positive, its exact effect is difficult to calculate, as τ_b, τ_e are the tax rates from marginal investors and hence remain unknown. Some might be tax-exempt while others fall into the highest tax bracket.

DEBT CAPACITY

The Tepper arbitrage approach relied on transparency. However, there is another way to increase shareholder value without even involving shareholder action. The idea is simply to reduce operative leverage (by switching between two NPV-equals-zero investments) in order to allow larger capital structure leverage that yields an additional tax shield. To put it differently, equity allocations within a firm's pension fund reduce debt capacity (even more so in the presence of bankruptcy or distress costs) and hence lower the tax shield below its optimal value. Reversing this is called *Black gain*.[8] Again, we want to be more precise on this. Reducing equity exposure at the pension fund level will lead to a change in earnings at the company (not shareholder) level of $l(r_b - \tilde{r}_e)(1-\tau_c)$ in every single year. The company issues new debt $\Delta d = l(1-\tau_c)$ and uses the proceeds to buy back equity. While payments to the debtholders rise by $\Delta d \cdot r_b$, payments to debtholders are reduced by $\Delta d \cdot \tilde{r}_e$. Payments to fixed-income and equity holders are reduced by $\Delta d (\tilde{r}_e - r_b)$. Corporate taxes are reduced by $\Delta d \cdot r_b \cdot \tau_c$ with a value of $\Delta d \cdot r_b \cdot \tau_c (1-\tau_e)$ for shareholders. Receiving this risk-free cashflow from now until forever guarantees a present value of (note that r_b cancels out)

$$PV_{Black} = \frac{l(1-\tau_c)\tau_c(1-\tau_e)}{(1-\tau_b)} \qquad (5.6)$$

We can again put a number on this. Under the above assumptions for corporate as well as private (marginal) tax brackets, the Black gain amounts to 32% of liabilities. Let us put this into perspective. Boots immunised its pension fund (reducing operative leverage) and bought about 300 million of its shares back (increasing financial leverage). The net effect under the above tax system would have been about £96 million in tax savings. It is also interesting to see that the net gain is independent of the level of interest rates.

While the mathematics of Black's approach is straightforward, we want to illustrate the effect of pension fund deleverage followed by balance-sheet leverage. The focus is on the riskiness of cashflows to shareholder.[9] Assume in the above framework that two states can occur, ie, equity returns can take on two values: $\tilde{r}_e \in \{-20\%, +50\%\}$, while $r_b = 5\%$. Suppose further a sample company (with enough operating profits to guarantee the existence of a tax shield) with €1,000 in assets equally financed with equities (€500) and fixed income (€500). The pension fund is half the size of the sponsoring company. It is fully funded with €500 in equities. How does an all-stock and an all-equity strategy compare? Remember again the basic steps in Black's argument

Table 5 Equity strategy and states of the world

	Bad state	**Good state**
Return on equities	-20%	50%
Sell equities	400	750
Retire pension obligation	525	525
Payoff from pension fund	-125	225
Tax	43.75	-78.75
Payoff to shareholder	-81.25	146.25

(1) Remove stocks from pension plan investments and replace them by matching fixed income instruments.

(2) Leverage the balance sheet by $\Delta d = l(1-\tau_c)$, ie, issue new bonds and use the proceeds to retire equity.

We start with a 100% equity strategy. The payoffs are summarised in Table 5. If equities do well, pension assets rise from 500 to 750. Pension liabilities accumulate to 525. This leaves a pension fund profit of 225 before and 146.25 after taxes. Taxes amount to 225 multiplied by the corporate tax rate of 35%. In case equities have been performing badly, the pension fund experiences a loss of 125 that can be fully offset against other earnings and hence yields a tax credit of 43.75. The range of possible outcomes amounts to 227.5 and is used as a measure of cashflow dispersion (risk).

Suppose now we switch to a 100% investment to matching fixed income. This actually leads to a massive decrease in the riskiness of our sample company. There is no payoff from the pension fund any more. Whatever equity markets do, pensions are always fully matched. In order to releverage the company we need to issue debt and retire equity. As we have calculated before, we need to retire equity by issuing bonds with total volume of $\Delta d = l(1-0.35) = 500 \cdot (1-0.35) = 325$. The new capital structure is now 825 bonds and 175 equity. After a year has gone by, we can issue equity in the market to create payoffs from the new capital structure. In case equities performed well we can reissue the 325 (book value) stocks at a price of 488 and retire the 325 in bonds. After paying interest of 16.25 and collecting the benefits provided by the tax shield of additional debt of $\Delta d \cdot r_b \cdot (1-\tau_c) = 325 \cdot 5\% \cdot (1-35\%) = 5.69$. The dispersion of cashflows equals $151.94 - (-75.56) = 227.5$. This is exactly the same as

Table 6 Bond strategy and states of the world

	Bad state	Good state
Return on equities	−20	50
Sell bonds	525	525
Retire pension obligation	525	525
Pay off from pension fund	0	0
Issue equity	260	488
Retire bond (reduce leverage)	−325	−325
Pay interest on bond	−16.25	16.25
Pay off from capital structure	−81	146
Tax shield (from leverage)	5.69	5.69
Pay off to shareholder	−75.6	151.9

in the pure equity case. However, while the dispersion is the same, cashflows are always higher than in the 100% equity case. Losses in the bad state are lower (–75.6 instead of –81.25) and gains in the good state are higher (151.9 instead of 146.25)

Note that the Black gain as well as the Tepper arbitrage reflect two different strategies. Which one delivers a larger increase in shareholder value? We can see this by creating the difference between both present values.

$$PV_{Tepper} - PV_{Black} = \frac{I(1-\tau_c)(\tau_b-\tau_e)}{(1-\tau_b)} - \frac{I(1-\tau_c)\tau_c(1-\tau_e)}{(1-\tau_b)}$$

$$= \frac{I(1-\tau_c)((\tau_b-\tau_e)-\tau_c(1-\tau_e))}{(1-\tau_b)} \qquad (5.7)$$

This difference will equal zero only if $(\tau_b - \tau_e)= \tau_c(1 - \tau_e)$, a condition ie, met only if

$$(\tau_b-\tau_e)=\tau_c(1-\tau_e)$$
$$(1-\tau_e)-(1-\tau_b)=\tau_c-\tau_c\tau_e$$
$$1-\tau_e-\tau_c+\tau_c\tau_e=1-\tau_b$$
$$(1-\tau_e)(1-\tau_C)=(1-\tau_b)$$

The left-hand side reflects the cost of corporate borrowing to the shareholder, while the right-hand side represents the cost of personal borrowing. If companies can no longer increase value from leverage (ie, to say, if the capital structure is optimal for their clientele) there is no difference between both approaches (see Gold 2000, p 35). Shareholders with different tax brackets will hence prefer different approaches. This is nothing more than another form of a clientele effect. Whatever strategy a plan sponsor chooses, it will benefit most from the described tax arbitrage if the level of funding is maximised. Given this analysis, it is surprising that pension funds are to a large degree both underfunded as well as invested in equities.

This section summarised the tax-related arguments for a 100% investment in immunising bonds. Bonds are taxed differently if held in the pension fund rather than in the private portfolio. Pension fund deleverage also frees tax-shield-generating debt capacity. This all is beneficial to shareholders. Note that a 100% bond investment in a defined benefit pension plan also increases the value to employees. The risk that defined benefits are not paid is substantially reduced. This effectively decouples pension risk from otherwise largely correlated job risk. Employees and shareholder win at the same time as the taxman loses out. This also applies to excise taxes upon plan termination if a substantial pension fund surplus has been generated by equity investments. In an empirical study, Landesman/Miller have shown that a contribution of US$1 into the pension plan increases shareholder value on average by US$1.2. This directly corresponds with previous arguments.

ASSET SUBSTITUTION

In contrast with the previous section, where a 100% investment in matching fixed income has been in the interests of both shareholders and employees, we can easily construct situations with conflicting interests. We will ignore tax effects for a moment. Suppose a company is close to its default point – ie, company net assets (asset minus debt) trade close to zero. While the sponsoring company will participate fully in any pension fund surplus in case it survives, it can walk away from pension deficits should it default. Maximising surplus volatility will now increase shareholder value. "If you are in trouble, double" will lead to a substitution of surplus risk-minimising assets (bonds) for surplus risk-maximising assets (equities).[10] Employees accepted to bear pension fund deficits in case of corporate default. We can value this put using option pricing theory.[11] If labour markets were perfectly flexible, any change in asset allocation would have a direct effect on the likelihood of benefits being paid that could be immediately offset by higher wage claims. Asset allocation changes motivated by asset substitution (effectively risk shifting) would become irrelevant, as employees cannot be fooled. However, if the plan sponsor is close to bankruptcy, wage increases might be difficult to enforce and even trigger default. In this scenario it is optimal for shareholders to invest 100% in a surplus risk-maximising strategy (equities).

So far, we assumed there was no pension insurance provided by a pension benefit guarantee company (called the PBGC in the United States, or PSV in Germany, to name but two). The costs of corporate default are yet borne by employees. In theory the introduction of pension insurance could transfer these costs from employees to shareholders. If plan sponsors pay an insurance premium that reflects the value of the put option provided by the PBGC, employees are made wealthier (they do not bear the costs of bankruptcy) while shareholders lose out. The positive effect of underfunding or surplus volatility will be offset by higher insurance premiums. Also employees will bid more aggressively for wage increases if their pension promise is guaranteed (see Ippolito 1986). However, the mechanics described above work correctly only if insurance premiums are fairly priced. In practice, premiums are changed on a percentage basis and reflect neither the plan sponsor's credit rating nor the riskiness of its asset allocation. As pension insurance is underpriced, the motives for asset substitution remain intact.

TRADE-OFF THEORY

So far we have been identifying two corner solutions. Tax arbitrage suggested that firms with stable earnings and high tax brackets should fund as much as they legally can and invest plan assets in matching fixed income. For successful firms, there is a gain to leverage (tax shield) that can be exploited without changing shareholder risk. One hundred per cent bonds are optimal. On the opposite end of this argument are deteriorating firms close to their default point. They should maximise the value of the pension (incorrectly priced) put provided by the PBGC by increasing surplus volatility via equity investments. For them, 100% equity is optimal. So far we have two corner solutions. Is there a middle ground?

First we need to evaluate the limits to financial leverage. Under what circumstances will increased leverage destroy shareholder value? The answer is simple: shareholder value is thrown away if increased volatility decreases the expected value of cashflows to shareholders. An increase in risk will yield negative return if the option-like claims from corporate outsiders also increase in value (see Grinblatt and Titman 2002, Chapter 21; Doherty 2000, Chapter 7). The most important sources of these kinds of claims arise from convexity. One source of convexity is bankruptcy costs. While direct bankruptcy costs (lawyers, management time and so forth) are not very large, indirect costs can be substantial.[12] Firms are essentially a nexus of contracts between labour, suppliers and customers – in other words, different stakeholders in general. Many contracting parties have made investments specific to the firm. Bankruptcy destroys the value of these investments. Hence contracting parties will either reduce investments or require compensation from firms with higher bankruptcy probability. For example, who wants to accumulate miles in a frequent-flier programme from an airline close to failure? Who wants to train employees in the use of a software system that is likely to disappear? Who wants to build highly specialised equipment for a customer that is close to bankruptcy? While it is clear that there are frictional costs from financial distress, indirect bankruptcy costs are difficult to measure. Empirical studies place them in the area of about 20% of market value (see Altman 1984; Opler and Titman 1994). A payoff profile from the shareholder perspective is shown in Figure 1.

This looks like the payoff diagram of a put option. We could calculate the present value of bankruptcy costs using the Black–Scholes formula. Why should management care? Because rational bondholders will also calculate expected bankruptcy costs and require a default premium as compensation for the games that management can play on them in times of financial distress. This again comes out of the shareholders' pockets. We can view bankruptcy costs as the costs of incomplete contracts from borrowing.

The second convexity arises from corporate tax schedules. For example, firms either pay taxes if they make profits (the more the higher profits are) or they don't (irrespective of the size of losses). Carrying losses backward and forward is typically limited. Hence there is a natural kink of the tax function creating convexity.

197

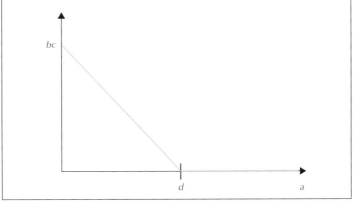

Figure 1 Bankruptcy costs. The costs of corporate bankruptcy (direct and indirect) indicated by *bc* rise if the asset value (*a*) falls below the value of corporate debt (*d*). Costs are measured at time of bankruptcy. Asset volatility will increase the value of this option

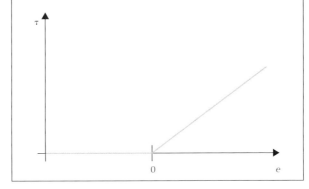

Figure 2 Nonlinear tax schedule. The value of total tax payments (τ) increases with earnings (*e*), but it does not become negative when earnings turn negative. Instead, it remains zero. This resembles a long call option on corporate earnings

If earnings (*e*) are 100 in one year and −100 next year, the tax base is on average zero (the company left its owner with zero profits after two years), while the company did pay 35 in taxes after Year One. Further convexity is introduced with a progressive tax system,

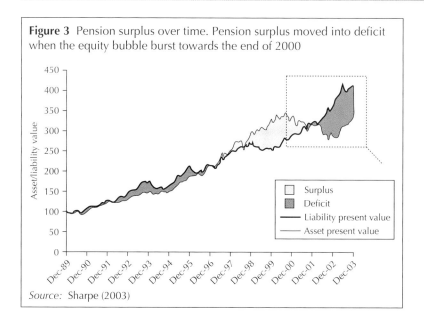

Figure 3 Pension surplus over time. Pension surplus moved into deficit when the equity bubble burst towards the end of 2000

Source: Sharpe (2003)

where the marginal tax rate rises with the tax base. The taxman (corporate outsider) is actually long this option. It rises in value with earnings volatility. Again we could use Black–Scholes-type analysis to calculate the value of this option. Shareholder value is created if we manage to reduce the governments contingent claim in a company.

In summary, a rise in earnings volatility induced by corporate leverage will reduce the expected value of the tax shield, as this can be used only if interest payments can be offset against profits.

Bicksler and Chen (1985) use the above convexity costs in their attempt to establish a trade-off theory of pension fund asset allocation. For bad firms an increase in financial leverage will still increase the tax shield but at a quickly decreasing rate. If marginal benefits from financial leverage are declining, there might be a trade-off point where marginal benefits from equities (creation of surplus volatility will increase the value of put options written by PBGC) show equal importance.[13] We can find little evidence at all that the trade-off theory applies to a large number of firms. In those years when the equity allocation was highest (such as 2000) pension surplus also was highest (see Sharpe 2003). We cannot explain these equity allocations with the trade-off theory. A high surplus always means that the pension put is deeply out of the money, in which case it has little sensitivity to surplus volatility. Consequentially, here was little value from trying to maximise the pension put.

Conversely, the pension put moved considerably in the money with increasing pension deficits. At market values, the average ratio of assets to accrued liabilities dropped from about 130% to 80% between 2000 and 2003. While the trade-off theory would indicate that plan sponsors should increase their equity allocation in order to react to the changed trade-off between pension put and tax shield, plan sponsors actually increased their debt allocations. At that point there is no convincing argument why benevolent (shareholder-value-maximising company managers) should opt for high or even modest equity allocations. While ignorance on managers' part is not an acceptable answer for classical economists (since it is not derived by first principles, ie, from a utility-maximising framework), it should not be ruled out given the amount of voodoo we have seen in the past from plan sponsors, equity analysts, consultants and asset managers. Instead, it seems more plausible to drop the assumption that managers act in the interests of shareholders. We will review the principal agency problem with respect to corporate pensions in a later section.

MANAGEMENT TIME, DIVERSIFICATION AND MONITORING COST

Tax-related arguments are always powerful. Corporations and individuals alike hate paying taxes and market economists dislike wealth transfer to the state, since it is the most inefficient participant in an economy. However, tax-related arguments are somewhat arbitrary and are merely the result of government actions in an attempt to distort economic solutions that are deemed unwanted. In this section I want to ask whether there are arguments against equity investments that do not rely on tax arbitrage.

Given the recent focus on pension funding and asset allocation, any deviation from a fully matched position will cost a considerable amount of management time. Senior management are forced to take their eyes off the ball in order to cope with sudden underfunding, and to discuss the appropriateness of the chosen asset allocation under current market conditions, the peculiarity of pension plans in different legal and geographical environments, the structure of pension fund governance, the appointment and monitoring of active asset managers (never mind the costs *versus* a matching strategy), the allocation of risk capital among different business units, the interpretation of asset liability studies and so on. Never mind the costs associated with ALM studies that directly (costs to ALM provider) and indirectly (wrong recommendations) reduce shareholder wealth. Contrasted with the transparency, cost-effectiveness and intellectual clarity of liability matching the above distractions to management weigh heavily against the standard solution of investing in an equity/bond mix with active manager selection and the involvement of asset-liability consultants.

Most companies would publicly state that they focus on the identification and management of their core business. However, the investment in an internationally diversified balanced fund is by definition the logical opposite of a focus on the core business. There is no consistency in combining both strategies. Diversification is nothing a company can claim compensation for. It can more cheaply replicated by investors. Moreover it will lead to inefficient internal capital markets (hierarchy *versus* market) and inefficient use of excess cash (empire building). There are two popular escapes from the above argument. First, manager selection is identified as a core business. While it is hardly credible for a saucepan manufacturer given specialised manager selection capabilities with global consultants, it does not justify mismatch, either. In order to tap an equity alpha, sponsors do not need to take directional equity exposure. Also, the argument has nothing to do with pension funds. If sponsors think they have found money machines (active managers) they would like to have them everywhere. We do not need pension funds for this purpose. Second, the diversification argument is directly attacked. In fact, there has been recent evidence that diversified firms earn a diversification premium rather than a discount.[14] However, if a diversification premium should exist, it is most likely related to concepts such as economies of scope that have nothing in common with pension fund investments.

Finally, liability matching could also make sense from an agency perspective, since it reduces monitoring costs. One of the key difficulties in principal agent relations is that effort is unobservable and results are contaminated by random events outside the responsibility of senior management. For example, a saucepan manufacturer might have had an excellent year in building a franchise with its clients, reduced costs and improved product quality. Too bad that interest rates dropped 200 basis points and wiped out the operative profit from an otherwise very successful year.

EXTERNAL *VERSUS* INTERNAL FUNDING

We have seen that the current practice of US companies to opt for external funding (assets and liabilities are held off balance sheet) is motivated by regulatory incentives. Pension expenses would not be tax-deductible if pension liabilities are held on balance sheet, and tax arbitrage would not be possible. Suppose a company needs to pay pensions l_i for $i = 1,...,\infty$. For simplicity we assume a constant payment $\bar{l}$. The present value of paying $\bar{l}$ in perpetuity is $\frac{l}{r_b}$. Firms can either pay $\bar{l}$ as the they go making after tax payments of $\bar{l}(1-\tau_c)$ in every single year, or they could invest the present value of all future liability payments into a pension fund and receive an immediate tax saving $\frac{l}{r_b}\tau_c$. While the pension fund would be able to generate the necessary cashflows to cover all future payments by investing in bonds $\frac{l}{r_b}r_b = \bar{l}$, the tax saving remains with the company. Note that we need matching bonds to generate equal cashflows and also note that bond returns are not taxed within the pension fund. This has nothing to do with the spurious claims often made for outside funding. International comparability is not even desirable given differential tax treatments. Instead, consultants as well as asset managers have a clear business incentive to recommend outside funding. As soon as the money leaves the company's balance sheet it cannot be repatriated. It is therefore no longer available to finance internal projects and will stay for ever (as long as the last plan member dies) off balance sheet, ie, in the hands of these lobby groups.

While external funding is beneficial to shareholders under a US tax code (only if the money is put into matching bonds) the same must not be true under tax neutrality. Let us investigate the disadvantages of outside funding if tax effects are absent. This also gives us an indication on how big tax savings must be to compensate for other effects. So is external finance the Holy Grail, increasing shareholder, bondholder and employee value at the same time, as rating agencies seem to imply? How can the pie become bigger by being sliced differently? The main objections to outside funding from a shareholder's perspective are the costs of liquidity. External funding will lead to a direct liquidity drain, while the legal obligation to satisfy the defined benefits will always stay with the sponsoring company. Cash outflows arise from the level of initial funding, from next year's accumulated benefits (service costs) and from conditional cash transfers in times of underperformance. In other words, the money goes but the obligation remains. If the pension fund's asset allocation has been inappropriate to ensure liability payments (as many pension plans now experience), the sponsoring company has to make up for the loss. Liquidity (cash in hand) is valuable to firms, because raising cash in the future might be expensive. The analytical framework for liquidity costs and the consequential hierarchy of financing decisions led by cash, followed by bonds and equities being last favourable (pecking-order theory), has been set out by Myers and Majluf (1984). They assumed perfect capital markets except asymmetric information. Liquidity costs (or more precisely adverse selection costs) arise because two types of firm might raise capital.

One type of firm (Type 1) needs to finance positive-NPV projects. Starting the project is good for existing investors; new investors get required rate of return. The other type of firm has overvalued shares and no positive-NPV projects. Raising capital transfers wealth (overvalued stocks) from new investors to existing investors. Investors know neither the true value of existing assets (are shares currently over- or undervalued?) nor the true value of the underlying project. Outside investors cannot distinguish between overvalued firms and those with positive-NPV projects. Suppose a firm announces a common stock issue. Investors will assume that stocks are overvalued. Existing managers act in the interests of existing shareholders (because of compensation contracts) and issue claims whenever they are overvalued or a positive-NPV project emerges. New investors would have, on average, a lower-than-required return. Potential investors understand this, and offer to pay less so that they earn their required rate of return on average. In the respective pooling equilibrium, firms can still issue new shares, but at a marked-down price. This is not due to price pressure or inelastic demand, but to the information content of equity issuance. We can compare this with Akerlof (1970) lemon paper. Buyers of used cars will anticipate that sellers of used cars are most likely those who are dissatisfied with their cars' performance. This will drive used-car prices so far down that it becomes unattractive to sell cars that are no lemons. This is why nobody likes the used-car salesman.

The stock market works in the same fashion. It will anticipate that companies with overvalued stocks will create the largest gain (to existing shareholders), issuing new stock. Since talk is cheap, managers known to pursue the interests of existing shareholders cannot justify equity issuance to credibly communicate that they have superior projects that need to be financed. In analogy, it would be much easier to sell your used car if you can credibly communicate that you lost your driving licence. If company managers cannot demonstrate the availability of positive NPV projects (information provided to capital markets would also reach competitors, who then just need to copy a good idea), these projects are not funded and investment opportunities are foregone. Suppose the management knows the intrinsic value of its assets (a) as well as the NPV of a new project (b). These values are not known to capital markets. In order to fund the project the company needs an amount of I. Let P and P^* be the market value of the old stockholders' shares before and after issuance. Note that P does not need to equal a. In fact we have argued that companies are reluctant to finance new projects if their stocks are undervalued $P < a$. The total value of the firm after issuance is the sum of the money raised from new shareholders and the market value of old stockholders' shares ($I + P^*$). Note that any price drop due to adverse selection is already included in P^*. Old shareholders now own only a fraction $\frac{P^*}{P^*+I}$ of company assets. The company will issue new stock if the old shareholders' participation on assets after issuance, namely $I + a + b$, is larger that the 100% participation in a. The condition for issuance becomes

$$\frac{P^*}{P^*+I}(I+a+b)>a \tag{5.8}$$

In order for us not to need to specify the mechanism to determine P^* in equilibrium, we simply assume that $a > P = P^*$. The company can issue shares at $P = P^*$. Suppose a company trades at $P = 50$ and can issues shares at $p^* = 50$. However, it knows the intrinsic value of its assets is $a = 90$ and it has a positive NPV project of $b = 10$, which needs funding of $I = 20$. In this setting, issuing equities is not good idea for old stockholders. While the value of the company would eventually increase to 120 (90 + 10 + 20), they get only a share of 71.4% (50/70), which totals 85.71. Not issuing equities and giving up the positive NPV project gives them 100% in the intrinsic value of 90.

The result of this form of adverse selection is underinvestment. Positive-NPV projects are not realised because necessary capital can be raised only at additional cost. One way to mitigate this problem is to issue fixed claims that do not generate a claim in the undervalued assets, because they minimise the inside-information advantage and hence by definition minimise the impact of asymmetric information (which still exists but can no longer be abused). Rising companies will work down the pecking order. First use internally generated cash, then use bonds (until increased frictional bankruptcy costs and decreased tax shield generation put a hold on additional leverage) and finally use equity. Cash reserves as such are valuable. Firms with future growth opportunities (real options) hold excess cash.

Essentially the above arguments are the ones that make corporate risk management a shareholder-value-generating task, as risk management preserves cash reserves. For example, Porsche AG hedging USD exposure is value generating, as 50% of revenues are in USD, while 100% of costs are in euros. A USD devaluation would drain cash quickly and force Porsche to raise expensive capital. There is little formal work to address liquidity costs. All we can do is to try to use somehow related studies to try to approximate the magnitude of adverse selection costs. One early thing to look at would be the underpricing of IPOs (initial public offering), since it involves a similar type of informational difference. It has been argued (see Rock 1986) that IPOs need to be underpriced (on average) to compensate uninformed investors for their participation with acceptable returns. The magnitude of IPO underpricing is about 16% of equity (see Ibbotson 1975).

How does funding affect the other stakeholders? We first start with bondholders. If pension money leaves the companies balance sheet (as a collateral for the employees pension claims) bondholders lose in two ways. First they see that creditors of equal seniority (employees) get a collateral assigned to them exclusively, which was before shared between bondholders and employees. However, more importantly

Table 7 External funding and corporate debt
Keeping assets and liabilities on balance sheet (company I) will provide holders
of normal debt a larger recovery value (35) than under outside funding (32.3)

Company I			Company E			
Asset		**Liabilities**	**Asset**		**Liabilities**	
oa	100	e 20	oa	60	e	20
		b 40			b	40
		p 40				
			Pension	**Asset**	**Pension**	**Liabilities**
			a	40	l	40

Company I			Company E (before transfer)			
Asset		**Liabilities**	**Asset**		**Liabilities**	
oa	70	e 0.00	oa	42	e	2
		b 35			b	40
		p 35				
			Pension	**Asset**	**Pension**	**Liabilities**
			a	28	l	40

Company E (after transfer)				
Asset			**Liabilities**	
Asset	Liabilities		e	0
oa	42		b	40
Transfr	−9.69			
	32.3			
Pension	**Asset**		**Pension**	**Liabilities**
a	28		l	40
Transfer	9.7			
	37.7			

the obligation to pay employees pensions still remains with the
employer. Collateral plus company promise must be worth more
than company promise alone. Assume two otherwise identical companies. The exempt numbers are provided in Table 7. Companies
I and II invest in the same operating assets, they have the same capital structures (20% equity and 80% debt, where debt is equally split
into pension promises and bonds) but differ with respect to outside
funding. If asset and liabilities are held on balance sheet a 30% drop in

operating assets will wipe out shareholders equity. The remaining assets (70) are equally split between two equally senior debt claimants. This leaves every party with 35. In case assets and liabilities are held outside the balance sheet, we observe the following. Company asset fell from 60 to 42. While this would leave the plan sponsor solvent, the pension fund would actually bring down the sponsor as it demands to fill up a deficit of 12 with equity of only 2. Assets of 42 are now split pro rata between two equally senior parties. The employees (pension fund) get about 23% ($\frac{12}{40+12}$) of 42. In total, the pension fund end with 37.7 in assets, which is a 2.7 advantage relative to what it would have got if assets and liabilities were held on balance sheet. Outside funding of existing pension claims will work against the interests of existing debtholders. The above problem becomes worse if claims that have originally been junior to debt also leave the balance sheet with collateral of equal size attached. For example, if non-vested pension liabilities are externally funded, this would have a very unsettling effect on bondholders. To the extent that there is a difference between what is funded and what is already vested, debtholders' interests are grossly violated.

Let's now have a close look at employees. First, unions will not be too impressed with external finance as long as payments to their clientele are already protected by a pension benefit guarantee company. Well, this leaves us with senior management and a principal agency issue. It is the well paid executives whose pension promises would remain uncovered in case of bankruptcy that would benefit most from (over-) collateralisation. So don't be surprised if some companies finance only the pension obligations of the board.

Let us summarise the position taken in the above section. External funding creates liquidity costs directly from the shareholders' pockets. It is therefore always bad news to the shareholders as otherwise internal funds disappear, while liabilities ultimately stay with the company. Straight debt is also likely to see part of their wealth eroded if collateral leaves the company to exclusively back claims of equal seniority. The economic position of most employees remains unaffected, apart from those whose pension claims remain unsecured by a pension benefit guarantee company, because these are above the maximum ceiling. While stakeholders in equity and debt see their position weakened, top-paid executives and the pension benefit guarantee company are the main beneficiaries of external funding.

Pension benefit guarantee companies win because they get now an assigned collateral (see example above). Additionally, in some legislations (eg, Germany) the sponsoring company still pays the same contributions as under internal funding.

PENSION FUNDS FROM A CORPORATE RISK MANAGEMENT PERSPECTIVE

Pension fund mismatch is a source of company risk. If the pension fund is large relative to the underlying company it can either trigger bankruptcy or put the company into financial distress. Given the costs of financial distress (see 'Trade-off theory' above) and those of raising new capital (see 'External *versus* internal funding' above), it seems reasonable to include company pension funds in a risk management framework.

Suppose we split earnings according to their sources. We distinguish between earnings from a company's core business ($\tilde{E}_{core}$) and from its pension fund ($\tilde{E}_{pf}$), which is assumed to be fully invested in equities. Partial matching of asset liability risk reduces pension fund earnings to $\tilde{E}_{pf}(1-h)$, where h denotes the ratio of hedged liabilities. If all liabilities are perfectly matched, there is zero earnings risk from the pension fund. For any given hedge ratio the company needs to set aside a capital reserve C, high enough to cover adverse earnings shocks. If we denote earnings risk (σ_E^2) as the sum of unrelated volatility of core business returns, $\sigma_{E_{core}}^2$, and partially hedged pension fund returns, $(1-h)^2 \sigma_{pf}^2$, we set the required capital reserve equal to traditional value-at-risk (VAR) $C = VAR = Z_{a\sigma}E$, where Z_α is the 95% quantile from a standard normal distribution. In other words

$$prob\left(\tilde{E}_{core} + (1-h)\tilde{E}_{pf} < C\right) = \alpha\% \qquad (5.9)$$

If earnings volatility, eg, is 200 million and financial distress is experienced in only one in 100 years $z_\alpha = -2.32$, the plan sponsor needs a capital reserve of 232 million to compensate for all but the worst 1% of losses. It is clear from the above arguments that liability matching reduces the required risk capital. As risk capital needs to be held in cash (which is also an NPV-zero investment) it carries opportunity costs in terms of lost business opportunities. Hedging releases capital reserves ΔC that can be invested into the core

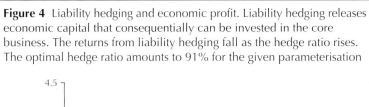

Figure 4 Liability hedging and economic profit. Liability hedging releases economic capital that consequentially can be invested in the core business. The returns from liability hedging fall as the hedge ratio rises. The optimal hedge ratio amounts to 91% for the given parameterisation

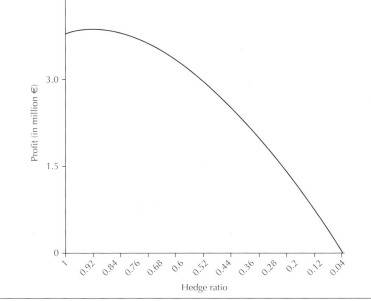

business, earning risk-adjusted return on capital (*raroc*), instead of being held in cash as risk capital

$$\Delta C \cdot raroc = -z_{\alpha} \left(\sigma_E - \sigma_{E|h} \right) \cdot raroc \qquad (5.10)$$

where $\sigma_{E|h}$, denotes total earnings volatility after liability hedging. We need to balance the gains from hedging in (10) against its costs given by, $h\sigma_{pf}\phi$ where ϕ reflects the marginal costs of hedging and $h\sigma_{pf}$ the hedging volume.

To clarify the mechanics of the simple model above we use the following parameterisation. Suppose earnings volatility from core operations as well as the unmatched pension fund amounts to €100 million each ($\sigma_{E_{core}} = 100, \sigma_{E_{pf}} = 100$). Hedging costs are assumed to be $\phi = 1\%$ of hedging volume. Also, we set raroc = 5% – that is to say investment opportunities in the plan sponsor's core business return a premium of 5% over risk-adjusted capital costs. The net profit from hedging is plotted against the respective hedge ratio in Figure 4.

Liability hedging unlocks capital reserves. A hedge ratio of 30% reduces earnings volatility from 141.42 million ($\sqrt{100^2 + 100^2}$) to 122.07 million ($\sqrt{100^2 + 70^2}$). Hence the change in earnings risk amounts to $\sigma_E - \sigma_{E|h} = 19.36$. This is equivalent to a decrease in the required risk capital of $\Delta C = 2.33 \cdot 19.36 = 45.03$. Assuming *raroc* = 5% freeing up capital reserve translates into an economic gain of 2.25 million, which needs to be counterbalanced by hedging costs of 0.3 million (30% of 100 million at 1% cost). Total profits amount to 1.95 million. Liability hedging increases shareholder value by transforming unrewarded (NPV-equals-zero) non-core risk into rewarded core business risk. The effect of liability hedging is smaller if pension fund earnings and corporate earnings are uncorrelated. In this case the additional earnings risk created by the pension fund is already small, due to diversification. Alternatively, we could have used the capital allocation rule provided by Perold (2001).

$$\frac{\Delta\mu}{\Delta C} - \theta > 0 \qquad (5.11)$$

The expected incremental profits $\Delta\mu$ (discounted at the risk-adjusted rate) are related to the risk-marginal risk capital ΔC, ie, defined in economic terms, ie, as the price of insurance against losses. Only if economic returns $\frac{\Delta\mu}{\Delta C}$ exceed the deadweight costs of volatility θ should a project be undertaken. Deadweight costs arise because volatility might reduce the total value of the firm (equity and bonds) due to the costs of financial distress, the nonlinearity of the tax schedule or liquidity costs. We see that capital market investments would not create economic profits (NPV of zero) but contribute to total asset volatility and as such impose deadweight costs.

MODIGLIANI–MILLER AND THE MACROECONOMY

The last line of defence for supporters of equity-based investments is often a macroeconomic argument: if everybody immunises liabilities, who would buy equities and provide the economy with risk capital? To answer this question we first need to establish a relation between the business and the household sector in an economy. Firms are investment vehicles that finance themselves with debt and equity, which in turn are held by end investors, namely households, in the

Table 8 Modigliani–Miller and the macroeconomy
Combining the corporate and household sector results in cancelling out
financing decisions and leaves us with the real economy

Corporate		Household sector		Economy	
Assets	**Liabilities**	**Assets**	**Liabilities**	**Assets**	**Liabilities**
Real capital	Debt equity	Debt equity	Real wealth	Real capital	Real wealth

form of direct ownership, individual securities or mutual funds. It
is the main insight of Modigliani–Miller's invariance proposition,
that a firm's capital structure does not matter. Changes in capital
structure can be undone on the investor's level. The same principle
applies to the economy as we can see in Table 8.

Firms are owned by the household sector. They ultimately bear
risk and reward. As I argued before, firms are only investment
vehicles through which investors get exposure to risk factors. The
corporate sector has no life of its own. To put it differently, the risk
in an economy does not arise from how an economy is financed: it
arises from its sectoral composition and from corporate competitiveness. If corporate pension funds decide to shift from equities
into bonds, this will make the same stocks less risky. Investors now
indirectly hold more bonds in their private portfolio. They can
adjust their portfolio by selling their bond holdings to companies
that look to increase their bond holdings and at the same time
increase their equity allocation. Companies would now end up
crossholding bonds rather than crossholding equities. In any case,
their participation in the real economy does not change. Neither
does exposure to systemic economic risks.

We can illustrate this with a fallacy that is widespread among
supporters of funded pension systems. They argue that funding a
privately funded pension system, where all individuals save with
the use of equity funds, is superior, because it would make everybody much wealthier. Their claim seems to be supported by long-
term stock returns. However, the problem with the we-can-all-be-
rich fallacy is that if everybody would buy stocks, and companies
would become less leveraged. As a consequence, returns on equity

investments would fall from historic levels to reflect this. The economy as a whole can earn returns only on the active side of the economic balance sheet – on real capital. It's the factories, service companies and so on that matter, not how it is financed.

Finally, a last argument to debunk. If everybody immunised with bonds, this would have an unsettling effect on markets, as there is not enough capacity. Actually, if it were true, sponsors should start immediately to gain the first-mover advantage. Everybody else who follows pushes the first mover into profits. However, it is more plausible to assume that, if 30-year rates fall dramatically below 10 year rates, issuance becomes attractive again.

CREDIT RISK AND EMPLOYEES

We concluded in the section entitled 'External *versus* internal funding' that external funding is beneficial to employees. While this is obvious, the more interesting question is: under which circumstances does outside funding and hence to a large degree the removal of credit risk improve shareholder value? After all, the only way to cheapen liabilities is to increase credit risk – in other words, decrease the probability of pension payments. Outside funding seems counter productive in this sense.

We start with a world without mandatory pension insurance. Our hypothetical company keeps assets and liabilities on balance sheet. If the company defaults, employees lose their jobs and their pensions. In fact, the company issued a corporate bond to their employees of equal seniority to the financial claims of other external bondholders. The difference is that, while default of this particular company is diversifiable to the broad capital market, it is not to employees (unless the pension is a small fraction of total wealth). In other words, for the employee the risk of this corporate bond is largely different from the risks of other corporate bonds. The employees already own too many company-specific risks tied up in their human capital. This risk can be neither diversified nor hedged. Hence the employees are not willing to pay the market price other investors (that could diversify) would be willing to pay. The amount of salary reduction in exchange for a future pension promise does not reflect the market value if issued to the capital market, as the company forces the corporate bond upon an unwilling buyer. In this situation external funding with matching fixed-income investments will decrease credit risk. The value to employees is larger than the costs to the plan sponsor. In this case it might well issue debt in order to raise the necessary money for full outside funding. Inefficient (underpriced) debt is replaced by efficient debt.

The problem with the above argument is simple. We need to ask the question: why do corporates provide pensions in the first place? Also, outside funding cannot completely reduce credit risk, and the inability to decorrelate risks inherent in employees' financial and human capital will leave corporate sponsors as inefficient providers of retirement benefits. It is more efficient to borrow directly from capital markets instead of from employees. Modern societies have two answers. The Dutch reaction to the above problem is industry-wide or economy-wide funds that provide pensions. The US answer is the setup of mandatory pension insurance via the pension benefit guarantee company (PBCG). The PBGC finances its operations by raising a flat fee from plan sponsors. By *flat*, I mean that the fee is independent of the quality of pension plan assets (Indian private equity or US Treasury bonds) and the plan sponsor's credit risk. Please note that the PBGC does not represent some external state-run lender of last resort: it merely operates as a collection agency financed by other plan sponsors. A pension promise covered by the PBGC is secure independent of funding considerations. Employees do not need to worry about the accumulation of company-specific risk in their pension plan. From this we conclude that funding in the presence of mandatory pension insurance does not benefit employees. Their position remains unchanged, with the exception of those employees whose claims are not covered by the PBGC, because they exceed a maximum amount. External funding transfers wealth in the form of a collateral to the PBGC. In the absence of mandatory funding requirements, every plan sponsor wants to fund as little as possible, while hoping that other firms fund as much as possible (prisoner's dilemma).

That collateral would very likely not have been available in the case of default, and can now be used to bail out the employees of failing competitors. In a world with pension insurance, any company would want to fund as little as possible, while it would wish that all other companies do the same.[15]

How should the PBGC itself invest? Given the current practice of putting a significant amount of pension collateral into equities, the risks insured by the PBGC are highly correlated. A meltdown in equity markets would hit all companies at the same time to a similar degree. In case of a global equity meltdown we also expect the probability of corporate defaults to rise, in which case the PBGC needs to provide the hoped-for security net. At the very minimum we would expect the PBGC not to engage in the same directional asset allocation bet. Sadly, this is exactly what happened. The PBGC recorded a surplus of US$9.7 billion at the peak of the equity bull market in 2000. After the collapse of the bull market at the end of 2002, the net position had fallen to a deficit of US$3.6 billion. The PBGC repeated the mistake that many US corporations did.

What is the shareholders' view of credit risk? We know from corporate finance theory that shareholders are not concerned about default per se. Default is diversifiable. Not to diversify is an individual failure we cannot expect compensation for. However, shareholders care about the frictional costs of default. This arises from a disruption of the business process. Customers don't like buying products from firms that are threatened by financial distress. If a pension fund is large enough relative to the sponsoring company, it can trigger default of the sponsoring company. British Airways, for example has cynically been called a hedge fund (short bonds, long risky but uncorrelated assets) that happens to own a couple of aeroplanes. From the shareholders' perspective, it is optimal if the pension fund suffers from a deficit in those countries where the company goes into default anyway, because it failed in its individual core business. A pension fund investing in its own corporate bonds would be theoretically ideal (from a shareholders' perspective) for this purpose. In fact, this is equivalent to an unfunded scheme, which is exactly what shareholders would prefer in the presence of a PBGC. Investing in a broadly diversified portfolio of AA corporate bonds comes close to this, but does not quite do the same thing. If the sponsor defaults, plan members might still get a considerable part of their pension claim, depending on how many other companies also default. However, other companies fail while the sponsor remains solvent, the defaults in the pension plan's corporate bond portfolio could eventually also bring down the surviving companies. All these considerations are meaningless in case a sponsoring firm's asset value comes close to its default point (value of external debt). It is then optimal for shareholders to maximise the volatility of pension fund assets by doubling up the same bets as are already on the sponsor's balance sheet. This strategy maximises the value of the PBGC pension put, while at the same time not diluting the risk-shifting transaction on the sponsor's balance sheet. If plan members were to choose among risky investments (they obviously prefer a matching portfolio without credit risk), they would opt for a risky investment that shows perfect negative correlation with company projects, to ensure that at least one wager pays off.

Next, I want to ask whether it is in the shareholders' best interests to buy credit default swaps on the sponsoring company. In the case of mandatory pension insurance there is little reason to do so. After all, pension claims are already insured by the PBGC (at too little cost). Buying a second insurance is not creating wealth to either shareholders or employees. It transfers wealth only to the PBGC. In fact the pension fund (and hence indirectly the sponsor) pays a premium that transfers wealth from countries where the company belongs to shareholders, to countries where the company belongs to creditors. Hardly in the interests of shareholders. Buying a credit default swap not only removes the exposure of pension claims to firm-specific risk, but also raises the rating of pension claims above ratings for other debt. Employees get more than what they could possibly expect, namely an AAA claim from an AA sponsor.

Finally it is not clear whether outside funding is renegotiation proof. In case of corporate bankruptcy, employees lose their jobs. Given the high degree of specialisation it is not clear that the human capital accumulated can be sold elsewhere in the job market. Nothing would stop a company from asking its employees to renegotiate the value of their pension claims in exchange for future employment. However, outside funding is not renegotiation proof: it is a direct wealth transfer to asset managers and lawyers.

EXTERNAL FINANCE AND COMPANY RATING

Suppose a company funds its pension liabilities externally. In the following we want to answer two questions.

(1) Does external funding *per se* improve the credit rating of a plan sponsor?
(2) Should companies care about credit ratings?

With respect to the first question, we have already made the point. If pension money leaves the company's balance sheet (as a collateral

LIABILITY HEDGING AND PORTFOLIO CHOICE

for the employees' pension claims) bondholders lose in two ways. First, they see that creditors of equal seniority (employees) get a collateral assigned to them exclusively, which was before shared between bondholders and employees. However, more importantly, the obligation to pay employees' pensions remains with the employer. Collateral plus company promise must be worth more than company promise alone. To test for this I suggest the following model. Suppose company A issued a € 45 debt as well as a €45 pension obligation to be due in one period. Operating assets amount to 100. They are invested in projects with 10% volatility. We apply risk-neutral valuation with 3% risk-free rate. If assets fall below the face value of debt (90) the remaining asset value is equally split between pension claims and bondholders. The market value of risky debt can be most conveniently calculated using Monte Carlo simulation

$$
\bar{b} = \frac{\frac{1}{10000}\sum_{i=1}^{10000} \min\left[\frac{(45+45)}{2}, \frac{100e^{0.03-\frac{1}{2}0.1^2+0.1z_i}}{2}\right]}{e^{-0.03}} \tag{5.12}
$$

where z_i is the i-th draw (out of 10,000) from a standard normal distribution. Our estimate of $\bar{b}$ (debt value) is 43.49, which translates into a yield of $\frac{45}{43.49}-1=3.47\%$. While we could have used Black–Scholes option pricing theory, calculations become increasingly complex as we move to outside funding. We now need to distinguish between the plan sponsor and an external pension fund. Plan sponsor's assets shrank to $a_c = 55$ At the year end, assets need to cover liabilities of 45. The remaining assets have been transferred to a pension fund, where they face liabilities of equal value (45). How did the value of risky bonds change? In order to pursue the above Monte Carlo simulation approach we need to identify cashflows in different states. If we denote the corporate surplus (operating assets minus liabilities) by s_c and the pension plan surplus (market value of investments minus pension obligation) by s_p we can distinguish four cases.

(1) $s_c > 0, s_p > 0$. Both debt and pension claims are paid off at the end of period, as assets cover liabilities on as well as off balance sheet.
(2) $s_c < 0, s_p > 0$. In this case pensioners get the face value of their liabilities paid out. The remaining assets cover bondholders'

claims first. If extra money is left it will be passed onto equity. Default is technically triggered in the sponsor company, but this does not mean that equity receives nothing. If pension assets have risen enough in value. they could even bail out equity.

(3) $s_c > 0$, $s_p < 0$. In this situation the pension fund could enforce bankruptcy on an otherwise perfectly healthy company. This will happen if the combined net asset values (assets minus liabilities) fall below zero ($s_c + s_p < 0$). We therefore need to distinguish between two cases

$$b = \begin{cases} 45 \\ a_c \left(\frac{1}{-s_c + 1} \right) \end{cases} if \quad \begin{matrix} s_c + s_p > 0 \\ s_c + s_p < 0 \end{matrix}$$

where a_c denotes the year-end value of operating assets. In the first case the combined assets are sufficient to satisfy all debt payments, while in the second case the pension fund triggered the plan sponsor's default and the remaining operating assets are shard on a pro rata basis between bondholders and those holding pension claims.

(4) $s_c < 0$, $s_p < 0$. Operating assets as well as pension plan assets do not cover their respective liabilities. Pensioners have a 100% claim against the remaining pension assets. Additionally, they have a claim against the assets of the sponsoring company totalling $-s_p$. However, they share this claim with bondholders and will receive pension assets only on a pro rata basis. The percentage of remaining operating assets allocated to satisfy pension liabilities amounts to $\frac{-s_p}{-s_p + b}$, while $1 - \frac{-s_p}{-s_p + b}$ belongs to bondholders.

In contrast to simulations in (see 'Credit risk and employees') we need to simulate the performance of both operating assets as well as pension fund investments. We assume a bivariate lognormal distribution in a risk-neutral world

$$\tilde{a}_c = e^{\left(r - \frac{1}{2}\sigma_{a_c}^2 \right) + \sigma_{a_c} \tilde{z}_1}, \tilde{a}_p = e^{\left(r - \frac{1}{2}\sigma_{a_p}^2 \right) + \sigma_{a_p} \tilde{z}_2} \tag{5.13}$$

where $\tilde{z}_1, \tilde{z}_2$ come from a bivariate standard normal with correlation ρ. Correlations and volatilities allow us to model alternative funding policies. The liability-matching solutions show low volatilities (as

Table 9 Yield on risky debt after pensions have been moved off balance sheet

The volatility on external assets varies between 5% and 25%.We assume the a fixed volatility of 10% for operating assets. Externally managed assets can also take on different correlations with operating assets. The shaded area marks combinations of correlation and volatility that increase credit risk for bondholders. As described in the text, yields on risky debt have been 3.47% before external funding took place

	Volatility of pension fund surplus				
	5%	**10%**	**15%**	**20%**	**25%**
Correlation with operating assets					
0.00	3.06	3.19	3.38	3.70	4.25
0.25	3.13	3.29	3.63	4.20	4.78
0.50	3.17	3.45	3.95	4.53	5.34
0.75	3.25	3.68	4.24	4.90	5.84
1.00	3.31	3.79	4.54	5.36	6.28

liabilities mature in one period) and little correlation with returns on operating assets, while investments into traditional equities exhibit high correlations with the underlying core business and volatilities in the range of 5% to 25%. The results are shown in Table 9.

The simulation results confirm our intuition. External funding will make bondholders worse off if we separate the capital structure decision from the investment decision. Investing in assets that replicate operating assets (correlation of one with equal volatility of 10%) leads to 3.79% bond yields relative to 3.47% with internal funding. Moving pension claims and collateral out of the plan sponsor's balance sheet destroyed bondholder value. You might now be tempted to argue that we cannot really separate investment and capital structure decisions and that moving to a diversified strategy with zero correlation between operating profits and investment returns would actually have improved bondholder value. However, this claim is misplaced, as a restructuring of assets could also have taken place on balance sheet. Reducing operating leverage will always increase bondholder value. In summary we have shown that:

(1) External funding will decrease bondholder value (bond yields rise), if the investment decision remains unchanged.

(2) Changing investment decisions can lead to an increase or decrease in corporate bond yields. It is, however, not external funding that can lead to a reduced default probability, but the change in combined asset volatility itself.
(3) Asset allocation changes have a direct effect on the risk of pension claims. A contingent claims framework, such as the one introduced above, can automatically deal with this complication.

We can now move to the second question: should companies care about credit ratings? The naïve view is that lower ratings will increase capital costs (anticipated direct and frictional costs of bankruptcy) and therefore reduce shareholder value. If this were true we would observe only AAA companies. However, corporate reality is distinctly different. The answer to this question is simpler than most people think. Each company chooses its rating itself as part of the capital structure decision. Increasing leverage will also increase the corporate tax shield. Only when the (marginal) frictional costs of default exceed the (marginal) tax benefits from bonds will there be an end to leverage.

One last caution. The fact that outside funding with perfectly liability-matched investments will reduce default risk is trivial. Effectively, we talk about deleverage, as it becomes virtually equivalent to buying back corporate debt. However, if the capital structure has been optimal before, the same company needs to issue new bonds to maintain the target capital structure. In the absence of tax effects this is not a good idea, as it incurs a doubling of transaction costs. External funding will create costs for lawyers and pension governance structures, too, since it requires management time as well as the costs of a new bond issue. However, if the main target of external funding is to reduce corporate leverage the same can be achieved more efficiently with debt buy-backs.

INCENTIVES AND PENSION ACCOUNTING

"With pension accounting people have an incentive to cheat"
Warren Buffet[16].

We will briefly review the basics of pension accounting under US GAAP and IAS in order to understand potential incentives for senior management to deviate from a liability-matching solution.

Table 10 Net periodic pension costs
Interest costs are calculated as discount rate times PBO (US GAAP) or DBO (IAS). While under US GAAP only expected returns are allowed to enter the P&L account, IAS rules offer a choice of including actual returns. Note that net periodic pension costs usually include the amortisation of unrecognised prior service costs. This item is excluded above as it contributes nothing to understanding the mechanics of pension costs

---

net periodic pension costs service costs
+ interest costs
− expected return on plan asets
± amortisation of recognised actuarial gains and losses

Note that accounting incentives are short-term in nature, as eventually accounting figures need to reflect economic value. After all, book values become market values as soon as cash flows.

The key to understanding management incentives from pension accounting is an appreciation of the mechanics behind the P&L account. Net periodic pension costs are calculated from different components, as can be seen from Table 10.

The first component of pension costs is so-called service cost. They reflect the present value of benefits attributed to employees for one years of service. Depending on the character of defined benefits, service costs will exhibit interest-rate as well as inflation sensitivity. Service costs arise because a company decides not to terminate its defined benefit program. Even a perfectly matched and fully funded pension plan needs each year additional funding equivalent to service costs. The payment of service costs cannot be hedged with current assets, as service costs arise only over the next year. In fact, we can define them as the change in PBO (projected benefit obligation) between now and year end at constant discount rates, but without interest costs.

Next, we need to add interest costs. These reflect the change in the existing PBO (or DBO (defined benefit obligation)), due to passage of time and are calculated as the PBO times the actuarial interest rate. Interest costs are known at the start of the year and can be seen as "carry" or equivalently as expected return on existing pension liabilities. Often, plan sponsors use interest rates that are too high relative to available rates in the market to downwardly adjust the year-end value of the PBO. In theory, the actuarial discount rate should reflect AA corporate bond rates with liability matching maturity (SFAS 87.44 and IAS 19.78). However, in practice there seems to be a great deal of manipulation around this rate, as it has a dominating impact on the development of pension liabilities. This essentially has two effects. First the accounting value of pension benefits will fall below its true economic value. This is equal to misrepresentation of corporate wealth. Effects can be substantial. A 50-basis-point deviation from market rates combined with a 20-year duration can result into a 10% drop in liabilities below their market value. Second, the expected return on pension liabilities is higher than the expected return on matching investments (lower market yields). Companies might wrongly conclude that hedging does not work or is too expensive. Neither is true. Even a certain loss is still the riskless position. Hedging is not too expensive, liabilities are simply undervalued. However, in an attempt to fix this situation plan sponsors engage into risky investments, as they feel obliged to match the wrong "carry" on pension liabilities.

Expected returns on pension assets will in turn reduce pension costs. Allocating into higher-yielding asset classes and maintaining high expectations will boost expected returns. After all, this element of the P&L is under perfect control of senior management and it might be tempting to assume profitability making the right assumptions rather than creating the appropriate returns within the core business. Note that this is a forward-looking formulation. Under US GAAP, all entries are estimates. If management is paid on the basis of accounting profits, it is in their interests to have high expectations with respect to the expected return on plan assets. High equity allocations and a high anticipated equity risk premium will help to downwardly manipulate net periodic pension costs.

The question that arises now is: what happens to differences in the expected and actual return on plan assets? These will be picked up by the last component, called amortisation of recognised actuarial gains and losses. The key words here are *recognised* and *amortisation*. What this means is that economic gains/losses are either not recognised at all (if accounting rules judge them as accidental, ie, if they are within an acceptable region, called *corridor*) or recognised with delay, but amortised over time (if the losses grow too large). This is a serious violation of economic principles.

Let us now look in detail at this last component of pension costs. Unexpected changes in pension expenses are caused by significant changes in market value of plan assets and changes in actuarial assumptions (discount rate, mortality and so on). For some reason unknown to economists, actuaries decided that this would lead to unwanted volatility in net income and decided to smooth the market outcome. At the root of this is a deep mistrust in market values that are deemed to be subjective due to their volatility. So return differences between expected and actual asset returns are recorded in the unrecognised net-gain or loss account. The same happens to PBO changes due to variations in actuarial assumptions. Unrecognised net gains or losses reflect a memo account. It is not included in the financial statements. If assets underperform liabilities this account might grow rather big. However, at some stage differential developments between assets and liabilities are deemed too large to be concealed off balance sheet without impact on P&L. I distinguish two levels of attention. The first level is defined in what has been called *corridor accounting* (SFAS 87.29 and IAS 19.92). Corridor accounting requires no amortisation of past unrecognised losses (I concentrate on losses, as this is the more interesting case; alternatively we might think of gains as negative losses) as long as their cumulative value does not exceed a threshold level of 10% of the maximum of pension assets and liabilities. More formally we can write

$$amortisation = \begin{cases} 0 & |CURAL| \leq corridor \\ \dfrac{|CURAL| - corridor}{T} & \text{if} & |CURAL| > corridor \end{cases} \quad (5.14)$$

where $CURAL$ denotes the cumulative value of unrecognised actuarial gains and losses. The number of years for amortisation (T) reflects the average service period of active employees. The corridor itself is given by,

$$corridor = 10\% \cdot \max[a, l] \quad (5.15)$$

Here a equals the market value of pension assets and l denotes the PBO. For example, if $l = 100$, $a = 75$ the corridor becomes 10% max $[100, 75] = 10$. If assets underperformed liabilities by more than 10% (reflected in cumulative actuarial losses) only the overshooting part will be amortised to pension expense over the average service

Table 11 Calculation of additional minimum liability
Note that the ABO, as well as the above mechanism, does not exist under
IAS. IAS calculates only the DBO (includes future anticipated wage growth)

additional minimum liability	=	accumulated benefit obligation	−	plan assets	−	unfounded accrued pension cost	+	prepaid pension expense

period of active employees. If we assume the average remaining
service period (T) to be 15 years, the above example will trigger a
required amortisation of 15. However, this will spread over 15
years. The recognition of 1 million per year over the next 15 years in
the P&L account creates a corresponding position on the balance
sheet (unfunded accrued pension costs) that rises by 1 million for
the next 15 years. At the same time accounting profits (EBIT) fall by
1 million a year. Together with overoptimistic assumptions on the
return on plan assets, net periodic pension costs can still be kept low
(or even negative, indicating a profit). Pension fund losses are only
partially recognised, while high expected returns still support the
P&L. I take General Electric as a prominent example. As long as
pension income has been positive, senior management strongly
favoured the inclusion of pension income in executive compensation. However, as pension income turned into expense for the first
time in 2003, it announced that it would decouple pension income
and executive compensation.

The second level of attention is more serious. If physical cash
transfer falls behind pension expenses a position called *unfunded
accrued pension cost* will show up on the passive side of the balance
sheet. However, this figure will not reflect the true funding gap, as
pension expenses may have been subject to substantial smoothing.
They can be kept artificially low, if the corridor approach is used to
amortise actuarial losses. So the difference between PBO and plan
asset value can vastly exceed the difference between cash payments
and pension expenses. Only if plan assets deteriorate further so as
not even to cover the ABO, US GAAP considers bringing the existing funding gap back to the balance sheet (showing it as a corporate
liability, which it is). For this to finally happen we also need the difference between ABO and plan assets (called *minimum liability*) to
exceed unfunded accrued pension costs. In the logic of US GAAP,

this makes sense, as unfunded accrued pension costs are already shown as liabilities. The difference between minimum liability and unfunded accrued pension cost is called *additional minimum liability* and immediately reduces shareholder equity (however, with no effect in the P&L account). In the case that past cash payments exceeded pension expenses the additional minimum liability increases by this amount. The additional minimum liability is calculated such that all liability-related balance-sheet positions reflect the amount of underfunding.

This is about the only time when an underfunding is correctly shown. No wonder that actuaries are busy projecting liabilities near year end in order to determine the necessary cash injections to prevent this situation from arising.

Accounting figures conceal the true economic situation. The question is whether high-equity allocations can consistently fool investors. This would assume massive capital market failure. Under the assumption that senior management works in the interest of existing shareholders, high-equity allocations could not only upwardly manipulate accounting earnings, but also increase the value of outstanding equity. While there is ample evidence that capital markets are efficient, there is little empirical evidence on how investors evaluate pension earnings. Studies by Barth, Beaver and Landsman (1993) found no evidence of market failure, while Coronado and Sharpe (2003) report evidence for such failure. The authors attribute at least parts of the stock market bubble to the effects of pension plan accounting.

It should be clear that accounting figures do not provide an early warning system. As a result pursuing the economically sensitive strategy (invest into lower yielding hedging instruments) will reduce earnings in the period of implementation. This might be a serious obstacle for the well meaning but not yet financially independent CEO.

WHY DO WE OBSERVE EQUITY ALLOCATIONS IN PENSION FUNDS?

So far I have argued that benevolent wealth-maximising managers should immunise their pension liabilities with matching fixed income and avoid external funding in the absence of positive tax effects. However, this considerably differs from reality. So why do we observe large equity allocations? It seems like a waste of corporate wealth, as the current regime ends in paying unnecessary fees to actuaries and asset managers who all have a vested interest in current malpractice.

While in the author's experience ignorance will probably explain a great deal, it is not an argument that rises to science. Believing in economic rationality, we need to look at the economic incentives that arise from incomplete contracts and self-interest. In other words, we have so far assumed benevolent company managers, asset managers and consultants. What if we drop this assumption? We will review the incentives of each of the groups involved.

Company management. From our analysis of accounting rules (IFRS and US GAAP) in the previous section, it is apparent that company management has a strong incentive to invest into equities. With corridor accounting and amortisation there is a large chance that accounting rules will allow us to show positive earnings arising from the pension plan, even though the pension deficit continues to increase. There is also a tendency towards outside funding, as claims by senior management are usually not fully covered by pension insurance, if kept on balance sheet. As long as all managers collectively deviate from the value-generating solution, there is no risk of being singled out among one's peers.

Consultants. Even though liability matching would be the economically sound strategy, pension consultants want to make things look rather complex in order to sell expensive asset-allocation studies. Moreover, liability hedging could be most efficiently undertaken by passive products or derivative products. This would dramatically reduce the fees from manager searches. Consultants are, for example paid to find the best equity manager for Japanese mid-caps as well as large caps, small caps, value stocks and so on. Instead this would be reduced to "Find me the best passive liability hedging manager". Fees from manager selection, manager monitoring and manager disinvestment would be largely reduced. However, things could be worse. If firms decided to leave pensions on balance sheet, pension consultants would be put back to their core business: boring actuarial calculations. To the degree that consultants provide insurance to corporate decision makers (paid by shareholders), they are inclined to bow to managers' interests. Rational consultants will, however, balance off the potential costs of legal action (should the plan sponsor suffer large losses) against their compensation.

Asset managers. They are not independent in their advice either. First they prefer high-margin equity products – or even better private equity and hedge funds – which all have nothing in common with pension liabilities. Winning new business by embracing faulty management practices is economically more important than arriving at the correct investment conclusions (underweight stocks from plan sponsors with large external unmatched pension liabilities). Asset managers will also have a natural preference for funded plans. Once assets are moved outside the balance sheet, they cannot be repatriated to the sponsoring company. They will always be managed by asset managers.

Managers, consultants and asset managers have large vested interests in the current system of pension fund malpractice. It is therefore safe not to anticipate drastic changes in the near future.

1   Legislations across Europe use the term *corporate pension funds* differently. Throughout the whole book the term refers to the US definition, ie, to corporate pension assets and liabilities that are segregated from corporate assets and liabilities and held off balance sheet.
2   CEO of Indian Head Mills in *Fortune*, May 1962, pp 129–30.
3   This statement assumes perfect competition in product markets and the absence of external effects. However, even in these circumstances it is better to increase competition or internalise externalities than abolish shareholder value maximisation.
4   Grinblatt and Titman (2002) has a review of key concepts.
5   These calculations hide a more general principle. Under correctly specified state price deflators, we will always observe that the product of state price deflator and excess return (either *versus* cash or *versus* any other asset) follows a Martingale process, ie, a driftless ransom walk.
6   Sometimes it has been argued that investing into active managers that are able to generate positive alphas (positive excess returns *versus* a benchmark) creates shareholder value. To satisfy corporate finance theorists we only need to make manager selection (identifying those with positive alphas) a core business. First it is well known to be extremely difficult to *ex ante* identify positive alpha managers and most companies have neither the skill nor the resources to engage in this activity. Second, alpha very often contains systematic risks, such that the benchmark does not serve as a proper risk adjustment. Systematically overweighting equities *versus* bonds creates positive alphas (as defined by the investment management industry), but zero NPV. Alphas arise from repackaged beta. This further narrows down the universe of successful managers. Third, everybody would like a money machine, but this argument has nothing to do with pension fund investments. If positive alphas existed *ex ante*, companies would also have them on their balance sheet.
7   See also Bader (2003) or Frank (2002) for more recent references.
8   For more recent discussions, see Black (1980), Ralfe, Speed and Palin (2003).
9   This section follows Copeland, Weston and Shastri (2005).
10 See Jensen (2000) on corporate incentives and agency costs.
11 Sharpe (1976) offers a conditional claims framework.

12 Warner (1977) estimates direct bankruptcy costs to be around 1% of a firm's market value (one year prior to default).

13 Harrison and Sharpe (1983) trade off Tepper arbitrage *versus* pension put and still find only corner solutions. However, they do not include convexity adjustments.

14 Villalonga (2003) and Campa and Kedia (2002) found a diversification premium *versus* previous studies from Lang and Stulz (1994).

15 One suggested way to resolve the situation is to charge a risk-based premium to the PBGC. Good companies (either fully funded in matching fixed income or with a very strong credit rating) would be charged less than bad companies. However, this would require the PBGC to evaluate asset allocation and funding status as well as corporate creditworthiness. This is a complex task, since the credit risk inherent in a pension plan depends on funding status (collateralisation), correlation with liabilities, correlation with core business and the sponsor's credit risk. Rather than duplicate the work of rating agencies, it seems more efficient to impose a mandatory 100% funding requirement.

16 Seattle Post – Intelligencer News Services, July, 21st, 2003.

REFERENCES

Akerlof, G.A., 1970, "The Market for 'Lemons': Quality and the Market Mechanism", *Quarterly Journal of Economics* **84(3)**, pp 488–500.

Altman, E., 1984, "A Further Empirical Investigation of the Bankruptcy Costs Question", *Journal of Finance*, pp 1067–89.

Bader, L., 2003, "The Case Against Stock in Corporate Pension Fund", *Pension Section News*, pp 17–19, February.

Barth, M., W. Beaver, and W. Landsman, 1993, "A Structural Analysis of Pension Disclosure Under SFRS 17 and Their Relation to Share Prices", *Financial Analysts Journal*, pp 18–26.

Bernstein, P., 1998, *Against the Gods*, (New York: John Wiley & Sons).

Black, F., 1980, "The Tax Consequences of Long Run Pension Policy", *Financial Analysts Journal*, **36(4)**, pp 21–8.

Brealey, R. and S. Meyers, 2003, *Principles of Corporate Finance*, 7th edn, (McGraw-Hill).

Campa, J. and S. Kedia, 2002, "Explaining the Diversification Discount", *Journal of Finance*, **57**, pp 1731–62.

Copeland, T., F. Weston, and K. Shastri, 2005, *Financial Theory and Corporate Policy* (Adison Wesley).

Coronado, J. and S. Sharpe, 2003, "Did Pension Plan Accounting Contribute to a Stock Market Bubble?", *Brookings Papers on Economic Activity*, forthcoming.

Doherty, N., 2000, *Integrated Risk Management* (McGraw-Hill).

Exley, J., S. Mehta, and D. Smith, 1997, "The Financial Theory of Defined Benefit Pension Schemes", *British Actuarial Journal*, pp 835–966.

Frank, M., 2002, "The Impact of Taxes on Corporate Defined Benefit Plan Asset Allocation", *Journal of Accounting Research*, **40(4)**, pp 1163–90.

Gold, J., 2000, "Accounting/Actuarial Bias Enables Equity Investment by Defined Benefit Pension Plans", Wharton Pension Research Council working paper, May.

Gold, J., 2003, "Creating Value in Pension Plans", *Journal of Applied Corporate Finance*, **15(4)**, pp 51–7.

Grinblatt, M. and S. Titman, 2002, *Financial Markets and Corporate Strategy*, 2nd edn (McGraw-Hill).

Harrison, J. and W. Sharpe, 1983, "Optimal Funding and Asset Allocation Rules For Defined Benefit Pension Plans", in Z. Bodie and J. Shoven (eds), *Financial Aspects of the United States Pension System* (University of Chicago Press), pp 91–105.

Hart, O., 1995, *Firms, Contracts and Financial Structure*, (Oxford University Press).

Ibbotson, R., 1975, "Price Performance of Common Stock New Issues", *Journal of Financial Economics*, pp 235–72.

Ippolito, R., 1986, "The Economic Burden of Corporate Pension Liabilities", *Financial Analysts Journal*, **42(1)**, pp 22–34.

Jensen, M., 1986, "Agency Costs of Free Cashflow: Corporate Finance and Takeovers", *American Economic Review*, **76**, pp 323–9.

Jensen, M., 2000, *A Theory of the Firm* (Cambridge, MA: Harvard University Press).

Jensen, M. and W. Meckling, 1976, "Theory of the Firm: Managerial Behaviour, Agency Costs and Ownership Structure", *Journal of Financial Economics*, **3(4)**, pp 305–60.

Lang, L. and R. Stulz, 1994, Tobins Q, "Corporate Diversification and Firm Performance", *Journal of Political Economy*, pp 1248–80.

Myers, S.C., and N.S. Majluf, 1984, "Corporate Financing and Investment Decisions When Firms Have Information That Investors Do Not Have", *Journal of Financial Economics* **13**, pp 187–221.

Opler, T. and S. Titman, 1994, "Financial Distress and Corporate Performance", *Journal of Finance*, **49(3)**, pp 1015–40.

Perold, A., 2001, "Capital Allocation in Financial Firms", Harvard University, URL: http://papers.ssrn.com/sol3/papers.cfm?abstract_id=267282.

Ralfe, J., C. Speed, and J. Palin, 2003, "Pensions and Capital Structure: Why Hold Equities in the Pension Fund?", Society of Actuaries, Vancouver.

Rock, K., 1986, "Why New Issues are Underpriced", *Journal of Financial Economics*, **15**, pp 187–212.

Sharpe, W., 1976, "Corporate Pension Funding Policy", *Journal of Financial Economics*, **3(1)**, pp 183–93.

Sharpe, W., 2003, "Asset Liability Management", URL: http://www.wsharpe.com.

Tepper, I., 1981, "Taxation and Corporate Pension Policy", *Journal of Finance*, **36(1)**, pp 1–13.

Villalonga, B., 2003, "Does Diversification Cause the Diversification Discount?", working paper, UCLA.

Warner, J., 1977, "Bankruptcy, Absolute Priority and the Pricing of Risky Debt Claims", *Journal of Financial Economics*, pp 239–305.

Wharing, B., 2004, "Liability Relative Investing II", *Journal of Portfolio Management*, pp 40–53.

6

External Asset Allocation in a Contingent Claims Framework

"Companies cannot commit to building new plants, launching new research projects or hiring new employees if that cash is needed to fund pensions."

Glen Barton, chairman and chief executive of Caterpillar Inc (*New York Times*, 22 June 2003)

We study the financial consequences of funding pension liabilities externally, in the absence of tax effects.* For some readers this might seem odd. After all, taxes are the main influential factors for corporate decision making. The reason why we think taxation is largely irrelevant is twofold. First, because it often *is* irrelevant. Moving into IFRS accounting does not change local tax laws. In fact, external funding will have no influence on the corporate tax situation for German pension funds, simply because tax regulations are still local. Second, because even if it *is* relevant it is largely arbitrary and depends on the state's will to distort market outcomes. However, a tax-free analysis allows us to specify the necessary tax advantage to create shareholder value from external financing.

External versus internal funding of pension liabilities is a problem of large practical relevance. At the end of 2003 a typical DAX-30 corporate had pension liabilities of, on average, €10 billion in book value. Given the fact that these numbers have been both based on a 6% discount rate and on actuarial mortality tables that dramatically underestimate longevity, the true economic value is

---

*It draws heavily on the common work of Scherer and Gintschel (2005).

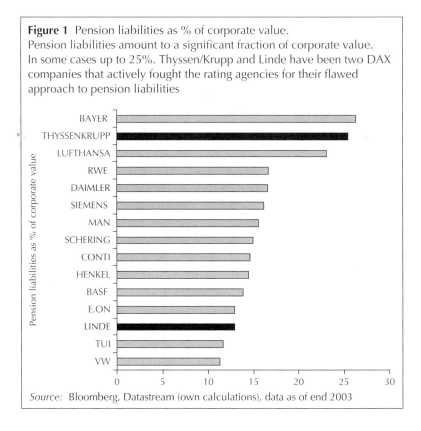

Figure 1 Pension liabilities as % of corporate value.
Pension liabilities amount to a significant fraction of corporate value.
In some cases up to 25%. Thyssen/Krupp and Linde have been two DAX companies that actively fought the rating agencies for their flawed approach to pension liabilities

Source: Bloomberg, Datastream (own calculations), data as of end 2003

considerably larger. In 2005 interest rates have fallen to 3.25% on 10-year bonds. In this environment many corporates consider external funding of pension liabilities.

This chapter will show that funding affects other debtlike claims by shifting seniority towards pension beneficiaries. This is in stark contrast to the rating agencies that ignore the seniority shift, as they do not take into account the value of contingent claims that arise from outside funding. Funding also affects the value of equity, since equity holders have no immediate claim on the surplus (of the assets underlying the pension liabilities) and can capture the surplus only at a (liquidity) cost. Thus, cashflows are different under internal and external funding.

First, we show that unfunded provisions dominate external funding from the equity holders' and bondholders' points of view. Both receive at best the same cashflows and in many cases smaller cashflows under external funding than under internal financing.

We proceed to value the major claims on the firms' cashflows using standard contingent claims methods. We find that, for the average DAX member, the cost of funding externally is between 10 basis points and 2.47% of market value of equity, depending on the legal vehicle chosen for the fund and the investment policy. These costs are borne almost entirely by equity holders. In general, bondholders lose very little and are affected only if leverage is substantial, so that shifts in seniority affect cashflows with non-trivial probability.

We show further that the loss due to funding externally increases in the volatility of the pension assets. For the DAX members, we find a fivefold increase in costs going from a low-risk, all-bond portfolio to a high-risk, all-equity portfolio. This part of our analysis is also relevant for US and UK corporations, which large tax benefits usually induce to fund externally. Our analysis suggests that conventional, return-maximising investment policies, which supposedly reduce pension costs, actually hurt equity holders.

Our results present a serious challenge for the rating agencies' treatment of pensions liabilities. Externally funded pension liabilities and the dedicated assets are completely ignored for rating purposes, implicitly assuming that pensions assets cover pension liabilities under all circumstances. *This approach obviously ignores the contingent claim that pension beneficiaries have on the non-pension assets of the firm.* It will also be shown, that outside funding is detrimental to shareholders wealth:

The main rationale for this view is the liquidity costs associated with outside funding (see Chapter 5 for a discussion of liquidity costs in this context). This view has been empirically validated. Investments into real projects exhibit negative correlation with mandatory contributions, triggered by unexpected underperformance in the underlying pension fund (see Rauh 2004). Pension fund deficits crowd out real investment opportunities. This can surely not be in the shareholders' interest.

DEBUNKING SOME COMMON PITFALLS

We start this chapter with a practical example of corporate behaviour. The company chosen was Lufthansa, but the arguments are fairly typical.

> Lufthansa's decision to create a CTA (collaterialised trust arrangement) had been anticipated since ex-chairman Jürgen Weber

announced at the airlines 2003 shareholder meeting that unless something was done, they would not meet its pension liabilities 20 years from that date.

"We have decided to set up a CTA to deal with these demographic changes at our company. With it, we expect to fully fund our liabilities," said Axel Tillmann, head of treasury at Lufthansa.[1]

Statements of this type are usually defended with spurious arguments. I will try to identify most of these below, although some companies are incredibly creative when it comes to defending a position that apparently is in the management's, but not in the shareholders', interest.

Precautionary saving. The first – quite responsible-sounding – argument is that "we have taken precautions". By this it is meant that Lufthansa does not want to liquidate operating assets in case future corporate cashflow will not cover pension liabilities. However, external funding will not increase cash available by a single penny. Whether assets are held on or off balance sheet, it will not affect their value. In fact, refinancing pension liabilities is equivalent to rolling over debt. One might argue that a debt rollover is very costly in case another 11 September 2001 type of catastrophe hits the airline industry, but this underlines the value of liquidity that is simply lost as soon as assets leave the balance sheet. Additionally, even if the precaution argument were true, it would also hold for already issued bonds. If Lufthansa thinks it shows too much operational leverage for its current level of debt, it would be well advised to reduce leverage the old-fashioned way: buy back bonds.

Shorter balance sheet. It is often said that moving liabilities off balance sheet is beneficial as it shortens the balance sheet under US GAAP.[2] While we find the only economic advantage of a shorter balance sheet is to save paper in annual reports, we will first review the argument. A shorter balance sheet arises from netting of plan assets and pension liabilities plus/minus the effects of corridor accounting (SFAS 87.36 and 87.29 or IAS 19.54 and 19.61). As a consequence the company will look less leveraged. A prerequisite for netting is that assets qualify as a plan assets, ie, they need to be segregated, separated and restricted (SFAS 87.19, IAS 19.7).

However, netting also affects the profit-and-loss account, where interest costs are netted against the return on plan assets plus/

Table 1 Balance sheet and external funding.
Outside funding will bring down leverage (liabilities/company value) from
75% (1,500/2,000) to 50% (500/1,000)

Before outside funding balance sheet				After outside funding balance sheet			
Assets	2000	Equity	500	Assets	1,000	Equity	500
		Bonds	500			Bonds	500
		Pensions	1,000				
				CTA			
				Assets	1,000	Pensions	1,000
Return on Financial Assets			60	Service Cost			40
Profit			100	Interest Cost			60

minus the effects of corridor accounting. This in turn will lead to
increased EBIT figures. Suppose we compare the balance sheet of a
hypothetical company, before and after funding in Table 1. Note
that the figures in Table 1 reflect only accounting numbers. Outside
funding has real effects as the different stakeholders' claims have
become conditional.

Outside funding will bring down leverage (liabilities/company
value) from 75% (1,500/2,000) to 50% (500/1,000). Pension costs
will drop from 100 (service costs + interest costs) to 40 (equalling
service costs as interest costs can be netted against return on plan
assets). Note that return on plan assets does not reflect actual but
rather expected (or better assumed) returns. Finally, EBIT rises
from 40 (profit minus return on financial assets) to 100 (financial
result is hidden in the pension fund). Accounting figures have
changed, but this does not change company cashflows. Economic
leverage is still the same, as the pension obligation will always
remain with the sponsoring company. Accounting profit has
increased, but economic profit is left unchanged. Personal costs
have dropped on paper, but neither the wages nor interest bill has
decreased. The real question is whether capital markets are so inefficient that even obvious manipulations remain undetected. Where
is the empirical evidence?

International transparency. This argument comes in two forms. First, it is argued that outside funding helps to compare the balance sheets between international firms particularly with Anglo-Saxon peers. It is true that if all companies did the same this would increase comparability between firms. However, this does not mean it is optimal that all firms do the same. The only reason why American firms pursue outside funding is that they are economically forced to do so. Otherwise they would not be able to deduct pensions expenses from their tax bill. This is hardly the case in other tax environments. Under German local GAP, outside funding does not affect tax treatment. Pension expenses (roughly 6% of last year's pension liabilities + service costs) will always reduce a company's tax bill. While outside funding helps US firms to use the tax shield from pensions as a form of corporate debt and hence increase corporate value, it is neutral under German GAP. The comparability argument seems not convincing.

Second, unfunded pension plans are perceived as not transparent and hence more risky. Pension obligations are said to be difficult to evaluate and forecast. A massive increase in pension-related cashflows will make investment programmes difficult to pursue and debt less likely to be serviced. Actually, outside funding will not change the nature of pension obligations, nor its market value. The complexity of actuarial calculations and the impact of changes in valuation assumption will not change, because assets and liabilities are transferred to an external pension fund. Yes, there is the danger that the burden of pension obligations will force corporate bankruptcy, but outside funding will not change this.

Cost reduction and return smoothing. It is argued that outside funding will reduce pension costs via efficient (maximising returns per unit of risk) and long-term (corridor accounting will help to dampen short-term fluctuations) allocation strategies. Smoothing is also perceived to lead to more stable company results and hence justify higher valuations. While these arguments might sound intuitive, they are all wrong. Asset allocation policies do not matter for valuation purposes. If they did, we would have to rewrite the theory of valuation. The only exception is where asset-allocation policies change credit risk (as reviewed in Chapter 5). Other than that we can only repeat the argument made in earlier chapters. All capital market investments have a net present value of zero. *This also applies to inefficient assets. An asset that is valued at a 100 is worth 100, even if it is well dominated by efficient frontier analysis.* Smoothing will only affect accounting profits, while economic profits remain unchanged.

Diversification. Most companies would publicly state that they focus on the identification and management of their core business. However, the investment in an internationally diversified balanced fund is by definition the logical opposite to a focus on the core business. There is no consistency in combining both strategies. Diversification is nothing a company can claim compensation for. It can be more cheaply replicated by investors. Moreover, it will lead to inefficient internal capital markets (hierarchy versus market) and inefficient use of excess cash (empire building).

There are two popular escapes from the above argument. First, manager selection is identified as a core business. While it is hardly credible for a saucepan manufacturer given specialised manager selection capabilities with global consultants, it does not justify mismatch, either. In order to tap an equity alpha, sponsors do not need to take directional equity exposure. Also, the argument has nothing to do with pension funds. If sponsors think they have found money machines (active managers), they would like to have them everywhere. We do not need pension funds for this purpose.

Second the diversification argument is directly attacked. In fact, there has been recent evidence that diversified firms earn a diversification premium rather than a discount.[3] However, if a diversification premium should exist, it is most likely related to concepts such as economies of scope, which have nothing in common with pension fund investments.

Positive impact on credit rating. Outside funding will decrease leverage and hence increase credit rating. As low ratings increase the burden of debt, shareholders should be interested in rating improvements. First of all, we should be absolutely clear that it is not within a firm's objective to maximise ratings. In a world without bankruptcy costs, default can be diversified in large portfolios and shareholders would be indifferent. With transaction costs shareholders need to trade off the benefits of debt (tax shield) against its disadvantages (contingent claim of corporate outsiders). Minimising default risk can never be an objective. Otherwise, we would observe only AAA issuers. In fact, every company chooses its rating itself by selecting the appropriate leverage (operative as well as financial) that maximises shareholder value. This is a question of finding the optimal capital structure.

Second, it is not even clear that outside funding will decrease economic leverage. It is true that a netting of assets and liabilities within a fully funded CTA does not leave net liabilities in accounting terms. However, this does not mean there is no substantial economic leverage. Moving assets and liabilities into an outside fund, but investing in volatile assets (equal or higher volatility than those real or financial assets the firm has invested in before), does not decrease a firm's risk of not meeting its pension or debt obligations. Remember that the obligation to meet its pension liabilities still rests with the plan sponsor.

Here we actually see that netting is the part of the problem. We can imagine infinitely many companies with fully funded pension plans, but widely differing asset allocations and hence completely different risk characteristics for shareholders, bondholders and pensioners. If outside funding took place on a fully funded and fully matched basis, this is as close as we can come to a debt buy-back (not exactly the kind of strategy we see in corporate finance namely equity buy-backs). If the capital structure has been optimal before, we need to reissue debt to maintain it. However, this would incur a doubling of transaction costs (on CTA structure as well as bond issuance). On the other hand, if the new capital structure is our target structure (too much leverage in the past), we could have achieved the same result by buying back outstanding bonds with much lower effort than it is required to implement a CTA and the corresponding governance structure.

Finally it is also not clear that externally financing pension liabilities with a fully funded and fully matched CTA should increase the rating of the remaining debt. Outside funding effectively means that pension claimants obtain a collateral (namely the assets within a CTA structure), while they still have a claim against the sponsoring company. If the sponsor goes bankrupt they still have their collateral left, while the remaining bondholders get less than their initial claim. To the extent that both groups (pensioners and bondholders) have been of equal seniority before outside funding took place, current bondholders are at a disadvantage. The price of their bonds should fall. Even more worrying from a bondholder's perspective is that outside funding of non-vested claims (these claims do not even legally exist, as they become effective only after a certain number of years in service has been reached) directly hurts their economic position. Collateral moves out of their reach that is used to back junior claims. The difference between PBO (projected benefit obligation) and VBO (vested benefit obligation) measures this effect.

Inefficient use of funds. The use of internal funds is said to lead to inefficient use of free cashflow. Managers tend to optimise their own perks (large company cars, fancy offices, private jets and so forth) rather than shareholder value. As a direct consequence, the agency costs from monitoring senior management rise. How does this argument apply to outside funding? Suppose a company has no more projects with positive NPV available. To be fair to this argument, we will ignore liquidity costs, which would make internal funding more appropriate in this setting. We also assume that cashflows cannot be distributed to equity holders in form of dividends or share buy-backs, as pension expenses reduce profits. Should the company invest externally (remove assets from management's discretion), in order to reduce agency costs? Even then it would be cheaper to use the excess cash to buy back bonds and achieve the same reduction in cashflow.

Defined benefit is insurance business. It is certainly true that providing retirement benefits is not part of a saucepan manufacture's core business. However, it is equally true that external financing does not change this proposition. If anything we need to distinguish between the actuarial and interest rate risk. While interest rate risk can be hedged in the capital markets, actuarial risk can only be insured. To the degree that this risk is meaningful and risk pooling does not work effectively, it would be in the plan sponsor's interest to unload these risks to reinsurance companies (which can then pool them). Outside funding, however, will not help.

Reduction of agency costs. It is well known that companies that carry excess cash (from free cash flows) are subject to agency costs. These costs arise as shareholders can not perfectly monitor the managements actions and managers have their own agenda. Managers might use this excess cash to invest into projects with zero (or negative) net present value that do not increase the value of the firm, but rather their personal well-being. Examples include spending shareholders money to help tsunami victims in exchange for an appearance on TV and increased personal respect,[4] a larger corporate jet or beauty operations for the chairmans secretary. Agency costs represent the difference between the actual value of a firm and the firm value in a perfect world where managers always act in the shareholders interest. External funding it is claimed to decrease these agency costs as they remove excess cash from managements discretion. However it is equally true that a debt buy back reduces agency costs in the very same way, but at much lower cost. The direct and indirect costs from setting up a CTA governance structure in terms of legal costs, additional personal and management time, very much exceed the costs of a debt buy back. Moreover a reduction of agency costs comes at the expense of liquidity costs with the later very likely exceeding the former.

Preferable taxation of equity returns. Assume a country with a strange tax rule (you might have guessed this country is Germany). Gains on equity are taxed at a mere 5% if held by a corporation, while bond returns (held by the same corporation) are subject to normal corporate tax (currently on average 39%). At the same time gains on equity investments for individuals are tax free (if the holding period exceeds one year). Suppose further a consultant (we know their incentives from Chapter 5) comes along and calculates the tax advantage of equities over bonds. Obviously this tax advantage is huge (getting bigger with any increase in time horizon), so the consultant argues you should hold about 40% in equities in your external pension fund. What would you do as CFO? First of all this has nothing to do with external funding. The same tax effects would prevail if assets were instead held on balance sheet. Second it is unclear how the consultant comes up with a 40% allocation (or any other percentage below 100%). Larger equity investments would carry even bigger tax savings. After all we need to trade off the tax advantage (if it really exists, see next point) against the increased liquidity and bankruptcy costs. Third the assumed tax advantage is illusive. What matters again is the shareholders position. Buying equities in his own account would result in 0% taxes (if held longer than a year), while buying equities indirectly through the pension fund results into a 5% tax disadvantage.

CONTINGENT CLAIMS ANALYSIS: THE MODEL

The trouble with traditional thinking in the asset management arena is that it is common belief that institutional investors (ie, plan sponsors) apply some type of risk return optimisation to decide upon the appropriate (surplus) risk return relationship for their pension investments. Corporations are not alive, they exhibit no risk-aversion coefficient and they do not use utility optimisation to decide upon the ranking of risky investments. All they do is to maximise corporate value. We know from the theory of corporate finance that cashflows to equity, fixed-income and pension claimants are contingent on the value of operating and financial assets. The value of these claims needs then to be modelled using option-pricing technology. Discounting techniques will fail, as we do not know the risk-adjusted discount rate for an option until we have calculated the option value. In fact, the beauty of this approach is that we do not need to care about the correct discount rate. We will infer it later. It is also important to realise that the discount rate cannot be fixed in isolation form either the asset allocation of the pension fund or its parent company. Traditional liability benchmarking will also fail for this reason. If pension assets are invested in leveraged Indian private equity, pension liabilities are unlikely to be discounted from a triple-A corporate bond curve.

In order to model the effect of internal versus external asset allocation (under alternative asset allocation strategies) on the value of the different stakeholders, we employ a simple model.

Our model company has three stakeholders, namely shareholders (limited liability), creditors and pensioners. Their claims are denoted by E, B, L. We first evaluate the contingent cashflows to each stakeholder in different countries. Cashflows are then valued using arbitrage-free pricing technology. The model is used to compare a plan sponsor with funded (external assets) and unfunded (internal assets) liabilities. In case pension liabilities are externally funded we need to model the pensioners' (contingent) claim against the plan sponsor in case assets in the external pension fund do not cover liabilities. For internally financed pension liabilities we assume equal seniority, that is pension liabilities and outstanding bonds rank equally in case of corporate default. There are no capital market imperfections. In particular we assume no taxes and zero transaction costs, with the exception of liquidity costs (see

Figure 2 Internal *versus* external funding.
While assets and liabilities are lifted outside the balance sheet, we have kept both capital structure (debt-equity ratio) and the investment programme constant. This allows us to focus on the contingent cashflows that arise from external funding

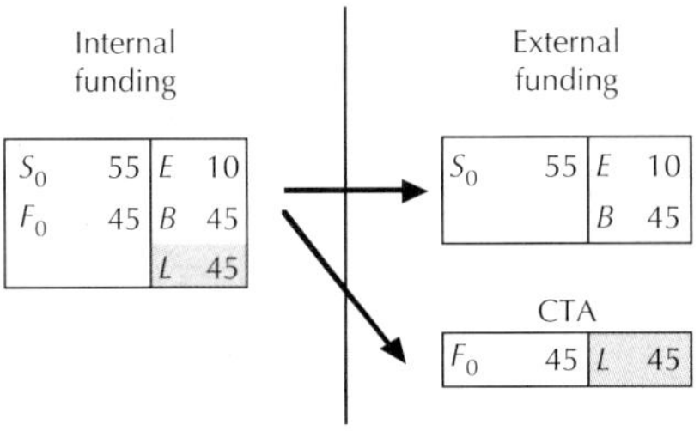

below). In this world the capital structure is irrelevant.[5] Therefore, an arbitrarily fixed capital structure is assumed.

At time $t = 0$ we choose between internal and external funding (CTA, ie, contractual trust agreement). Company funds are invested in real assets (S_0) or financial assets (F_0), either on balance sheet or off balance sheet. The process of outside funding is described in Figure 2.

At $t = 1$ we observe cashflows from the plan sponsor's operating business, S_1 as well as from financial assets F_1. The plan sponsor needs to repay outstanding debt with face value B and pay off pension claims L. We distinguish two cases.

❑ If liabilities are externally financed, the plan sponsor promises to fill any gap in the external pension fund. In other words, if externally held financial assets do not cover pension liabilities, pensioners have got a conditional claim on the (operating) assets of the plan sponsor.

❑ If operating assets do not cover outstanding debt payments, the plan sponsor can retrieve money form the CTA, provided it shows a surplus ($F_1 > L$). Due to liquidity costs, the plan sponsor's residual claim amounts to $\theta(F_1 - 1)$, where $0 < \theta \leq 1$ reflects the liquidity costs. For example, if $\theta = 0.8$ the plan sponsor can retrieve only 80% of the existing surplus. In other words, there is a deadweight loss of $1 - \theta$, ie, 20%.

Where do these deadweight costs come from? It is well known that liquidity is costly. An important strand of the corporate finance literature investigates the determinants of optimal capital structure policies (see De Matos 2003), hedging policies (see Nance, Smith and Smithson 1993) and the interplay between investment programmes and capital structure (see Froot, Scharfstein and Stein 1993). Apart from taxes (see Modigliani and Miller 1958; Graham 1996) and insolvency costs (see Warner 1977; Bris, Welch and Zhu 2004), adverse selection costs are the main influence factors. While the literature uses the above arguments to discuss optimal capital structure choice, the same arguments equally apply to the practice of risk management, ie, to what extent risk management is value-generating. To put it differently, for a given capital structure, the number of liquid assets as well as their volatility (risk management) will crucially impact the insolvency probability (costs of financial distress) as well as liquidity requirements. Liquidity shortfalls will therefore create costs. Rather than deriving liquidity costs exogenously, we choose a simpler specification. Liquidity costs are modelled as exogenously given transaction costs that always arise in case the plan sponsor tries to access external funds. We believe that these costs can be conservatively estimated as the costs of forfeiting a surplus. Given that in reality a forfeit of the surplus will be rather costly (plan sponsor controls the asset allocation policy and the forfeit is likely to be very long-term) the resulting discount must be substantial.

CONTINGENT PAYOFFS

We first evaluate the contingent cashflows to each stakeholder in different states of the world. This will later allow us two types of analysis.

❏ *Dominance analysis*. If we can prove that cashflows to individual stakeholders under internal funding are always larger or equal to cashflows under external funding, we have generally proved that external funding destroys value for a given stakeholder. The beauty of this approach is that it is distribution-free.
❏ *Pricing*. While dominance analysis tells us the direction of potential value creation (destruction), it says nothing about its size or its influence factors. For assessments of this kind we need to price the contingent claims of alternative stakeholders and analyse associated sensitivities.

Contingent cashflows are provided in Tables 2 to 7. All tables are split into four main quadrants. The differentiating factor is whether

Table 2 Contingent payoffs to bondholders under *internal* funding. If operating assets and financial assets both cover their "earmarked" liabilities ($S_1 \geq B$ and $F_1 \geq L$), the payoff to corporate debt is B. The same is also true if the company survives in general ($S_1 + F_1 \geq B + L$). In all other cases (plan sponsor defaults on its debt obligations), bondholders will receive a pro rata (assumption of equal seniority) share ($B/(B + L)$) of total assets ($S_1 + F_1$)

	$F_1 \geq L$	$F_1 < L$
$S_1 \geq B$	B	(i) B if $S_1 + F_1 \geq L + B$
		(ii) $(F_1 + S_1)\dfrac{B}{B+L}$ otherwise
$S_1 < B$	(i) B if $S_1 + F_1 \geq B + L$	$(F_1 + S_1)\dfrac{B}{B+L}$
	(ii) $(F_1 + S_1)\dfrac{B}{B+L}$ otherwise	

Table 3 Contingent payoffs to bondholders under *external* funding. If operating assets and financial assets both cover their "earmarked" liabilities ($S_1 \geq B$ and $F_1 \geq L$), the payoff to corporate debt is B. If the external fund exhibits a deficit ($F_1 < L$), but combined assets outgrow liabilities ($S_1 + F_1 \geq L + B$), creditors will also receive B. The same is true as long as the surplus in external assets is large enough to cover operating losses, even after liquidity costs have been subtracted ($S_1 + \theta(F_1 - L) \geq B$). Otherwise bondholders receive the remaining operating assets plus a fraction of any pension fund surplus: $S_1 + \theta(F_1 - L)$. In case external assets are not large enough to cover pension liabilities and operating assets are not large enough to avoid bankruptcy, bondholders will receive a fraction ($B/(B + L - F_1)$) of operating assets

	$F_1 \geq L$	$F_1 < L$
$S_1 \geq B$	B	(i) B if $S_1 + F_1 \geq B + L$
		(ii) $S_1\dfrac{B}{B+L-F_1}$ otherwise
$S_1 < B$	(i) B if $S_1 + \theta(F_1 - L) \geq B$	$S_1\dfrac{B}{B+L-F_1}$
	(ii) $S_1 + \theta(F_1 - L)$ otherwise	

Table 4 Contingent payoffs to pensioners under *internal* funding. If operating assets and financial assets both cover their "earmarked" liabilities ($S_1 \geq B$ and $F_1 \geq L$), the payoff to pensioners is L. The same is also true if the company survives in general ($S_1 + F_1 \geq B + L$). In all other cases (the plan sponsor defaults on its debt obligations), pensioners will receive a pro rata (assumption of equal seniority) share ($L/(L + B)$) of total assets ($S_1 + F_1$)

	$F_1 \geq L$	$F_1 < L$
$S_1 \geq B$	L	(i) L if $S_1 + F_1 \geq L + B$
		(ii) $(F_1 + S_1) \dfrac{L}{L+B}$ otherwise
$S_1 < B$	(i) L if $S_1 + F_1 \geq L + B$	$(F_1 + S_1) \dfrac{L_1}{L+B}$
	(ii) $(F_1 + S_1) \dfrac{L}{L+B}$ otherwise	

Table 5 Contingent payoffs to pensioners under *external* funding. If operating assets and financial assets both cover their "earmarked" liabilities ($F_1 \geq L$ and $S_1 \geq B$), the payoff to pensioners is L. The same is also true if the pension fund shows a surplus, in which case it does not matter how well the operating assets perform. Even if the pension fund is in deficit, pensioners can still expect a full pension payment, as long as financial assets and operating assets together exceed the total value of corporate debt ($S_1 + F_1 \geq L + B$). If the plan sponsor is bankrupt, however, pensioners can exercise their additional claim against the operating assets of the plan sponsor. They receive not only F_1 but they additionally get a pro rata share $(L - F_1)/((L - F_1) + B)$ of the plan sponsors operating assets. Note, that $1 - (B)/(B + L - F_1) = (B + L - F)/(B + L - F) - (B)/(B + L - F_1) = (L - F_1)/(B + L - F_1)$. The main difference between Tables 4 and 5 is the improvement in seniority of pension claims. Pensioners not only obtain a collateral (F), but also hold a claim on the plan sponsor's assets. The size of this claim depends on the pension fund deficit in relation the claims of other creditors

	$F_1 \geq L$	$F_1 < L$
$S_1 \geq B$	L	(i) L if $S_1 + F_1 \geq B + L$
		(ii) $(F_1 + S_1) \dfrac{L - F_1}{L - F_1 + B}$ otherwise
$S_1 < B$	L	$(F_1 + S_1) \dfrac{L - F_1}{L - F_1 + B}$

Table 6 Contingent payoffs to equity under internal funding. If operating assets and financial assets together cover at least total liabilities, the payoff to equity amounts to the difference between assets and liabilities, ie, shareholders receive the residual income

	$F_1 \geq L$	$F_1 < L$
$S_1 \geq B$	$S_1 + F_1 - B - L$	(i) $S_1 + F_1 - B - L$ if $S_1 + F_1 \geq B + L$ (ii) 0 otherwise
$S_1 < B$	(i) $S_1 + F_1 - B - L$ if $S_1 + F_1 \geq B + L$ (ii) 0 otherwise	0

Table 7 Contingent payoffs to equity under *external* funding. Payoffs to equity are similar to Table 6. The difference is that access to a pension fund surplus can be achieved only by incurring dead-weight costs of $1 - \theta$, ie, only a fraction θ can be repatriated

	$F_1 \geq L$	$F_1 < L$
$S_1 \geq B$	$S_1 - B + \theta(F_1 - L)$	(i) $S_1 + F_1 - B - L$ if $S_1 + F_1 \geq B + L$ (ii) 0 otherwise
$S_1 < B$	(i) $S_1 - B + \theta(F_1 - L)$ if $S_1 + \theta(F_1 - L) \geq B$ (ii) 0 otherwise	0

operating assets exceed corporate debt $S_1 \geq B$ or not $S_1 < B$ (vertical split) and whether financial assets exceed liabilities $F_1 \geq L$ or not $F_1 < L$ (horizontal split). We distinguish between internally and externally funded liabilities. To increase readability I will explain one Table in more detail. All other tables follow the same logic, Table 3 describes the contingent payoffs to corporate debt in case pension liabilities have been externally funded. If operating assets and financial assets both cover their liabilities ($S_1 \geq B$ and $F_1 \geq L$), the payoff to corporate debt amounts to B. The company simply survived. There is equity capital left and so pensioners as well as creditors receive their respective payments in full. If the external fund exhibits a deficit ($F_1 - L < 0$), that is fully covered by the operating result

$$(S_1 - B) + (F_1 - B) \geq 0 \qquad (6.1)$$

creditors will also receive B. What happens if the pension fund survives but the operating performance is negative? In this case the existing surplus $F_1 - L$ can be used to avoid corporate bankruptcy. However, due to the above-described deadweight costs a fraction $1 - \theta$ will be lost. Bondholders will receive their nominal claim in full, only if

$$(S_1 - B) + \theta(F_1 - L) \geq 0 \qquad (6.2)$$

In case condition (6.2) is not met, ie, the plan sponsor defaults on its corporate debt, corporate bondholders get whatever is left.

$$S_1 + \theta(F_1 - L) \qquad (6.3)$$

In case the operating business is sound, but the gap in the pension is sufficiently large to trigger bankruptcy, bondholders need to share their claim on the operating assets with pensioners' demands to make up for a pension fund deficit. The pro rata claim amounts to

$$\frac{B}{B + (L - F_1)} \qquad (6.4)$$

Note that the fraction owned to pensioners can be directly calculated from

$$1 - \frac{B}{B + (L - F_1)} = \frac{B + (L - F_1)}{B + (L - F_1)} - \frac{B}{B + (L - F_1)} = \frac{(L - F_1)}{B + (L - F_1)} \qquad (6.5)$$

Pensioners and creditors split operating assets according to (6.5). We can now move to the next section, where we will compare the cashflows to all three stakeholders under alternative funding regimes.

DOMINANCE

Dominating solutions will result in cashflows that equal or exceed cashflows under alternative solutions in all scenarios. This makes dominance a very robust and distributional free concept. I will show in this section that unfunded liabilities dominate funded liabilities from the perspective of shareholders. External funding will – in the absence of other effects (or example taxes) – never improve but some-times worsen the financial situation of these stakeholders. At $t = 1$ we denote the claim (A) on a given stakeholder under a particular fund-ing regime $k = \{funded, unfunded\}$ by $A_1^k(S_1, F_1)$. Alternative i domi-nates alternative j for stakeholder A if we can write for all (S_1, F_1).

$$A_1^i(S_1, F_1) \geq A_1^j(S_1, F_1) \qquad (6.6)$$

and $A_1^i(S_1, F_1) > A_1^j(S_1, F_1)$ for at least one economic scenario. Two alternatives are equivalent if

$$A_1^i(S_1, F_1) = A_1^j(S_1, F_1) \qquad (6.7)$$

for all (S_1, F_1). Finally, we can establish no dominance relationship between two alternatives if there are some (S_1, F_1) such that $A_1^i(S_1, F_1) < A_1^j(S_1, F_1)$ and others such that $A_1^i(S_1, F_1) > A_1^j(S_1, F_1)$. If an alternative dominates the other it must have a bigger value. However, without a distributional assumption we cannot make a judgment about the magnitude.

Proposition 1. From the shareholders' point of view, unfunded lia-bilities dominate funded liabilities for $\theta < 1$. Both alternatives are equivalent for $\theta = 1$.

Changing the fixed-income seniority structure does not affect the shareholders' position. After all, shareholders have no interest in what happens after the residual claim has been wiped out. Shareholders' interests are touched only if externally funded assets show a surplus. Funding will result in transaction costs $\theta < 1$. It is exactly these transaction costs that make internal funding superior to external funding. In order to prove dominance we need to com-pare each single cell in Table 6 and Table 7. This is particularly easy, if we view contingent cashflows from the shareholders perspective. As external funding will introduce transaction costs θ, the share-holders' position will have deteriorated in all scenarios for which access to external funds is required (in case $F_1 > L$). An alternative way of thinking about the above specification is an option analogy. The corporate sponsor effectively wrote a put option on the sur-plus of the external funds. At the same time it holds $\theta < 1$ call options on the surplus. For any positive volatility of financial assets, the value of the short put exceeds the value of θ calls.

Equality only occurs at $\theta = 1$, in which case put call parity tells us that long call and short put are of equal value in case the common strike is at the money forward (strike exceeds current funds by the risk-free rate).

Proposition 2. From the bondholders' point of view, unfunded liabilities dominate funded liabilities.

For internally funded pension claims, pensioners as well as holders of corporate debt exhibit equal seniority. Outside funding changes this. Pensioners obtain collateral (asset pool to fund liabilities) as well as a contingent claim on the corporate assets. Holders of corporate debt on the other side need to share their claim on corporate assets (on a pro rata basis) with the pensioners' deficit claim. First we need to prove that

$$\left(F_1 + S_1\right)\frac{B}{B+L} \geq S_1 \frac{B}{B+\left(L-F_1\right)} \tag{6.8}$$

ie, payoffs under internal funding are larger than under external funding. Expanding (6.8) and collecting term yields

$$F_1 \left(B + L - F_1 - S_1\right) \geq 0 \tag{6.9}$$

Condition (6.9) is only satisfied if $B + L \geq F_1 + S_1$. ie, as long as the combined assets exceed total liabilities. Note that this condition applies only as long as $F_1 < L$.

$$\left(F_1 + S_1\right)\frac{B}{B+L} \geq S_1 + \theta\left(F_1 - L\right) \tag{6.10}$$

Again expanding and collecting terms yields the condition for (6.10) to be met, which is exactly the description for the cells involved.

$$S_1 + \theta\left(F_1 - L\right) \leq B \tag{6.11}$$

Debtholders lose out because of their seniority shift. Note that we need not introduce deadweight costs θ to arrive at this result.

Proposition 3. From the pensioners' point of view, external finance creates a gift to pension beneficiaries.

We have proved so far that equity and bondholders lose. By definition pensioners as the remaining party must gain. Again, this arises due to the seniority shift in the pensioners' claim. Collateral plus a contingent pro rata claim must be more valuable than a pro rata claim alone. It is left to the reader to work through the cells in Tables 4 and 5.

CONTINGENT CLAIMS PRICING

If capital markets are complete and arbitrage-free we can uniquely price uncertain cashflows to all stakeholders involved. We assume that real assets (S_1) and financial assets (F_1) are multivariate lognormally distributed. Expected returns are distributed with mean μ_S and μ_F with volatility σ_S (dependent on the nature of chosen projects) and σ_F (dependent on the nature of chosen financial assets) as well as with correlation ρ_{SF}. The risk-free rate is r.

We can define now the value of an arbitrary stake in the company at $t = 0$ as the expected value under the equivalent martingale distribution.

$$A_0^k = e^{-r}E^Q\left[A_1^k\right] \qquad (6.12)$$

where A_1^k denotes random cashflows to stakeholder A at $t = 1$ for funding regime k. The expected value under the risk-neutral distribution is given by E^Q, where Q denotes the equivalent martingale distribution. While this method is standard in the use of derivative pricing (see Harrison and Kreps 1979; Duffie 2001), it also applies to the valuation of any conditional claim in general. For some claims, closed-form solutions are available, particularly for unfunded liabilities. For more complex claims under external funding, closed-form solutions become much more difficult to obtain. Instead we will use Monte Carlo integration to evaluate (6.12).

As a base case we evaluate the stakeholder claims for unfunded pension liabilities. The results are provided in Table 8. For readability we use shareholder (corporate bond, pension claim) instead of $E_0^k(B_0^k, L_0^k)$. We have set $\rho_{SF} = 0$, $\sigma_S = 12.5\%$ and the riskless rate to $r_f = 3\%$. Rising (financial) asset volatility does not change the value of the firm (€100 in a 100% volatility asset has the same value than €100 in a zero-volatility asset, namely €100) but it changes the value of both equity and debt in opposite positions. While the equity stake is equivalent to a long call option on the firm's value that naturally increases with volatility, debt positions equal a risk-free

Table 8 Contingent claim value for alternative stakeholder under *internally funded* assets (on balance sheet).
Volatility on real assets is assumed to be $\sigma_s = 10\%$. Correlations between assets and liabilities are set to zero. The riskless rate is assumed to be 3%. Stakeholder values are calculated according to (6.12). A rising volatility of financial assets yields an increase in shareholder value (equity equals long call on the firm's assets with strike equal to the nominal debt value). The numbers above are used as reference values

σ_F	Shareholder	Corporate bond	Pension claim	Firm value
2.5%	12.7	43.6	43.6	100.0
7.5%	12.8	43.6	43.6	100.0
12.5%	12.9	43.6	43.6	100.0
17.5%	13.1	43.5	43.5	100.0
22.5%	13.4	43.5	43.3	100.0
27.5%	13.8	43.1	43.1	100.0

bond plus a short position in a put option on the firm's assets. Both options share the same strike: the nominal value of outstanding debt.

We can now look at funded pension liabilities and how funding affects stakeholder value. First, let us introduce an extreme case for externally funded pension liabilities in which $\theta = 0$ and $\rho_{SF} = 0$. A correlation of zero between operating assets and financial assets assumes that there is no relationship between a company's core business and economy-wide risks. Essentially, all risks are idiosyncratic. We will remove this assumption as we go along. Setting $\theta = 0$ assumes that the whole surplus cannot be captured by equity holders. It somehow completely disappears. This assumption will also be removed later. In this case the valuation of stakes is given in Table 9. First, note that the total firm value is always smaller than in Table 8. This effect rises with volatility and is hardly surprising, as deadweight costs are a positive function of volatility. As shareholder and bondholders lose out, pension claimants win. They see their pension claim to end always higher than under an unfunded system.

We see support of our intuition in the previous sections. External funding destroys shareholder value and reduces debt seniority.

Table 9 Contingent claim value for alternative stakeholder under *externally funded* assets (off balance sheet).
Assumptions: $\sigma_S = 10\%$, $\rho_{SF} = 0$, $r = 3\%$, $\theta = 0$. A rising volatility of financial assets results in a decrease in shareholder value. The value of short put increases with rising volatility

σ_F	Shareholder	Corporate bond	Pension claim	Firm value
2.5%	11.4	43.6	43.7	98.7
7.5%	10.6	43.6	43.7	97.9
12.5%	10.0	43.5	43.6	97.2
17.5%	9.4	43.4	43.6	96.4
22.5%	8.8	43.2	43.5	95.6
27.5%	8.2	43.0	43.4	94.6

This alone will eventually lead to higher borrowing costs, if we keep the investment programme unchanged.

ALTERNATIVE FINANCING SCHEDULES: CHANGE IN INVESTMENT PROGRAMME

So far we have kept the investment programme constant. Financial assets have been held on balance sheet before external funding took place. Exactly the same financial assets are then reinvested within the CTA structure. However, we could think of an alternative situation where a fraction of real assets are sold. The proceeds are then used to buy financial assets to back the externally financed pension liabilities. This situation is depicted in Figure 3.

Again, we will first evaluate the value of equity, bonds and pension claims under internal funding. Assuming that all assets consist of real assets with 12.5% volatility, we arrive at

$$E_0^{\text{intern}} = 13.5, \; B_0^{\text{intern}} = 43.3, \; L_0^{\text{intern}} = 43.3 \qquad \textbf{(6.13)}$$

Note that investing in 100% real assets makes the company a more risky place than in the previous section. The diversification between 55% real assets and 45% financial assets ($\rho_{SF} = 0$) is lost. Shareholders' wealth is therefore larger, while debt trades at lower prices than in Table 8.

Let us now move to external funding. Liabilities are lifted out of the balance sheet, while real assets are sold and the proceeds

Figure 3 Change from real assets into financial assets. The plan sponsor disinvests real assets and invests in externally held financial assets. External funding does not only change contingent claims, but also the investment programme. An investment in real assets (with positive net present value) is replaced by investing in financial assets (zero net present value, ie, negative after costs) with different volatility

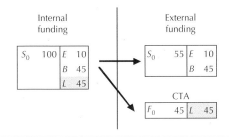

are invested in financial assets. The results are summarised in Tables 10 to 12.

As long as deadweight costs are low, shareholders will benefit from an investment in risky financial assets (asset substitution). Low volatilities on financial assets (riskless cash is the one-period, liability-risk-minimising asset) will shift wealth to pension claimants as well as bondholders, simply because the company reduced its operative leverage. For large liquidity costs the company value is substantially reduced. Again, shareholders bear the burden of this adjustment.

Finally, we can look at correlation in isolation. The results are summarised in Table 13. What will a diversifying strategy result in?

We see that the firm value remains stable as volatility costs are independent of correlation. It is financial asset volatility that matters. However, a correlation of 1 is similar to funding with one's own assets – that is, the sponsor walks away from its pension obligations exactly at the same time as the core business also fails. This is particularly attractive to shareholders. Diversification is not. Shareholder value is reduced by diversifying into financial assets with zero correlation. It is in the shareholders' interest to move (conditional) contributions to external assets (when the CTA shows a deficit) into those countries where the company is bust anyway and no contribution needs to be made.

Table 10 External funding, followed by a change in investment programme.
Zero deadweight costs. Assumptions: $\theta = 100\%$, $\rho_{SF} = 0.5$

σ_F	Shareholder	Corporate bond	Pension claim	Firm value
2.5%	12.77	43.58	43.67	100.0
7.5%	12.85	43.45	43.65	100.0
12.5%	13.15	43.23	43.60	100.0
17.5%	13.50	42.95	43.50	100.0
22.5%	14.03	42.64	43.38	100.0
27.5%	14.48	42.28	43.21	100.0

Table 11 External funding, followed by a change in investment programme.
Medium deadweight costs. Assumptions: $\theta = 50\%$, $\rho_{SF} = 0.5$

σ_F	Shareholder	Corporate bond	Pension claim	Firm value
2.5%	12.1	43.6	43.7	99.4
7.5%	11.8	43.4	43.6	98.9
12.5%	11.7	43.2	43.6	98.5
17.5%	11.6	43.0	43.5	98.1
22.5%	11.6	42.6	43.4	97.6
27.5%	11.7	42.3	43.2	97.2

Table 12 External funding, followed by a change in investment programme.
High deadweight costs. Assumptions: $\theta = 0\%$, $\rho_{SF} = 0.5$

σ_F	Shareholder	Corporate bonds	Pension claim	Firm value
2.5%	11.33	43.60	43.67	98.60
7.5%	10.73	43.45	43.65	97.83
12.5%	10.21	43.23	43.60	97.04
17.5%	9.81	42.98	43.51	96.30
22.5%	9.25	42.65	43.38	95.28
27.5%	8.87	42.30	43.21	94.39

ALTERNATIVE FINANCING SCHEDULES: CHANGE IN LEVERAGE

The previous section assumed that real assets that carry positive NPV projects are closed down, while the proceeds are used to buy financial assets with zero net present value. Instead, companies

Table 13 Contingent claim value for alternative stakeholder under externally funded assets (off balance sheet).
Assumptions: $\sigma_S = 12.5\%$, $\sigma_F = 12.5\%$, $r = 3\%$, $\theta = 0.5$. A rising volatility of financial assets results in a decrease in shareholder value. The value of short put increases with rising volatility

ρ_{SF}	Shareholder	Corporate bonds	Pension claim	Firm value
0.0	11.4	43.5	43.6	98.6
0.2	11.5	43.4	43.6	98.5
0.4	11.6	43.3	43.6	98.5
0.6	11.8	43.2	43.6	98.5
0.8	11.9	43.1	43.6	98.5
1.0	12.0	43.0	43.5	98.5

Figure 4 Increase in leverage.
The plan sponsor finances external funding with additional debt issuance. The proceeds of bond issuance are invested in the CTA structure. Core business remains unaffected with a (additional) CTA added

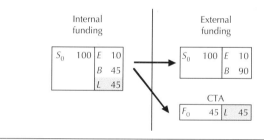

might wish to issue new bonds and use the raised money to externally fund a given stream of pension liabilities. A graphical representation of this can be found in Figure 4. Two effects of this become immediately apparent.

❏ First, the plan sponsor would double transaction costs for setting up a CTA structure (paying asset management fees) and issuing corporate bonds (paying investment banking fees).
❏ Second the CTA resembles a long short portfolio combining NPV-equal zero investments and has an NPV of zero itself.

I will not elaborate both arguments further, as they have already been discussed in Chapter 5. Instead I will focus on the valuation of contingent claims and on the effect of external funding on credit risk.

Removing pension liabilities from the balance sheet with the help of debt issuance as described in Figure 4, will create a bigger company. Assets now total 145, while nominal debt obligations have risen to $135/145 = 93\%$, rather than $90/100 = 90\%$ as in the unfunded case. The stakeholder values for the an internal funding solution can be read from (6.13). The value of equity amounts to 13.5 while the remaining debt value must equal $100 - 13.5 = 86.5$. We can now compare these values with those for external funding, provided in Tables 14 to 16. We will focus on the correlation between financial assets and real assets.

First we see that corporate bondholders will have to bear negative wealth effects, simply because leverage increased. Their stake falls below 86.5 (total value for unfunded debt) for all correlations between zero and 1. Note that the risk created by the CTA structure is always on top of the risks inherent in the company's core business. Only if the CTA worked as a hedge against the core business (correlation were significantly negative) would bondholders gain.

For large transaction costs, shareholders lose out relative to an internally funded solution (see Table 14). However, if transaction costs become smaller (Table 15), equity holders start to benefit from an increase in leverage. Note that total firm value is not affected by a change in correlation, because deadweight costs only depend on the volatility of financial assets (and therefore the likelihood of additional contributions without symmetric withdrawals).

Pension claims are largely unaffected by a change in correlation. Only if correlation approaches 1 and the shareholder successfully transfers pension fund default into those countries where the operating company defaults anyway do we see a slight deterioration in the economic value of pension claims. The total value will still be above the unfunded stake (43.3).

This section finishes with a final word of caution. All the above results depend quantitatively on the specific parameterisation. For example, bondholders of companies that have a large equity cushion will be much less affected as in the examples above. However, all results will remain qualitatively the same.

Table 14 Bond-financed external funding.
Assumptions: $\sigma_S = 12.5\%$, $\sigma_F = 12.5\%$, ρ_{SF} varies, $\theta = 0\%$

ρ_{SF}	Shareholder	Corporate bonds	Pension claim	Firm value
0.0	12.2	86.4	43.6	142.2
0.2	12.4	86.2	43.6	142.2
0.4	12.5	86.0	43.6	142.2
0.6	12.7	85.8	43.6	142.2
0.8	12.8	85.7	43.6	142.2
1.0	13.1	85.5	43.5	142.2

Table 15 Bond-financed external funding.
Assumptions: $\sigma_S = 12.5\%$, $\sigma_F = 12.5\%$, ρ_{SF} varies, $\theta = 50\%$

ρ_{SF}	Shareholder	Corporate bonds	Pension claim	Firm value
0.0	13.6	86.4	43.6	143.6
0.2	13.7	86.2	43.6	143.6
0.4	14.0	86.0	43.6	143.6
0.6	14.2	85.8	43.6	143.6
0.8	14.3	85.7	43.5	143.6
1.0	14.6	85.5	43.5	143.6

Table 16 Bond-financed external funding.
Assumptions: $\sigma_S = 12.5\%$, $\sigma_F = 12.5\%$, ρ_{SF} varies $\theta = 100\%$

ρ_{SF}	Shareholder	Corporate bonds	Pension claim	Firm value
0.0	14.9	86.4	43.6	145.0
0.2	15.2	86.2	43.6	145.0
0.4	15.4	86.0	43.6	145.0
0.6	15.6	85.8	43.6	145.0
0.8	15.9	85.7	43.5	145.0
1.0	16.1	85.5	43.5	145.0

EMPIRICAL ASSESSMENTS

In this section I will try to investigate the impact of external funding for realistic parameter constellations. As a corporate universe I have chosen the DAX 30 companies as of end 2003. All parameters (leverage, pension claim, firm value, volatility of real assets) are taken from Bloomberg/Datastream. The volatility of real assets is assumed to be the volatility of equity returns adjusted for leverage.

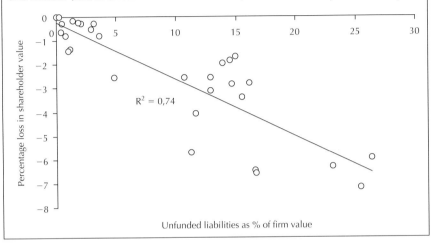

Figure 5 External funding and shareholder value.
Companies with large unfunded pension liabilities destroy up to 7% of
shareholder value, when lifting pension assets off balance sheet ($\theta = 0\%$).
The figure also displays a sad reality. Many DAX 30 companies have already
moved to external funding (points clustering around zero). Considerable
shareholder (and to a lesser extent bondholder) value has already been destroyed

$$\sigma_S = \frac{E_0}{B_0 + L_0} \sigma_E \qquad \text{(6.14)}$$

where σ_E reflects the volatility of equity returns based on 60 observations of monthly data between January 1999 and December 2003,
B_0 and L_0 are taken from balance sheet data, and E_0 reflects the
market value of a yet internally funded scheme. We assume $\rho_{SF} = 0$
and $r = 3\%$ ($e^r = 1.03045$).

Having collected all necessary inputs to apply (6.12), we can
briefly visualise the effect of lifting pension assets into an external
pension funds on shareholder value. The results are summarised in
Figure 5.

As we expected, external funding would potentially destroy
considerable shareholder value. Interestingly, DAX 30 companies
decide differently. While Thyssen/Krupp correctly choose not to
externally fund their total pension liabilities (they funded only
pension liabilities of senior management), corporates such as
Lufthansa, Daimler, Siemens and Deutsche Bank decided in favour
of external funding. This has been in violation of bondholders' and

shareholders' interests. The case of Heidelberger Zement (not a DAX 30 company) shows how realistic theses arguments really are. Although management would have wanted to externally fund pension liabilities in 2005, covenants of a previously issued bond did not allow them to do so. In this context it might be interesting (and worthwhile) to research the covenants of companies that externally funded their pension liabilities!

CONCLUSION

We have shown (dominance analysis) that external funding reduces the contingent claims of shareholders and bondholders in at least some countries, while it never increases payments relative to internal funding. While equity and normal debt stakes get diluted, the opposite is true for pension claims.

If employees were the net gainers we could make the case that reduced wage claims make up for the calculated losses. In this case pension funding could actually increase total firm value as employees would value the increase in pension security more highly than it would cost the sponsoring firm to provide it. This argument has already been made in the previous chapter. External funding (with matching fixed income) would allow employees to effectively diversify job and pension risks. However, this argument does not apply if (mandatory) pension insurance (for a flat, ie, risk-insensitive fee) exists. In this case, pensioners are not made better off under external funding. The only party benefiting is the pension guarantee company. Under external funding they will get collateral (external funds), while still receiving insurance premiums.

The costs of external funding are twofold. We distinguished between liquidity costs (transaction costs, deadweight loss) affecting shareholders and changes in seniority structure hitting bondholders. Liquidity costs (θ) have been exogenously given. They are a proxy for a complicated multi-period process. In perfect capital markets these costs would be zero ($\theta = 100\%$). The plan sponsor could raise money any time at competitive rates without transaction costs. Alternatively, it could sell any surplus at fair value. Access is necessary (and costly) only in imperfect capital markets. These imperfections are most likely to arise from imperfect information between management and capital markets (see Myers and Majluf

1984). Seniority changes arise from the collateralisation of pension debt, which violates bondholders' interests.

1   European Pension News, May, 24th, 2004.
2   There are no changes under local GAAP if it differs from US GAAP.
3   See Villalonga (2003) and Campa and Kedia (2002), who found a diversification premium, *versus* previous studies from Lang and Stulz (1994).
4   If the monetary value of increased customer loyalty or brand recognition exceeds the value of the donation, this would be entirely in the shareholders interest, but it is not the social responsibility that should drive it.
5   See Modigliani and Miller (1958). However, changes in seniority are relevant.

REFERENCES

Black, F., 1980, "The Tax Consequences of Long-Run Pension Policy", *Financial Analysts Journal* **360(4)**, pp 22–28.

Black, F., and J. C. Cox, 1976, "Valuing Corporate Securities: Some Effects of Bond Indenture Provisions", *Journal of Finance* **31**, pp 351–367.

Black, F., and M. S. Scholes, 1973, "The Pricing of Options and Corporate Liabilities", *Journal of Political Economy* **81**, pp 637–654.

Blome, S., and H. J. Zwiesler, 2003, "Asset Funding in der betrieblichen Altersversorgung", *Zeitschrift für Versicherungswissenschaft* **92**, pp 9–34.

Bodie, Z., 1990, "The ABO, the PBO, and Pension Investment Policy", *Financial Analysts Journal*.

Bris, A., I. Welch, and N. Zhu, 2004, "The Costs of Bankruptcy – Chapter 7 Cash Auctions vs Chapter 11 Bargaining", Working Paper, Yale University.

Campa, J., 2002, "Explaining the Diversification Discount", *Journal of Finance*, **57**, pp 1731–1762.

De Matos, J. A., 2003, *Theoretical Foundations of Corporate Finance* (Princeton, NJ, and Oxford, UK: Princeton University Press).

Duffie, Darell D., 2001, *Dynamic Asset Pricing Theory* (Princeton, NJ: Princeton University Press).

Duffie, Darrell, and K. J. Singleton, 2003, *Credit Risk: Pricing, Measurement, and Management* (Princeton, NJ: Princeton University Press).

Epn, 2004, 24 May.

Froot, K. A., D. S. Scharfstein, and J. C. Stein, 1993, "Risk Management: Coordinating Corporate Investment and Financing Policies", *Journal of Finance* **48**, pp 1629–1658.

Gerke, W., and B. Pellens, 2003, Pensionsrückstellungen, Pensionsfonds und das Rating von Unternehmen – eine kritische Analyse. Universität Erlangen – Nuremberg.

Gold, J., and N. Hudson, 2003, "Creating Value in Pension Plans (or, Gentlemen Prefer Bonds)", *Journal of Applied Corporate Finance* **15**, pp 51–57.

Graham, J., 1996, "Debt and the Marginal Tax Rate", *Journal of Finance* **41**, pp 41–73.

Harrison, Micheal, and Kreps, David, 1979, "Martingales and Arbitrage in Multiperiod Securities Markets", *Journal of Economic Theory* **20**, pp 381–408.

Lang, L., and R. Stulz, 1994, "Tobins Q, Corporate Diversification and Firm Performance", *Journal of Political Economy*, pp 1248–1280.

Leland, H. E., 1998, "Agency Costs, Risk Management and Capital Structure", *Journal of Finance* **53**, pp 1213–1243.

Merton, R. C., 1973, "Theory of Rational Option Pricing", *Bell Journal of Economics and Management Science* **4**, pp 141–183.

Merton, R. C., 1974, "On the Pricing of Corporate Debt: The Risk Structure of Interest Rates", *Journal of Finance* **29**, pp 449–470.

Merton, R. C., 1977, "On the Pricing of Contingent Claims and the Modigliani–Miller Theorem", *Journal of Financial Economics* **5**, pp 241–249.

Modigliani, F., and M. H. Miller, 1958, "The Cost of Capital, Corporation Finance, and the Theory of Investment", *American Economic Review* **48**, pp 261–297.

Myers, S. C., and N. S. Majluf, 1984, "Corporate Financing and Investment Decisions When Firms Have Information That Investors Do Not Have", *Journal of Financial Economics* **13**, pp 187–221.

Nance, D. R., C. W. Smith, and C. W. Smithson, 1993, "On the Determinants of Corporate Hedging", *Journal of Finance* **48**, pp 267–284.

Rauh, J., 2004, "Investment and Financing Constraints: Evidence from the funding of corporate pension plans" 2005 Philadelphia Meeting.

Reichel, C., and H. J. Heger, 2003, *Betriebliche Altersversorgung* (Munich: Verlag C. H. Beck).

Scherer, B., and A. Gintschel, 2005, "External Funding and Stakeholder Value", unpublished working paper, Deutsche Asset Management.

Tepper, I., 1981, "Taxation and Corporate Pension Policy", *Journal of Finance* **36**.

Treynor, J., alias W. Bagehot, 1972, "Risk in Corporate Pension Plans", *Financial Analysts Journal*.

Villalonga, B., 2003, "Does Diversification Cause the 'Diversification Discount'?", *Financial Management*, **33(2)**, Summer 2004.

Warner, J. L., 1977, "Bankruptcy Costs: Some Evidence", *Journal of Finance* **32**, pp 737–747.

Index